Soldiers on the Santa Fe Trail

Leo E. Oliva
Soldiers on the Santa Fe Trail

UNIVERSITY OF OKLAHOMA PRESS : NORMAN

Library of Congress Catalog Card Number 67–15579

Copyright 1967 by the University of Oklahoma Press, Publishing Division of the University. Composed and printed at Norman, Oklahoma, U.S.A., by the University of Oklahoma Press. First edition.

To Raymond Leo Welty

Preface

This book is the outgrowth of an interest in the military forts formerly established along the Santa Fe Trail. They were occupied by soldiers who served on the overland route, one of the most important in the history of America. These troops performed important services aiding in the expansion and development of the West, and their colorful experiences are a part of that enduring phenomenon, the "Western," which has engaged and held the interest of Americans and many other peoples.

Various aspects of the history of the Santa Fe Trail have been described by extensive and wide-ranging literature, and the soldiers on the Trail have shared in this coverage. Military escorts, Indian campaigns, and military posts, as well as the activities of of soldiers on the route during the Mexican and Civil wars, have been treated in many formal histories, popular books, articles in journals and magazines, and reminiscences by participants.

However, despite the number of outstanding works dealing with different phases of the history of the Santa Fe Trail, no one has heretofore attempted to relate the total military history of the route. The long period during which the Trail was used, the various types and relative importance of military actions, and the vastness of the source materials available have resulted in the production of histories treating only isolated facets of the story of the soldiers on the Trail. These factors have encouraged me to undertake an inclusive account, an integrated military history of the Santa Fe Trail from the first escort in 1829 to the arrival of the railroad at Santa Fe in 1880. My aim has been to reveal the importance of the Trail as a military road and the value of the soldiers in the development of the American West.

This study is based upon an extensive sifting of primary sources, but it could not have been completed without earlier investigations. My reliance upon these for data and interpretation is demonstrated throughout the text. I wish to acknowledge here my indebtedness to all whose writings provided me with insight and information.

Many persons have been most generous with their assistance, without which this story could not have been told. I wish to acknowledge particularly the valuable aid rendered in locating pertinent materials, furnishing microfilm, photocopies, photographs, and maps, granting permission to microfilm published and unpublished manuscripts and documents with private equipment, and other special privileges. For this help I am obligated to the staffs of the Western History Department and Documents Division of Denver Public Library; the Army and Air Corps Branch and Diplomatic, Fiscal, and Legal Branch of the National Archives; the United States National Park Service; the State Historical Society of Colorado; the Museum of New Mexico; the Kansas State Historical Society; the Missouri Historical Society; the Missouri State Historical Society; the Southwest and Genealogy departments of Fort Worth Public Library; and the Reference and Documents departments of Washington University Library, Fort Hays Kansas State College Library, Texas Christian University Library, and the University of Denver Library. Words cannot express my gratitude to these courteous helpful librarians and archivists.

I also express my thanks to the Denver Posse of The Westerners for permission to use material published in my article concerning Fort Dodge, Kansas, in the *1960 Brand Book*.

Invaluable advice and encouragement has been given by Professor Harold H. Dunham of the University of Denver, to whom I shall be forever grateful.

LEO E. OLIVA

Fort Hays Kansas State College
January 23, 1967

Contents

	Preface	*page vii*
I	The Santa Fe Trail	3
II	Military Escorts, 1829–1845	25
III	Effects of the Mexican War, 1846–1848	55
IV	Military Protection, 1848–1861	93
V	Effects of the Civil War, 1861–1865	131
VI	The Soldiers' Life on the Trail, 1865–1880	167
	Bibliography	202
	Index	217

Illustrations

Map of Santa Fe Trail and surrounding region, 1847   *after page* 52
Fort Zarah, 1864
Fort Zarah (New Post), 1867–1869
Fort Larned, 1867
Company C, Third U.S. Infantry, at Fort Larned, 1867
Sod officers' quarters at Fort Dodge, 1868
Officers' quarters at Fort Dodge in 1879
Philip St. George Cooke
Manuel Armijo
March of the Caravan

Sutler's store, Fort Dodge, 1867   *after page* 148
Fort Union, late 1850's
Fort Union hospital
Edwin V. Sumner
Bennet Riley
Fort Lyon (New Post), 1875
John M. Chivington
Winfield S. Hancock

Maps

Map of battle area, Glorieta Pass   *page* 133
Man of the Santa Fe Trail   *after page* 164

xi

Soldiers on the Santa Fe Trail

1

The Santa Fe Trail

The Santa Fe Trail was probably the oldest regular land route across the Great Plains, and it was one of the most important overland trails in the history of America. Established during the 1820's, the Trail witnessed the growth and changes occurring in America during six decades, and was directly involved in several important international and national events before it was superseded by the railroad in 1880. Beginning as an international road and later serving as a vital national link between the eastern and southwestern United States, the Santa Fe Trail was much more than a local or regional phenomenon. An understanding of the origin and development of the Santa Fe Trail is necessary background to the military history of that great road.

Given the northward expansion of the Spanish residents of New Spain, who founded Santa Fe in late 1609 or early 1610, and the westward expansion of the Anglo-Americans, who had their permanent beginnings on the Atlantic seaboard two or three years earlier, it seemed inevitable that these two civilizations would someday meet, establish permanent contact and commercial intercourse, and ultimately intermingle. This joining of two cultures was accomplished more than two centuries later, with the establishment of the Santa Fe Trail.[1]

During those two centuries, there were occasional overland contacts by adventurers, fur traders, missionaries, and explorers, but

---

[1] At the same time the Santa Fe Trail was being opened, 1821–22, Stephen F. Austin was leading a group of Anglo-Americans into Texas. Thus, in the same year, two permanent contacts were established between the same two civilizations.

a permanent route was slow in being born. Years, decades, and generations passed before there was a determined effort by Anglo-Americans to establish commercial relationships with the New Mexicans at Santa Fe. This delay resulted from the fact that there were a number of obstacles to overcome.

Spanish authorities were suspicious of foreigners, and they placed almost prohibitive restrictions on foreign trade. There was neither road nor navigable river between the two areas of settlement. Also, the region between them was occupied by Indians who attacked northern Spanish settlements and western American settlements as well as the men who traveled between. Even the profit motive, and it was yet uncertain that profits could be obtained, failed to induce large-scale, permanent trade when loss of property and possibly loss of life were at stake.

The early nineteenth century witnessed the breakdown of the barriers and the establishment of contacts leading to continuing relationships. But even then the beginnings were slow and somewhat indefinite. Josiah Gregg declared in the opening sentence of his invaluable account of the Santa Fe trade:

> The overland trade between the United States and the northern provinces of Mexico, seems to have had no very definite origin; having been rather the result of accident than of any organized plan of commercial establishment.[2]

Following the transfer of Louisiana to the United States, one of the earliest-known attempts to open New Mexico to profitable trade occurred in 1804, when William Morrison, an enterprising merchant of Kaskaskia, Illinois, sent a French Creole, Jean Baptiste La Lande, to Santa Fe with commodities to trade. Although arrested and sent to Chihuahua upon his arrival, La Lande was permitted to return to Santa Fe the following year. His venture was profitable, but he never left New Mexico nor returned to Morrison the proceeds from his sales.[3] If nothing else was accomplished by

[2] *Commerce of the Prairies*, 9.
[3] *Ibid.*, 10; Hiram Martin Chittenden, *The American Fur Trade of the Far West*, II, 490–92.

The Santa Fe Trail

this undertaking, it did prove there was a demand for American products at Santa Fe.

Spain was unable to supply the New Mexicans with essential manufactured goods, but this did not mean that the citizens of the province had no desire for such items. Not only did they have the need for many things Americans could provide, but they had valuable products, such as gold, silver, furs, donkeys, and mules, to barter for them. Once this situation was understood by enterprising adventurers and the political barriers were removed, the law of supply and demand was certain to bring about the Santa Fe Trail. But before the commercial vision could be fulfilled, other problems had to be overcome.

In spite of the rigid Spanish restrictions on foreign trade, other traders attempted to penetrate into New Mexico during the early nineteenth century, but they were either kept out or arrested by Spanish troops.[4] It was not until the return of Lieutenant Zebulon Montgomery Pike, who had been a prisoner in northern Mexico in 1807, and the publication of his *Expeditions* in 1810, that the possibility of profitable Santa Fe trade attracted much attention.

Pike pointed out the wealth derived by traders from Mexico who brought their wares to Santa Fe by mule train. With a little reflection upon his statement that "The journey with loaded mules from Santa Fe to Mexico, and returning to Santa Fe, takes five months,"[5] it was obvious that Missouri was closer to the New Mexican capital than the leading Mexican market at Vera Cruz. Pike's account of the high prices obtained for imported cloth and other commodities was enough to cause some American adventurers to believe that the risk of Indian threats and the possibility of a reserved cell in a Mexican jail might be offset by the profits that could be realized.

During the same year that Pike's *Expeditions* was published, an incident occurred in Mexico that provided added attraction

---

[4] For an exception, see Joseph J. Hill, "An Unknown Expedition to Santa Fe in 1807," *Mississippi Valley Historical Review*, Vol. VI (March, 1920), 560–62.

[5] *The Expeditions of Zebulon Montgomery Pike* (ed. by Elliot Coues), II, 740.

for would-be Santa Fe traders. A premature revolt against Spanish rule, led by Miguel Hidalgo, created the false belief that the Spanish prohibitions against foreign commerce had been rescinded. Although the Hidalgo revolution failed with the capture and execution of its leader in Chihuahua, the rumors that traders would be now welcomed in New Mexico persuaded some to set out from Missouri for Santa Fe.

One trading party, led by Robert McKnight, arrived in Santa Fe in 1812. Apparently having received no word that Hidalgo had long since been executed, they were openly violating Spanish law. Instead of being heartily welcomed and paid high prices for their merchandise, the traders were arrested, and their goods confiscated. They were transported to Chihuahua and imprisoned until the successful Mexican revolution in 1821.[6] This was not an encouraging reward for attempting to provide for the needs of the Mexicans.

Because the boundary separating Spanish-America and the United States was not clearly defined between the time of the Louisiana Purchase (1803) and the Adams-Onís Treaty (1819), a group of St. Louis fur traders, who had no intention of trading with the New Mexicans, was captured in disputed territory in 1817. These traders, led by Jules de Mun and Pierre Chouteau, had been trapping along the upper Arkansas River, which the arresting officials claimed was Spanish territory. The trappers were taken to Santa Fe and tried for violation of Spanish law, the official conducting the trial maintaining that the Mississippi River was the boundary between the United States and Spanish territory. The convicted traders were finally released, but not until their approximately $30,000 worth of furs and trading goods had been confiscated.[7] In addition, David Meriwether, an Indian trader, was captured and taken to Santa Fe in 1820. He was imprisoned for a

[6] Gregg, *Commerce of the Prairies* 11–12; 26 Cong., 1 sess., *Sen. Doc. 472*, p. 6.

[7] *Ibid.;* 18 Cong., 1 sess. *Sen. Doc. 7*, p. 3; Chittenden, *American Fur Trade*, II, 496–98. The value, $30,000, was reported by Chittenden, 498, but De Mun and Chouteau later claimed $50,000. 24 Cong., 1 sess., *Sen. Doc. 400*.

The Santa Fe Trail

time and finally released. The signs were obvious; Americans were not welcome in New Mexico.

The Mexican revolution of 1821, led by Augustín de Iturbide, eliminated Spain as an obstacle to American trade with Mexico's northern province. During that same year, William Becknell, a Missouri trader, led an expedition which accidentally ended in Santa Fe and won him the title, "Founder of the Santa Fe trade and father of the Santa Fe Trail."[8]

When Becknell and his party of about thirty men set out from Arrow Rock, Missouri, on September 1, 1821, they had no intention of going to Santa Fe or trading with the New Mexicans. They planned, at the outset, to trade with the Indians, trap fur-bearing animals, and procure wild horses. The traders accidentally encountered some Mexican soldiers near the upper Canadian River and, impressed by their hospitable disposition even though unable to converse because of the language differences, accompanied them to Santa Fe. Arriving there on November 16, 1821, they learned, through a Frenchman who served as interpreter, of Mexico's independence from Spanish rule. With the Spaniards and their restrictions on foreign trade removed, American traders were now welcomed in New Mexico. Becknell profitably disposed of his few trading goods and returned to Missouri in January, 1822. He carried with him a message from New Mexican Governor Facundo Melgares that American traders would henceforth be welcome in Santa Fe, and this information was sufficient to make the Santa Fe Trail, which Becknell had traversed, become a reality.[9]

Curiously enough, Becknell had been the first American trader into an independent Santa Fe by only two weeks; two other parties were close behind his profitable venture. One of these, led by Thomas James, arrived in Santa Fe with a cargo of textiles on De-

[8] Chittenden, *American Fur Trade*, II, 499.
[9] 18 Cong., 2 sess., *House Doc. 79*, p. 6; "The Journals of Captain Thomas [William] Becknell from Boone's Lick to Santa Fe and from Santa Cruz to Green River," *Missouri Historical Review*, Vol. IV (January, 1910), 76–79; Max L. Moorhead, *New Mexico's Royal Road*, 60.

Soldiers on the Santa Fe Trail

cember 1, 1821. It had embarked for Santa Fe without any knowledge of the Mexican revolution. John McKnight, brother of Robert McKnight, intent on going to New Mexico to investigate the whereabouts of his brother, had persuaded James to take his commodities and accompany him. They secured a passport from the Spanish minister to the United States, Don Luis de Onís, and left St. Louis on May 10, 1821. They were informed of the revolution by Mexican troops before reaching the New Mexican capital. These men found the trading situation in Santa Fe unsatisfactory and lost a large amount on their venture.[10] James arrived in Santa Fe before Becknell left, but neither mentioned the other in his account of the 1821 expedition. James did make contact with another group of traders who arrived in New Mexico early in 1822.

Hugh Glenn and Jacob Fowler, with their party of trappers and Indian traders, were encamped in southeastern Colorado, near the site of present Pueblo, when they were visited by Mexican troops on December 29, 1821. When the soldiers departed for Santa Fe on January 2, Glenn and four other traders accompanied them. The soldiers either did not know of the successful Mexican revolution, or, if they did, they did not tell the Americans. But Glenn sent word back to the remainder of the party on January 29, informing them in the unique words of Jacob Fowler:

> We now under Stand that the mackeson [Mexican] provence Has de Clared Independance of the mother Cuntry and is desirous of traid With the people of the united States [.] Conl glann [Glenn] also advises me that He Has obtained premition to Hunt to trap and traid In the Spanish provences. . . .[11]

The party hurried to Taos and enjoyed a profitable trading season, Glenn making at least two visits to Santa Fe. They left New Mexico on June 1, 1822, accompanied by the James party and several recently freed prisoners who had been captured with Robert McKnight in 1812, and arrived home in July.

[10] Thomas James, *Three Years among the Indians and Mexicans*, 49-95.
[11] *The Journal of Jacob Fowler* (ed. by Elliot Coues), 95.

The Santa Fe Trail

These three trading expeditions, led respectively by Becknell, James, and Glenn and Fowler, had almost simultaneously opened the Santa Fe Trail. Many had preceded them in their efforts, but this time the situation was different because the Trail stayed open.

Before the Santa Fe Trail could assume importance, a mode of transportation better than the pack-mule had to be found and a passable wagon trail had to be located. Becknell's contributions toward solving both these problems were as important as his successful trading venture of 1821.

Becknell, on his second expedition to Santa Fe, in 1822, introduced wagon transportation to the Trail, and ceased being a trapper and Indian trader and became a Santa Fe trader. Leaving Franklin, Missouri, on May 22, with twenty additional men and three wagons, he established the real Santa Fe trade. Realizing that the wagons could not be taken over the rocky Raton Pass which he had crossed the previous year, he followed the Arkansas River to a point a few miles west of present Dodge City, Kansas. There the party crossed the river and headed southwest on a more direct route to Santa Fe. After a severe trial crossing the Cimarron Desert, they succeeded in reaching Santa Fe with wagons, entering the city via San Miguel instead of Taos, a route that proved to be more popular with future traders.

Also during 1822, an important year in the history of the Trail, at least two other trading expeditions left for Santa Fe. In April, Colonel Benjamin Cooper and his nephews, Braxton and Stephen Cooper, led a group of traders who took no wagons and yet enjoyed a successful season, returning to Missouri in the autumn. In the fall, Samuel Chambers and James Baird left Missouri for Santa Fe. They were caught on the Arkansas River by a severe snowstorm and were forced to spend the winter in camp on an island there. Most of their animals failed to survive the cold season, making it impossible for them to transport their goods when spring arrived. They cached their commodities on the north bank of the Arkansas above the island where they had spent the winter, journeyed to Taos and purchased mules, and returned to pick up their

Soldiers on the Santa Fe Trail

concealed property. The spot where they had hidden their goods became known as the "Caches," and Gregg reported in 1844: "Few travellers pass this way without visiting these mossy pits, some of which remain partly unfilled to the present day."[12]

The Santa Fe Trail was now firmly established. The Spanish restrictions had been eliminated, a route had been opened, profits had been realized, adequate means of transportation had been developed, and traders were quick to take advantage of the opportunities. Despite this favorable beginning, a new kind of difficulty soon began to appear. The nomadic Indians of the Great Plains began stealing the horses and supplies of travelers. When trade over the Trail became regular during the 1820's, the Indians attacked wagon trains traveling in either direction.

While continued Indian raids were eventually to bring the use of military escorts and the establishment of military posts for protection, in the beginning the traders themselves found it necessary to take steps to meet the Indian problem. Several years were to elapse before the United States government recognized the need for, and provided, such protection. The traders' answer to the Indian raids was the caravan. It was believed that if all, or at least a large number of, the traders who intended to reach Santa Fe in any one year were united into one train, their strength in men and arms would insure their safety.

The first trade caravan went to Santa Fe in 1824, leaving Mt. Vernon, Missouri, on May 25, and returning on September 24. Regarding the organization of that Marmaduke-Storrs expedition, Augustus Storrs wrote:

> The company consisted of eighty-one men, who had one hundred and fifty-six horses and mules; twenty-three four-wheeled vehicles, one of which was a common road wagon, and one piece of field artillery. The company adopted rules and regulations for its government; which rules created three offices, and specified the duties of the incumbents. They also regulated the conduct of the members toward each other, and their intercourse with the Indians.[13]

[12] *Commerce of the Prairies*, 47.   [13] 18 Cong., 2 sess., *Sen. Doc. 7*, p. 3.

The Santa Fe Trail

This expedition made the journey to Santa Fe and the return trip without Indian interference. It also added a new feature to the trade. In order to find adequate markets, some of the traders went beyond Santa Fe and visited the Mexican states of Chihuahua and

GREGG'S ESTIMATES OF THE VALUE AND VOLUME
OF THE SANTA FE TRADE, 1822–43*

Year	Cost of Goods in the U.S.	Number of Wagons	Total Number of Men	Number of Proprietors	Value of Goods to Chihuahua
1822	$ 15,000	[3]	70	60	$ 9,000
1823	12,000		50	30	3,000
1824	35,000	26	100	80	3,000
1825	65,000	37	130	90	5,000
1826	90,000	60	100	70	7,000
1827	85,000	55	90	50	8,000
1828	150,000	100	200	80	20,000
1829	60,000	30	50	20	5,000
1830	120,000	70	140	60	20,000
1831	250,000	130	320	80	80,000
1832	140,000	70	150	40	50,000
1833	180,000	105	185	60	80,000
1834	150,000	80	160	50	70,000
1835	140,000	75	140	40	70,000
1836	130,000	70	135	35	50,000
1837	150,000	80	160	35	60,000
1838	90,000	50	100	20	80,000
1839	250,000	130	250	40	100,000
1840	50,000	30	60	5	10,000
1841	150,000	60	100	12	80,000
1842	160,000	70	120	15	90,000
1843	450,000	230	350	30	300,000

* Gregg, *Commerce of the Prairies*, 332.

Sonora, thus inaugurating what was to become a standard practice. It was an exceptionally profitable year, the traders realizing a return of approximately $190,000 on an investment of about $35,000. Thus the trading pattern for the Santa Fe Trail was established.

With few exceptions, such as the entrance of Mexicans into the trade in 1826 and the periodic protection afforded by United States and Mexican troops, the only marked change in the Santa Fe trade before the Mexican War was its increase in volume. The accompanying table details value and volume from 1822 to 1843.

Convinced that the Santa Fe trade was permanently established and presented promising opportunities for continued expansion, the Missouri traders requested the United States government to survey and mark a permanent road and provide military protection from the Indians. The Missouri legislature took up their cause, as did Senators Thomas Hart Benton and David Barton from Missouri. The state legislature memorialized Congress in behalf of the merchants, Senator Benton sponsored a bill to authorize a survey, and Senator Barton introduced a resolution calling for an inquiry "into the expedience of establishing a fort on the route."[14]

Military protection had to wait a few years, but Congress authorized a survey of the Trail in 1825. A survey from Fort Osage, Missouri, to Taos, New Mexico, was completed the next year.[15] Additional government assistance was provided in 1825, when Augustus Storrs and James W. Magoffin were appointed to serve as United States Consuls at Santa Fe and Saltillo, respectively.[16]

The Santa Fe Trail had several points of departure. Most of the earliest traders departed either from Arrow Rock or Franklin, Missouri, the latter being the more important. Franklin, located across the Missouri River from Boonville, was founded in 1816. It was

---

[14] Frederic A. Culmer, "Marking the Santa Fe Trail," *New Mexico Historical Review,* Vol. IX (January, 1934), 78. Petitions requesting legislation and other information supporting the need for assistance are in 18 Cong., 2 sess.,. *Sen. Doc. 7,* and 18 Cong., 2 sess., *House Doc. 79.* For Senator Benton's views on the Santa Fe trade and his role in securing authorization of the survey, see Thomas Hart Benton, *Thirty Years' View,* I, 41–44.

[15] The story of the survey, including diaries, letters, editorial comments, and the final report of the commissioners, is contained in Kate L. Gregg (ed.), *The Road to Santa Fe.*

[16] Robert L. Duffus, *The Santa Fe Trail,* 90; Adams to Magoffin, March 3, 1825, Consular Dispatches, Secretary of State, MSS, State Department (Record Group No. 59), Diplomatic, Legal and Fiscal Branch, National Archives.

The Santa Fe Trail

one of the most flourishing towns west of St. Louis until 1828, when the Missouri changed its course and washed the town away.[17] Fort Osage, where the survey began in 1825, also served as a point of debarkation for some traders, as did Blue Mills, Missouri. The

Major Points and Distances on the Santa Fe Trail*

Independence to	Miles	Total Miles			
Round Grove	35	—	Cimarron River		
Narrows	30	65	(Lower Spring)	8	445
110-Mile Creek	30	95	Middle Spring	36	481
Bridge Creek	8	103	Willow Bar	26	507
Big John Spring	40	143	Upper Spring	18	525
Council Grove	2	145	Cold Spring	5	530
Diamond Spring	15	160	M'Nees's Creek	25	555
Lost Spring	15	175	Rabbit-Ear Creek	20	575
Cottonwood Creek	12	187	Round Mound	8	583
Turkey Creek	25	212	Rock Creek	8	591
Little Arkansas River	17	229	Point of Rocks	19	610
Cow Creek	20	249	Río Colorado (Upper		
Arkansas River	16	265	Canadian)	20	630
Walnut Creek	8	273	Ocaté	6	636
Ash Creek	19	292	Santa Clara Spring	21	657
Pawnee Fork	6	298	Río Mora	22	679
Coon Creek	33	331	Río Gallinas		
Caches	36	367	(Las Vegas)	20	699
Ford of Arkansas			Ojo de Bernal Spring	17	716
(Cimarron Crossing)	20	387	San Miguel	6	722
Sand Creek	50	437	Pecos Village	23	745
			Santa Fe	25	770

* Gregg, *Commerce of the Prairies*, 217 n.

major point after the destruction of Franklin was Independence, rivaled after 1833 by Westport, which finally superseded it about 1840. Fort Leavenworth was another point of origin for some caravans. At these various places the caravans were outfitted, although

[17] Gregg, *Commerce of the Prairies*, 22n.

they were organized at a rendezvous down the Trail. Gregg's estimate of the distance from Independence to Santa Fe was 770 miles.

Outfitting for the long trip to Santa Fe was one of the most important parts of every expedition. The big wagons had to be operating satisfactorily, adequate supplies for the march had to be stored in them along with the merchandise intended for market, and the draft animals had to be in good condition and trained before setting out on the Trail. Since the mules and oxen were dependent upon the prairie grass for their nourishment during the journey, expeditions had to wait until the fresh spring grass was sufficiently high before starting, and they could not delay very late in the autumn for the return trip.

The departure of a caravan for Santa Fe was a time of excitement, hilarity, singing, and celebration.[18] Gregg claimed: "even the mules prick up their ears with a peculiarly conceited air, as if in anticipation of that change of scene which will presently follow."[19]

Leaving Independence, the loaded wagons and their skillful drivers moved thirty-five miles westward to Round Grove, "a regular stopping place and also something of a rendezvous."[20] About eight miles beyond Round Grove, the Oregon Trail branched off northwestward, after it was established in the early 1840's. The Santa Fe traders moved on to the Narrows, thirty miles from Round Grove, so called because the camp was on a narrow ridge separating the Kansas and Osage rivers. About ninety-five miles from Independence, the traders reached 110-Mile Creek (110 miles from Fort Osage). After crossing this and several other creeks and the headwaters of the Osage River, they reached the Neosho River at Council Grove, 145 miles and usually about ten days from Independence. This was one of the most significant campsites along the entire Trail.

Here was the usual rendezvous for the wagon trains. Situated in a timber belt along the Neosho River, Council Grove was a

[18] *Ibid.*, 26; Richard L. Wilson, *Short Ravelings from a Long Yarn*, 1-5.
[19] Gregg, *Commerce of the Prairies*, 26.
[20] Chittenden, *American Fur Trade*, II, 533.

major point at which hardwood for wagon repairs could be procured. Thus some time was usually spent cutting and trimming oak, hickory, ash, or walnut shafts and tying them underneath the wagons for future emergencies, both going and returning. The place was named "Council Grove" by the commissioners of the survey in 1825, being the point where they concluded a treaty with the Osage Indians.

The designation was also appropriate for the Santa Fe traders; there, in the grove of trees, they held their own council to choose officials, agree upon a system of government, and organize the caravan. In a situation similar to that faced by many frontiersmen who had passed beyond the reach of the law, some organization was necessary to provide for the protection of life and property. When organization work was completed, the caravan was ready to move across the plains; its rate of travel was apt to be ten to fifteen miles a day, although occasionally eighteen or twenty were covered. In 1846 the caravan which preceded the Army of the West to New Mexico marched the unprecedented distance of forty-five miles a day during the last half of the journey.

Proceeding westward from Council Grove, the caravan usually spent the first night at Diamond Spring, fifteen miles out. Sometimes caravans did not organize until reaching this campsite. Beyond Diamond Spring there followed Lost Spring, Cottonwood Creek, Turkey Creek, the Little Arkansas River, Cow Creek, and the Big Bend of the Arkansas River, the last-named measuring 265 miles from Independence.

As the caravans plodded toward the Arkansas, the prairie grass region was left behind and the short grass of the semiarid plains was entered. Buffalo were usually encountered between Council Grove and the Arkansas River. Those beasts of the plains were always a welcome sight, since they provided the staple diet and major source of fresh meat during the remainder of the journey. Entrance into the buffalo range meant, also, that hostile Indian country had been reached.

When the Trail was opened, Indians might appear anywhere

along the entire route from Independence to Santa Fe. Those found east of the Council Grove region were often termed "friendly" Indians, as opposed to the more hostile "wild tribes" found along the remainder of the route.

The commissioners of the survey concluded peace treaties with the Kansas and Osage Indians in 1825, and these "friendly" Indians caused no more than minor problems for traders after that time.

The major "wild tribes" having contact with the Trail were the Pawnees, Arapahoes, Cheyennes, Kiowas, Comanches, and Apaches. These were nomadic Indians, depending upon the buffalo for their livelihood. Horses were important to each of these groups, and the stealing of horses was considered an honorable deed. Consequently, they were a constant threat to travelers over the Trail. Often their sole aim was to procure horses, and they fought only when necessary to obtain these valued possessions.

With these hostiles roaming the region of the Trail, traders were wise to remain constantly alert. The Little Arkansas River was considered the place to begin keeping a careful eye out for Indian "sign." From that point, the caravan marched in four columns, and the night camp was formed into a small fortification, each column forming one side, the wagons parked with their big wheels interlocking. The enclosure thus formed could be used as a corral for protecting the animals when necessary, and was considered a secure position in the event of an Indian attack. The wagons could be driven quickly into this formation during the day if an Indian attack seemed imminent.[21]

Upon reaching the Arkansas River, the caravans moved up its north bank, crossed Walnut Creek, and passed the famous landmark, Pawnee Rock, about 290 miles from Independence. Beyond this point they crossed Ash Creek before arriving at Pawnee Fork, where the Trail split into two branches, the Wet Route and the Dry

---

[21]Wilson, *Short Ravelings from a Long Yarn*, 34–35; Gregg, *Commerce of the Prairies*, 43, 72.

The Santa Fe Trail

Route. The former closely followed the Arkansas River, part of it winding through sand hills. The latter followed the upland divide and rejoined the Wet Route and the Arkansas a few miles below the Caches. The Dry Route was often without water the whole distance, but it was approximately fifteen miles shorter, and was thus attractive to traders and other travelers. A camping ground developed just west of where the two branches rejoined, on what later became the site of the military post of Fort Dodge.[22]

When the caravans reached this camping site, they had at least four alternate routes to Santa Fe. Three crossed the Arkansas and proceeded to the Cimarron River, traversing part of present Oklahoma; the other followed along the Arkansas to Bent's Fort, in present Colorado, and then turned south into New Mexico.

The three major crossings of the Arkansas that led to the Cimarron River were (1) Lower Crossing (Mulberry Creek Crossing), where Mulberry Creek entered the Arkansas near the extreme point of its southern bend; (2) Middle Crossing (Cimarron Crossing), located about forty miles upriver from Lower Crossing and approximately twenty miles above the Caches; and (3) Upper Crossing at Chouteau's Island.[23] The Cimarron Crossing was the most popular of the three, and the Cimarron Route was used almost entirely during the pre–Mexican War era.

Beyond the Middle Crossing the Cimarron Route passed through sand hills and the Cimarron Desert for a distance of fifty-eight miles before reaching the Lower Spring on the Cimarron River (also called "Lost River"). This was one of the most difficult sections of the Trail, usually without water the entire distance and with no visible trail until after 1834, an uncommonly wet year during which the wagons left permanent ruts that could be followed. From

---

[22] Fort Dodge was occupied from 1865 to 1882. Fort Larned, 1859–78, was established on Pawnee Fork near the eastern point where the Wet and Dry routes divided.

[23] Chouteau's Island was named for Auguste P. Chouteau following an attack by Pawnee Indians upon his trading party in 1816. The traders retreated to the island and survived the attack. Gregg, *Commerce of the Prairies*, 19–20n.

Soldiers on the Santa Fe Trail

Lower Spring the Trail followed the sandy valley of the Cimarron for eighty-five miles, passing Middle Spring, Willow Bar, and Upper Spring, and leaving the valley at Cold Spring.

It was a little over two hundred miles to Santa Fe from Cold Spring, and major landmarks along the arid route were Round Mound and Point of Rocks. At the upper Canadian River (often called the Río Colorado by traders), about 140 miles from Santa Fe, the caravan usually broke up for the remainder of the journey, proceeding as it had been before the organization at Council Grove. Settlements were reached at Las Vegas, and the route continued through San Miguel and Pecos Village, over Glorieta Pass, and into Santa Fe, approximately 770 miles from Independence.

The Bent's Fort route, known as the Mountain Route, was popular during and after the Mexican War. Traders were unable to make good use of it until wagons could be taken over Raton Pass. It is not known when the first wagon train used this branch of the Trail. The earliest report found stated that a party of traders returned to Missouri over Raton Pass in 1843, but they had only a few empty wagons.[24] Lieutenant J. W. Abert, of the Topographical Engineers, traveled the route in 1845 and reported that it was only "recently commenced."[25] Concerning the pass, he continued:

> Our road now became exceedingly rough, leading along a tortuous valley, sometimes passing on one side of the Raton fork, sometimes on the other, whilst occasionally the narrowness of the banks forces us to seek a passage in the rocky bed of the creek itself.[26]

The caravan that followed the Army of the West from Bent's Fort to Santa Fe in 1846 had an extremely difficult time negotiating the pass.[27]

Those traveling the Mountain Route stayed on the north bank of the Arkansas, passed the Big Timbers, and proceeded to Bent's

[24] Philip St. George Cooke, *Scenes and Adventures in the Army*, 255–56.
[25] 29 Cong., 1 sess., *Sen. Doc. 438*, p. 12.
[26] *Ibid.*, 15.
[27] *Down the Santa Fe Trail and into Mexico: The Diary of Susan Shelby Magoffin, 1846–1847* (ed. by Stella M. Drumm), 78–84.

The Santa Fe Trail

Fort. The soil became rockier or sandier and the grass thinner as they moved toward that outpost on the plains. From Bent's Fort the route continued westward about six miles, crossed the Arkansas River, proceeded south-southwesterly, crossed Timpas Creek and the upper Purgatoire River, and went over Raton Pass. From this pass the route followed along the eastern side of the Sangre de Cristo Mountains. At a point east of Taos, it was possible to cross over to Taos and proceed from there to Santa Fe. Most traders preferred to continue south, join the route from the Cimarron at Santa Clara Spring, and follow it into Santa Fe. The distance from Independence to Santa Fe via the Mountain Route was about 825 miles.

The men celebrated at the end of their journey just as vigorously as, if not more so than, they did at the time of their departure from Missouri. But the proprietors' celebration was usually brief; they had come to Santa Fe to sell merchandise and had to be about their business. After settling with the customs officials, they set up shop. The Santa Fe Trail originated and survived as a commercial route; trade was the vital factor in its pre–Mexican War history.

Cloth was the most important of the items transported to New Mexico and comprised the bulk of most proprietors' merchandise. All types of cottons were popular, as were imported silks and linens. Other dry goods, hardware, cutlery, notions, and jewelry figured in the exports to New Mexico and beyond. The major items returned to the United States were gold and silver Mexican dollars, silver bullion, and gold dust. Other prominent goods were mules, donkeys, furs, a few buffalo rugs, some wool, and Mexican blankets.

Traders who stopped at Santa Fe often had disposed of their merchandise, either retail or wholesale, by late summer or early autumn, and were ready to return to Missouri. Autumn was the most common season for the journey back to the United States, the traders leaving Santa Fe around September 1 and arriving in Missouri about October 10. Because the wagons were not so heavily loaded, the return journey could be accomplished much more quickly than the outbound trip. Since the grass on the plains was drying up and winter was approaching, the traders necessarily traveled with celerity.[28]

The returning caravans were generally smaller than those departing in the spring and thus were easier prey for hostile Indians. Some traders stayed in New Mexico permanently, and others, not so fortunate with their sales or for other reasons, remained through the winter before returning. Those who went farther south, instead of returning through Santa Fe and over the Trail, often returned through Texas or dragged their wagons to Matamoros, at the mouth of the Río Grande, where they were loaded on packet boats from New Orleans and transported back to Missouri by water.[29]

Such was the beginning, growth and development, character, and pattern of the Santa Fe trade until the Mexican War.

The coming of the Mexican War ended forever the pattern of trade that had existed up to that time. After the war, the Santa Fe trade was no longer foreign commerce, and the small proprietors were soon replaced by larger freighting companies. The commercial value of the Trail did not decline; rather, it continued to expand. But the old Santa Fe trade had come to an end.

When war came, more wagons than had appeared in any previous year moved toward New Mexico. However, not all belonged to Santa Fe traders; the bulk of them were government supply trains.[30] Army freighting continued to be a major enterprise of the Trail until the railroad terminated its necessity. But even war could

[28] Gregg, *Commerce of the Prairies,* 212-13. Not all caravans followed this general pattern of a spring departure from Missouri and an autumn return to that state. After Mexican merchants entered the trade, they often left Santa Fe in the spring, procured their goods in the summer, and returned to New Mexico late in the season. It would appear that by the 1840's traders moved along the Trail in both directions throughout the season when grass for draft animals was available, although the largest caravans continued to move to Santa Fe during the spring. This practice was later discontinued as a result of changes in trading patterns which occurred during and after the Mexican War.

[29] *Ibid.;* 22 Cong. 1 sess., *Sen. Doc. 90,* p. 32.

[30] The trade caravans alone comprised 363 wagons in 1846. Moorhead, *New Mexico's Royal Road,* 75. By November 24, 1847, over fifteen hundred wagons had been sent over the Trail carrying military supplies. 30 Cong. 1 sess., *House Exec. Doc. 8,* p. 545.

The Santa Fe Trail

not stop the persistent traders; a large caravan preceded the United States troops into Santa Fe in 1846.[31]

During the war, the Santa Fe Trail became a great avenue of expansion, as well as a route of conquest. Throughout the summer of 1848, Lieutenant Colonel William Gilpin, commanding at Fort Mann on the Arkansas River, counted approximately three thousand wagons and at least twelve thousand persons and fifty thousand head of livestock moving westward over the Trail.[32] The California gold rush, beginning a year later, turned that stream into a flood. The Colorado gold rush of a decade later increased the use and importance of part of the route. Westward migration transformed the old Trail into a great road, and as the numbers of travelers increased, Indians became an increasing problem.

As Americans acquired possession of the Southwest, they felt a need for a more rapid system of communication with the East. The army established a monthly express service in May, 1849, but it was not sufficient. A government mail contract was awarded to Waldo, Hall and Company of Independence in July, 1850, providing for monthly mail and stagecoach service to Santa Fe. Jacob Hall, who received the contract, was granted additional contracts in 1854 and 1858; beginning in the latter year, trips were made semi-monthly.[33]

The company often sent two or more vehicles over the Trail together for protective purposes. The train on which W. W. H. Davis journeyed to Santa Fe in 1853, to assume his position as United States attorney to the Territory of New Mexico, consisted of a wagon for mail, a wagon for provisions and baggage, and an ambulance for passengers. Including the drivers, guards, and four passengers, the party numbered ten well-armed men. While on the road, they met an eastbound mail, which consisted of just one wagon under the guard of four men.[34]

[31] James J. Webb, *Adventures in the Santa Fe Trade, 1844–1847* (Vol. I of *The Southwest Historical Series*, ed. by Ralph P. Beiber), 179–98.
[32] 30 Cong., 2 sess., *House Exec. Doc. 1*, p. 139.
[33] LeRoy R. Hafen, *The Overland Mail, 1848–1869*, 73.
[34] W. W. H. Davis, *El Gringo*, 4, 18.

Soldiers on the Santa Fe Trail

By the early 1860's a daily stage service was established between Independence and Santa Fe. The advent of the stagecoaches brought additional changes to the Trail. Although the service operated without way stations in the heart of Indian country in the beginning, the stage line soon established stations at regular intervals along the route. These small stations were the object of Indian raids and increased the need for military protection along the Trail.

Freighting also changed as the small proprietors gave way to the large freighting companies immediately following the Mexican War. General Stephen Watts Kearny's Army of the West had attempted to provide its own supply trains, but had not been completely successful. At the close of the war, with occupation troops and military posts to supply, the army granted contracts to private freight lines. The first great freighting concern of the Far West, Majors, Russell and Waddell, got its start and developed in the Santa Fe trade.[35] This company, along with others such as Wells, Fargo and Company, dominated the trade over the Trail until the railroad replaced them all.

As freighting companies grew in size and number, the amount and value of goods carried to New Mexico necessarily increased. In 1846, about $1,000,000 worth of merchandise and army supplies were sent over the Trail, more than twice as much as Gregg reported in 1843, the largest prewar year. The total trade for 1855 was worth approximately $5,000,000, and in 1860, while no dollar value is known, about 16,500,000 pounds were sent out in over three thousand wagons. Robert L. Duffus estimated that the freight charges alone for that year would have approximated $1,300,000.[36] By the end of the Civil War the physical volume of trade, compared to 1860, had almost doubled. In 1866 between five and six thousand wagons followed the Trail.[37] The Santa Fe trade was big business by the close of the Civil War.

By the time the Civil War ended, military posts had been estab-

[35] Raymond W. Settle and Mary L. Settle, *Empire on Wheels*, 7–10.
[36] *Santa Fe Trail*, 244.
[37] L. L. Waters, *Steel Trails to Santa Fe*, 20.

lished at strategic points along the entire length of the Trail. The Santa Fe trade continued, but the Trail was being shortened as the railroads built westward. During this final era of the Trail's history, 1865–1880, the Indians were finally overpowered and confined to reservations.

The Union Pacific Eastern Division, which became the Kansas Pacific Railroad in 1869, began building westward from Kansas City in 1863. By June, 1867, it was in operation to Ellsworth, Kansas. This town then became the departing point for the Santa Fe trade, eliminating the eastern end of the old Trail, including such famous stopping places as Round Grove, the Narrows, Council Grove, Diamond Spring, and Cottonwood Creek. The traders left Ellsworth and took the Trail at the Arkansas River. A year later the railroad reached Hays, Kansas. By 1871, with the completion of the Kansas Pacific, the point of departure for the Santa Fe trade was Kit Carson, Colorado, all points in Kansas having been eliminated. Only army supply trains and mail coaches traveled the old Trail east of Las Animas, Colorado, provisioning and providing communication for the forts where soldiers remained to protect settlers, help remove the Indians to their reservations, and protect the builders of the railroads.

Meanwhile, the Atchison, Topeka and Santa Fe Railroad line was being constructed, and it soon replaced the Santa Fe Trail. Beginning at Topeka in 1868, the Santa Fe Railroad reached Dodge City in September, 1872, the Colorado boundary line five months later, and arrived at Granada, Colorado, in July of 1873. The days of the old wagon route were numbered. The Santa Fe reached Las Animas in September, 1875, and Trinidad, Colorado, three years later; its tracks were laid over Raton Pass in 1879, and extended to Las Vegas on Independence Day of that year.[38]

Although the value of trade was shrinking during the final years of the Trail's history (it was estimated at only $2,000,000 in 1876), enterprising merchants did not abandon it. One of the last signifi-

[38] The building of the Atchison, Topeka and Santa Fe is treated in *ibid.* and in James Marshall, *Santa Fe; the Railroad that Built an Empire*.

Soldiers on the Santa Fe Trail

cant traders, Don Miguel Antonio Otero, moved his eastern headquarters seven times in eleven years as the railroads built westward (from Hays, Kansas, in 1868 to Las Vegas in 1879).[39] Las Vegas was the last point of departure for the Santa Fe traders. From there the railroad was extended to Lamy, and the first train entered Santa Fe, February 16, 1880, on a branch line built the eighteen miles from Lamy.

The Santa Fe Trail, first of the great transcontinental highways, came to an end after six decades of service. It had joined two civilizations, had witnessed a significant, although by no means gigantic, carrying trade, had served as an avenue of expansion and conquest, and had played an important role in the Mexican and Civil wars. As a commercial route, it had contributed to the economic development of the Southwest, of Missouri, and of the nation. Hostile Indians plagued the Trail during most of its life, and military forces were important in keeping the Trail open and the commerce moving, as well as in protecting the railroads that replaced it.

[39] A. A. Hayes, *New Colorado and the Santa Fe Trail,* 140.

2

Military Escorts, 1829-1845

THE FIRST UNITED STATES military aid extended to the Santa Fe traders was in the form of escorts, the troops accompanying the traders through Indian country, but remaining permanently stationed in Missouri, Indian Territory, or at Fort Leavenworth on the Missouri River. In other words, instead of guarding the Trail, as the later military posts did, the military escorts guarded only the trade caravans which they accompanied.

There were at least six such United States Army escorts during the pre–Mexican War era:[1] (1) 1829—Major Bennet Riley and four companies of Sixth Infantry, (2) 1833—Captain William N. Wickliffe and a few soldiers of the Sixth Infantry and Captain Matthew Duncan's company of United States Mounted Rangers, (3) 1834—Captain Clifton Wharton and a company of the Regiment of Dragoons, (4) Spring, 1843—Captain Philip St. George Cooke and four companies of First Dragoons, (5) Autumn, 1843—Captain Cooke and six companies of First Dragoons, and (6) 1845—return escort provided by Colonel Stephen Watts Kearny and the First Dragoons, following their expedition to South Pass on the Oregon Trail.[2]

[1] The Mexican government also provided armed escorts from time to time. Gregg reported that almost every spring the caravans were met near the upper Canadian River, about 140 miles from Santa Fe, by a military escort. The primary purpose was to prevent smuggling, but it also provided protection from the Indians for the traders. Gregg, *Commerce of the Prairies,* 75. Mexican soldiers provided a return escort to the United States boundary in 1829 and met the caravan going to Santa Fe, at the Cimarron Crossing, in the autumn of 1843. See below.

[2] There were other bodies of troops on the Trail during this period, using it only as a means of travel and not of directly protecting traders. The most important of

Indians, as mentioned above, began to harass the Santa Fe traders soon after the Trail was opened. Nevertheless, it was relatively peaceful along the route until 1828. In that year the large number of traders who journeyed to Santa Fe experienced frequent Indian attacks and sustained heavy losses. Two eastward-bound caravans alone lost several men and $40,000 worth of property.

These Indian outrages led to demands by the traders, Missouri Governor John Miller, and the Missouri legislature for the federal government to furnish military protection for the Santa Fe trade.[3] Senator Benton pushed for passage of a bill to provide escorts, but Congress adjourned in March of 1829 without enacting the requested legislation.

It appeared that the traders would receive no escorts, and many of them, reflecting upon the losses of the previous year, were unwilling to take the risks without some protection from the Indians. It seemed that the recently established Santa Fe trade might be terminated; however, some of those who had profited most were determined that the Indians would not close the Trail. A small group of leading proprietors, including Samuel C. Lamme and David Waldo, sent a direct appeal to the newly inaugurated president, Andrew Jackson, for military escort for the caravans as far as the boundary between the United States and Mexico.

An old Indian fighter himself, President Jackson brought the request to the attention of the War Department, and orders were soon issued directing Brevet Major Bennet Riley and four companies of the Sixth Regiment, United States Infantry, to move from

---

these was Colonel Henry Dodge's expedition to the Rocky Mountains in 1835, which returned via the Arkansas route. For the Dodge expedition, see 24 Cong., 1 sess., *House Doc. 181*. In addition to the six escorts along the Trail, an escort was provided for the caravan led to Santa Fe by Josiah Gregg in 1839, which did not follow the regular route. Departing from Van Buren, Arkansas, the traders followed a route along the Canadian River. Henry Putney Beers, "Military Protection of the Santa Fe Trail to 1843," *New Mexico Historical Review*, Vol. XII (April, 1937), 126-27.

[3] 20 Cong. 2 sess., *Sen. Doc. 52*.

[4] Macomb to Eaton, November, 1829, *American State Papers: Military Affairs*, IV, 155. Companies A, B, F, and H comprised the escort.

Military Escorts, 1829-1845

Jefferson Barracks at St. Louis to escort the 1829 caravan.[4] An announcement of the army's plans was published in Missouri newspapers, so that traders desirous of protection could take advantage of it.[5]

Even after the federal government had come to the aid of the traders, many proprietors were hesitant about venturing into Indian country again. They doubted the effectiveness of infantry (the United States Army had no cavalry in 1829) in dealing with mounted Indians.[6] Also, they were concerned about the safety of the caravan while traveling without military protection from the Arkansas River through Mexican territory to Santa Fe.[7]

Even with the promise of military protection halfway to Santa Fe, fear of losing life and property made the caravan of 1829 much smaller than the one a year earlier. In 1828 there had been about one hundred wagons and the value of merchandise was estimated at $150,000; in 1829 there were only thirty-eight wagons and merchandise worth $60,000. Only one-fourth as many proprietors and men made the journey in 1829 as had gone the previous year.[8]

The four companies of infantry left Jefferson Barracks on May 5, 1829, and sailed on the steamboat *Diana* to Fort Leavenworth. This post had been founded in 1827 as part of the defense line along the Missouri River.[9] The escort departed from Leavenworth on June 3 to join the traders at their rendezvous, Round Grove, ar-

[5] See, e.g., *Missouri Intelligencer* (Fayette), May 1, 1829.

[6] Although no cavalry existed in 1829, General Alexander Macomb intended for the escort to be mounted. His plans were abandoned because no appropriation was available to purchase horses for the infantry. Macomb to Eaton, November, 1829, *American State Papers: Military Affairs*, IV, 156. The officers of the escort battalion had horses to ride, but the troops marched to the Arkansas and back.

[7] In response to this fear, Governor Miller attempted to raise a company of Missouri militia to accompany the traders all the way to Santa Fe, but the effort failed. Major Bennet Riley's Journal of the 1829 Escort, printed with notes in Fred S. Perrine, "Military Escorts on the Santa Fe Trail," *New Mexico Historical Review*, Vol. III (July, 1928), 269 (hereafter cited as Riley's Journal); Otis E. Young, *The First Military Escort on the Santa Fe Trail, 1829*, 40–41.

[8] Gregg, *Commerce of the Prairies*, 332.

[9] For a history of this post, see Elvid Hunt, *History of Fort Leavenworth, 1827-1937*.

Soldiers on the Santa Fe Trail

riving there on June 11. Besides Major Riley, there were ten officers and about two hundred men in the battalion.[10]

Transportation for the troops' twenty wagons of provisions and four carts of camp equipment presented a problem, because the battalion lacked funds to purchase enough horses and mules for them. It was finally decided to experiment with oxen (cheaper than horses or mules by about three to one), which had never been used for draft purposes on the Great Plains. Thus, the first military escort introduced these animals to the Trail. Moreover, after the caravan had reached the Arkansas crossing, the captain, Charles Bent, borrowed one yoke of oxen and used them the rest of the way to Santa Fe. Bent was pleased with their performance, even though on the return trip from Santa Fe the oxen strayed and were lost.

The experiment proving successful, oxen became a regular sight on the Trail, although they never entirely replaced mules. By the time of the Mexican War, approximately half the draft animals used on the Trail were oxen, and, after the war, with army freighting and developing commercial freighting companies, oxen became the most frequently used means of locomotion. If the first escort did nothing more, it made a significant contribution by proving the efficiency of oxen on the plains.

The troops and the caravan arrived at Council Grove on June 18 and departed two days later. They reached the Arkansas on

[10] Riley's Journal, 267–71, 273; Cooke, *Scenes and Adventures,* 40–41; Major Bennet Riley's Report of the 1829 Escort, 21 Cong., 1 sess., *Sen. Doc. 46,* p. 2 (hereafter cited as Riley's Report). The latter document has been reprinted in Perrine, *New Mexico Historical Review,* Vol. II (1927), 178–92. Besides Riley, other officers of the expedition were Second Lieutenant James Farley Izard, adjutant; Second Lieutenant Francis J. Brooke, acting assistant quartermaster and commissary of subsistence; Assistant Surgeon William H. Nicoll; Captain William N. Wickliffe, ranking junior officer and commander of Company F; Captain Joseph Pentland, commander of Company B; First Lieutenant George Washington Waters, commander of Company H; Second Lieutenant Joseph Van Swearingen, commander of Company A; and Second Lieutenants Gustavus Dorr, Robert Sevier, and Philip St. George Cooke. Riley's Journal, 268. Cooke served as Major Riley's chronicler for the expedition and has provided much information, in addition to the official records, concerning the escort in his *Scenes and Adventures,* 40–93.

Military Escorts, 1829–1845

June 27, and arrived at the Upper Crossing near Chouteau's Island on July 9. The traders had delayed crossing the river until reaching the westernmost route to the Cimarron in order to have the protection of the escort as far as possible. From Council Grove to Chouteau's Island, a march of twenty days, Indian signs appeared occasionally and six horses were lost, supposedly by Indian theft, but no direct contact occurred with the Indians of the region. As intended, the Indians apparently were overawed by the presence of the troops.

The caravan crossed the Arkansas on July 10 and departed without the escort the following day. The traders hoped that Riley would accompany them into Mexican territory, but, as Cooke later reported, "Our orders were to march no farther; and as a protection to the trade, it was like the establishment of a ferry to the mid-channel of a river."[11] Before the two groups parted, Major Riley wrote a letter for the traders to present to the governor of New Mexico, informing him of the location of the troops and their orders. Pointing out that the trade was important to Mexico as well as the United States, Riley asked the Mexican government to provide an escort for the caravan's return to the Arkansas in the autumn.[12]

Following the departure of the traders, the soldiers began to settle down into camp and to enjoy what they anticipated would be a period of restful waiting. The traders had estimated their return date at some time between October 5 and 10, so it appeared that the troops would have about three months of buffalo hunting and relaxation. However, the sojourn on the Arkansas proved to be much more taxing and dangerous than the long march to Chouteau's Island or the return march to Fort Leavenworth in the autumn.

Before the first afternoon of welcome rest for the tired infantrymen had passed, a small party of traders rode hurriedly into their camp and announced that the caravan had been attacked in the sand hills about six miles south of the river, and that one of the

[11] *Ibid.*, 46.
[12] Copy of letter reproduced in Young, *First Military Escort*, 181–82.

Soldiers on the Santa Fe Trail

proprietors, Samuel C. Lamme, had been killed. The frightened traders requested Riley and his troops to come to their aid, and, although it meant taking United States soldiers into Mexican territory, Riley did not delay. He led his command across the river and proceeded to the besieged caravan. Arriving at the train during the night and establishing a suitable guard, the soldiers witnessed the withdrawal of the Indians the following morning. The traders, fearing to continue without escort, begged Riley to accompany them onward. He complied, and escorted them for two days, to Drunken Creek (twenty-four miles from the scene of the attack), and then refused to go farther into foreign territory. After resting in camp for one day, the troops returned to the Arkansas and remained on the Mexican side for ten days before recrossing the river and going into camp opposite Chouteau's Island.

For the duration of their encampment, the soldiers moved camp when necessary for cleanliness or to find grass for the oxen or buffalo for food. They were almost constantly harassed by Indians until August 11, but the remaining two months of their stay on the Arkansas were passed practically without incident. Since they were infantry, Riley and the soldiers found it extremely frustrating not to be able to give chase to the hostile Indians. As Riley reported, following the attack upon their camp on August 3:

> Think what our feelings must have been to see them going off with our cattle and horses [the officers had horses], when if we had been mounted, we could have beaten them to pieces; but we were obliged to content ourselves with whipping them from our camp. We did not get any of the killed or wounded, but we saw the next day where they had dragged them off. They have said since that our fire from the big gun [six-pound cannon] killed five or six.[13]

---

[13] Riley's Report, 5. Riley recorded that the number of Indians attacking the camp was between three and four hundred. He estimated the Indians' losses at eight or ten killed and wounded, and later learned it was eight. Riley's Journal, 286, 293. It is interesting to note that eight years later the opposing force had increased considerably. In a letter to Senator Lewis F. Linn, August 28, 1837, Major Riley, recalling the battle, stated the number of Indians was eight hundred and their losses were forty killed and wounded. *American State Papers: Military Affairs*, VII, 958.

About the last Indian attack upon the encamped infantrymen, August 11, Cooke later complained:

> It was a humiliating condition to be surrounded by these rascally Indians, who, by means of their horses, could tantalize us with hopes of battle, and elude our efforts; who could annoy us by preventing all individual excursions for hunting, &c., and who could insult us with impunity. Much did we regret that we were not mounted too.[14]

Despite the limitations placed upon them because they were not mounted, the soldiers withstood the Indian attacks. The command lost only four men during the entire expedition. For defensive purposes they were effective and successful, but their experiences demonstrated the need for cavalry if they were ever to take the offense against the Indians. This lesson apparently had its effect, because the next escort was comprised of United States Mounted Rangers.

From August 11 to October 11 the soldiers were busy preparing the wagons and carts for the return trip, standing guard, and obtaining their meat rations from the abundant buffalo herds. In addition to supplying their current needs for food, they were able to garner thirty-two days' provisions of dried buffalo meat for the return march.

Major Riley had agreed, at the time of the traders' departure, to wait until October 10 for their return. When that day arrived and no caravan was in sight, he decided to remain in camp one more day. Early in the morning of October 11 the troops fired their cannon once and departed without the traders. They had not advanced far when they were overtaken by a party of riders from the caravan, who related that the train, accompanied by a command of Mexican soldiers, was only about one day's march behind them. Riley halted his command, went into camp, and sent Captain William N. Wickliffe and Lieutenant Francis J. Brooke back with a trader to escort the caravan to the camp. The traders and the Mexican troops arrived the following day.

It was learned from the traders that, after leaving Riley's force

[14] Cooke, *Scenes and Adventures*, 59.

Soldiers on the Santa Fe Trail

on July 14, they had been harassed by Indians for forty days as they continued toward Santa Fe. But no more traders were killed and no property was stolen. Finally, a large number of Mexican buffalo hunters had joined the caravan for its protection, and additional assistance was sent out from Taos. As the number traveling in the train increased, the Indians became less daring, allowing the traders to proceed to Taos and on to Santa Fe.

At Santa Fe, the traders' account of their difficulties plus the letter of request from Major Riley led an inspector general of the Mexican Army, Colonel José Antonio Vizcarra, to offer the services of a mounted escort for the return trip to the Arkansas. During their journey, the Mexican command lost three men during an Indian attack on the Cimarron River, but the traders suffered no losses.

On October 14 the Mexicans departed for Santa Fe, and Riley's command, with the caravan, started for Missouri. The return march was free from Indian attack, and the caravan broke up and the escort ceased at the Little Arkansas River. Marching quickly because of the approaching winter, the soldiers reached Fort Leavenworth on November 8. They were a tired and tattered bunch of men, but, as a result of their experiences, much wiser about Plains Indians and military needs for escort duty along the Santa Fe Trail.

Even though the 1829 escort was limited in its military operations against the Indians because it was not mounted, certain accomplishments indicate that the expedition was a success. It proved the efficiency of oxen on the plains. The trade caravan had experienced no Indian hostilities while under the charge of the soldiers. The command had adequately protected itself from Indian attacks while encamped on the Arkansas. A show of force at the Arkansas camp, while not completely restraining the Indians, finally taught them a healthy respect for American troops and artillery and caused them to leave the command unmolested for two months. The soldiers had subsisted upon buffalo meat and the small amount of provisions carried along. And it had been clearly demonstrated that mounted troops would be necessary to deal appropriately, especial-

Military Escorts, 1829-1845

ly offensively, with the hostile Indians who harassed the traders and travelers on the Trail. The expedition also demonstrated the need for securing co-operating Mexican escorts in conjunction with any such efforts in the future.[15]

The effects of the expedition were felt in Washington, where Senator Benton submitted Major Riley's report to the Senate in 1830 in support of legislation to provide further protection for the Santa Fe trade. The report may have been influential in securing passage of an act, in 1832, establishing the United States Mounted Rangers.[16] Regardless of the report's influence, or lack of it, along these lines, the next escort on the Trail, in 1833, was comprised of mounted soldiers.

After the successful escort venture of 1829, Secretary of War John H. Eaton immediately began planning for future protection of the Trail.[17] Commanding General of the Army Alexander Macomb also favored additional escorts, and he advocated converting eight companies of infantry into a mounted force to provide protection along the western frontier in general, as well as along the Santa Fe route.[18]

In addition to this support from top officials in the War Department and the army, the people of Missouri again memorialized Congress to authorize military protection for the Trail, but no responsive action was taken. There appeared to be some thought that sending infantry again would be inadequate; at any rate, no more protection was provided until the army had a mounted force.

[15] This fact, perhaps, was best recognized by Colonel Vizcarra, who stated in a letter to Major Riley, summarized as follows by Secretary of War John H. Eaton: "... experience has taught him that unless there be a perfect understanding between the United States and his government to protect their commerce, that it will not be safe for any merchant to undertake any kind of traffic; he therefore requests to urge with the Congress of the United States the importance of such an understanding, and engages to do his best, on his return to the capital of New Mexico, to do the same." *American State Papers: Military Affairs*, IV, 277. Despite the determined efforts of interested parties in both countries, no arrangements for co-operative protection were ever worked out. This problem is further discussed below.

[16] Otis E. Young, *The West of Philip St. George Cooke, 1809-1895*, 54.

[17] *American State Papers: Military Affairs*, IV, 154.

[18] Macomb to Eaton, January 4, 1830, *ibid.*, 219.

Soldiers on the Santa Fe Trail

Indian hostilities along the Trail probably helped to bring about the creation of a mounted force. Although no lives were lost during 1830, several men were killed along the route during 1831, including the famous fur trader and pathfinder, Jedediah Smith. In December of that year, Senator Benton introduced a bill to provide for a command of mounted volunteers to serve in the American West. Several reports pertaining to the fur trade and the trade with Mexico, submitted to the Senate early the following year, lent support to the bill.[19]

Lewis Cass, recently appointed secretary of war, referring to Indian hostilities along the Trail, stated that "the only remedy for this, is to restrain the depredation of these Indians by an exhibition of our strength, or by prompt chastisement."[20] This and similar recommendations, plus the fact that the Black Hawk War was in progress, led to the creation of a new militia unit, the United States Mounted Rangers, June 15, 1832.[21] This six-company battalion of volunteers, which was authorized for only one year, served as a significant link between a United States Army with no mounted troops and an army with a permanent branch of cavalry, beginning in 1833.[22]

The sixth and last company of the Rangers, commanded by Captain Matthew Duncan, was enlisted in October and November of 1832 and sent immediately to Fort Leavenworth. At about the same time the troops arrived at that post, the Indians again became active along the Trail. On January 1, 1833, twelve traders returning from Santa Fe to Missouri were attacked by a band of Kiowas on the Canadian River. The traders lost their string of pack mules, all supplies, two men, and most of the $10,000 to $12,000 in specie

---

[19] 22 Cong., 1 sess., *Sen. Doc. 90*.

[20] *Ibid.*, 4. Cass favored sending an escort, and apparently one company of troops was sent out in 1832. They started so late in the season, however, that they met the traders coming back from Santa Fe before they had advanced as far as the Arkansas River. Beers, *New Mexico Historical Review*, Vol. XII (1937), 123.

[21] Albert Gallatin Brackett, *History of the United States Cavalry*, 54.

[22] Otis E. Young, "The United States Mounted Ranger Battalion, 1832–1833," *Mississippi Valley Historical Review*, Vol. XLI (December, 1954), 453–55.

Military Escorts, 1829–1845

they carried. After being under siege for nearly thirty-two hours, the survivors managed to escape during the night. Five went in a northwesterly direction and finally arrived at a Creek Indian camp near the Arkansas River, where they were treated hospitably. The other five headed east; only two survived, and they did not reach a white settlement for forty-two days. By this time they were nearly starved.[23] This incident, which was reported in *Niles' Register* on March 23, 1833, probably helped secure the authorization for an escort for the 1833 caravan.

Secretary of War Cass decided to provide protection for the spring caravan, and since the infantry had suffered limitations in handling the Indians, Captain Duncan's company of Rangers, assisted by two officers, twenty-five privates, and one piece of field artillery from the Sixth Infantry, was selected for the escort. Captain Wickliffe, Sixth Infantry, who had served with the 1829 escort, was placed in command of the expedition.

Initially, Major Henry Dodge, commanding officer of the Mounted Rangers, had ordered Captain Duncan to proceed with the caravan to the Arkansas Crossing and remain there for its return in the autumn. However, General Henry Atkinson, commanding the Department of the West, after taking charge of provisioning the escort, changed the orders. Instead of requiring the troops to remain on the Arkansas, he instructed them to accompany the traders to the Mexican boundary and then return immediately to Fort Leavenworth. He also placed Captain Wickliffe in charge of the escort and sent the accompanying soldiers from the Sixth Infantry.[24]

Major Bennet Riley, who had led the 1829 escort and had since been advanced to the position of commander of Fort Leavenworth,

[23] Gregg, *Commerce of the Prairies*, 253–56.
[24] Henry Dodge, A Frontier Officer's Military Order Book, MS, Iowa State Historical Society Library, Iowa City, 29–30, cited in Young, *Mississippi Valley Historical Review*, Vol. XLI (1954), 462; General Orders, No. 1, Headquarters Department of the West, April 15, 1833, MS, Adjutant General's Office (Record Group No. 94), Army and Air Corps Branch, National Archives (hereafter cited as AGO, AACB, NA).

put the escort troops through two weeks of training. Then on May 22, 1833, he instructed Captain Wickliffe to take his unit to Round Grove and join the caravan. The total command was made up of 144 officers and men, five supply wagons, and the piece of field artillery and its accompanying ammunition wagon. The soldiers arrived at Round Grove on May 23, and found that the rendezvous was scheduled for Council Grove. They marched on immediately, but did not reach their destination until June 13 because rainy weather forced them to limit their daily marches. There they found the caravan, which consisted of 184 men, 103 vehicles, and commodities valued at approximately $100,000.[25]

The proprietors of the caravan were unable to agree upon a captain for the journey while at Council Grove, so, after a few days delay, they moved to Diamond Spring. Arriving there on June 20, the traders finally resolved their differences and selected Charles Bent as captain. From Diamond Spring to the Arkansas River, with the escort preceding the caravan, nothing of note occurred, and no Indians were met. The party reached the Great Bend of the Arkansas on July 2. Attempting to follow the Dry Route beyond Pawnee Fork, the soldiers wandered from the Trail and did not reach the river again until July 6. On July 10 they arrived at the Lower Crossing, where the traders decided to cross, and the following day the caravan proceeded toward Santa Fe while the soldiers began their return journey. Experiencing no difficulties, they arrived at Fort Leavenworth on August 4.

Since the 1833 escort had apparently prevented the Indians from harassing the caravan, plans were made to repeat protection of the Trail the following year.[26] General Henry Leavenworth, soon after his arrival at Fort Gibson, Cherokee Territory, in April, 1834, in-

[25] Riley to Wickliffe, May 18, 1833, and Wickliffe to Riley, August 4, 1833, Letters Received, MSS, *ibid*.

[26] The battalion of Mounted Rangers passed out of existence in 1833, but Secretary of War Cass requested the creation of a permanent cavalry force to replace it. Congress responded favorably, and on March 2, 1833, a bill was enacted which authorized the creation of a regiment of Dragoons as part of the regular service. Brackett, *History of the United States Cavalry*, 35.

structed the commanding officer of the newly organized Regiment of Dragoons, Colonel Henry Dodge, to furnish the 1834 caravan with an escort.

General Leavenworth sent Lieutenant John Henry K. Burgwin to Missouri to communicate with the traders, inquire whether or not they desired an escort, and find out when they planned to depart for New Mexico. Meanwhile, Colonel Dodge ordered Company A, Regiment of Dragoons, commanded by Captain Clifton Wharton, to proceed to the Cow Creek crossing of the Santa Fe Trail and to escort the caravan from that point to "the supposed boundary of the U. States."[27]

About fifty Dragoons departed Fort Gibson on May 13 and headed for Cow Creek. While en route they met Lieutenant Burgwin, who informed Wharton that the traders desired the escort and, if he did not suffer serious delays, he should intercept the caravan on the Trail. Wharton decided to take a more direct route to the Trail rather than continue toward Cow Creek, and his command arrived at the crossing of Cottonwood Creek on June 3.

The caravan, consisting of 160 men and 80 wagons, with goods valued at $150,000, had traveled under the captaincy of Josiah Gregg, arriving at the crossing on June 8. The traders and the soldiers proceeded the following day. Nothing out of the ordinary occurred between Cottonwood Creek and Walnut Creek, where the party arrived on June 17.

Unlike the mounted escort of the previous year, the Dragoons had some contact with Indians. At Walnut Creek Indians were sighted approaching the camp during the night. They were fired upon by the guards, and the command prepared for an attack, but none occurred. The next day a band of Kansas Indians visited the encampment. Captain Wharton talked with them, even though some of the traders insisted that the troops should fire upon the Indians and others demanded that the band not be allowed to come

---

[27] Captain Clifton Wharton's Report of the 1834 Escort, July 21, 1834, printed with notes in Perrine, *New Mexico Historical Review,* Vol. II (1927), 269-70 (hereafter cited as Wharton's Report).

Soldiers on the Santa Fe Trail

near the caravan. The Indians, who displayed a copy of the treaty made with them in 1825, asked Wharton to read it to them and pledged their continued observance of its stipulations. Although the Indians denied having approached the camp the previous night, Wharton was certain they were the same ones. The presence of the troops and their alert guards had frustrated what might have been an attempt to rob the caravan and had averted a possible attack. The presence of the escort was probably responsible, also, for the friendly visit and peaceful pledges of the following day.

The traders and soldiers continued their march on June 19, and no Indians were sighted until they approached the Cimarron Crossing of the Arkansas on the morning of June 26. There a band of approximately one hundred Comanches were encountered, who exhibited a friendly attitude. Hoping to hold council with the Comanches, Captain Wharton, Captain Gregg, another Dragoon officer, and an interpreter crossed the Arkansas to meet with five Indians who had motioned to them to cross over. The Indians invited the party to their encampment for a feast, but, before the conversation had proceeded very far, the crossing of a number of curious onlookers from the caravan alarmed the Indians. Finding that the Indians were uneasy and that their principal chief was absent at the time, Captain Wharton proposed that, later in the day, "five individuals of each party and only five, should meet on their side of the river with a view of having a friendly talk and a Smoke."[28]

The Indians consented to the proposed meeting, and Captain Wharton terminated the interview and returned to his camp. Although he had no authorization to hold council or make promises to any Indians while on the expedition, Wharton hoped to impress upon the Comanches the peaceful intentions of the government of the United States and its people, urge them to remain at peace with other tribes, and attempt to secure their promise to be friendly and peaceful toward travelers in the region. He also hoped to induce them to meet with Colonel Dodge, who at the same time was leading

[28] *Ibid.,* 274–75.

five hundred Dragoons toward the villages of the Pawnee Picts north of the Red River.[29]

The traders prevented Wharton from carrying out his plans. Many men with the caravan were displeased because the soldiers were friendly with the Indians, and they urged driving the Comanches away, with gunfire if necessary. Their confidence increased by the presence of the troops, a group of the traders became belligerent. Soon after Captain Wharton had returned to his tent, while a large number of Indians were still congregated across the river, some of the traders moved up a piece of field artillery and made preparations to fire upon the Indians. Informed of this action, Wharton went immediately to protest to Gregg. At the same time he was remonstrating against the intended action, one of the Dragoon officers went to the place where the cannon was being prepared for firing. The officer protested, warning the traders that an attack upon a small band of Indians might jeopardize their future safety along the route. In return, he was cursed and threatened with physical harm for "interfering." Fortunately, at this point Captain Gregg intervened, and the cannon was not fired.

This incident was only the beginning of Captain Wharton's disappointments. Gregg, who had been present when the proposed meeting with the Comanches had been set, selected four other traders to complete the agreed-upon number for the meeting, and crossed over to the Indians while Wharton was attending to other duties. Gregg informed the Comanches that the traders wanted to be friendly, but he also threatened that the soldiers would attack their camp if they did not move away. Concluding with this warning, the traders returned to their camp, and the Indians withdrew to a safe distance. Thus the traders destroyed any possibility for Wharton to carry out his intentions through the conversations he had proposed.

[29] *Ibid.*, 276–78; Beers, *New Mexico Historical Review*, Vol. XII (1937), 124–25. For an account of Colonel Dodge's expedition, see "The Journal of Hugh Evans, Covering the First and Second Campaigns of the United States Dragoon Regiment in 1834 and 1835" (ed. by Grant Foreman and Fred S. Perrine), *Chronicles of Oklahoma*, Vol. III (September, 1925), 175–215.

Soldiers on the Santa Fe Trail

That same day, June 26, Wharton informed Gregg by letter that at Cimarron Crossing they had reached what he considered to be the Mexican boundary, beyond which his orders prevented him from proceeding. However, when the caravan crossed the Arkansas the following morning, the escort, for what reason is not clear, accompanied it. Later that day Gregg replied to Wharton and requested the escort to continue "to the utmost limits of your discretion." The captain of Dragoons immediately replied that he would accompany the caravan to the Cimarron River, but could go no farther because of his limited provisions and because he did not wish to violate his orders. The reason for this unusual action cannot be determined from the available records.

Meanwhile, Gregg resigned as captain of the caravan and was succeeded by I. G. Smith.[30] Smith, respecting the Dragoons' orders and the problem of provisions, expressed hope that the escort would go as far as the upper Canadian River, where the traders usually met the Mexican escort and where the soldiers could obtain supplies. He informed Wharton that unless the troops could go that far, the traders would decline the offer to proceed to the Cimarron. This decided the arrangements—the escort would go no farther.

This series of exchanges pointed up a most serious problem regarding protection of the Santa Fe trade. Until Mexico could be persuaded to provide escorts as far as the Arkansas River, or the United States to send troops beyond the Arkansas to the upper Canadian River, for approximately 250 miles, through a region roamed by hostile Indians, caravans would be left unprotected. And, if the traders could travel in caravans large enough to insure their own protection through that region, there would be no need for escorts on the remainder of the Trail. Considering the Arkansas River the boundary, Mexico should have provided military assistance between that point and Santa Fe. But, except for the escorts of 1829 and 1843, no records have been located showing Mexican

---

[30] The reason for Gregg's resignation is not clear, although he stated in a communication to Wharton that he considered himself "unworthy" of the office. Wharton's Report, 304.

protection beyond the upper Canadian. Thus the problem was not solved until the Mexican War placed the entire route within United States territory.

Despite the apparent disagreement resulting from the controversy over extending the Dragoons' escort, the traders and soldiers parted amicably on June 28. The Dragoons crossed to the north side of the Arkansas and headed for Fort Gibson. Because their supply of flour and pork was extremely limited, the soldiers were placed on reduced rations. The command, having abandoned its wagon in order to make better time, pushed the weakened horses to the practicable limit and reached the fort on July 19, one day after the last of the flour was issued. During the return march the soldiers encountered bands of Pawnee, Kansas, and Little Osage Indians. Captain Wharton talked with each of these groups; all declared their peaceful intentions and professed their friendship.

Finding the Indians so peaceful on this expedition, Wharton concluded that an escort to the Arkansas crossing was hardly necessary, especially when there was no escort beyond. He pointed out that the traders became careless while they could depend on troops for protection, and this made it more difficult for them to exercise vigilance after losing the escort, when negligence could be disastrous. Thus, under the circumstances, the escort might do more harm than good. He recommended that some arrangement be worked out with Mexico to provide protection for the caravans from the Little Arkansas River to the New Mexican settlements.[31] No such arrangement was made, however, and no escort was again provided over the regular route of the Trail until 1843.

Although Indian hostilities occurred along the Trail from time to time following 1834, they were not the primary reason for the next effort at federal protection on that route.[32] Actually, the military expedition ordered in the spring of 1843 was sent primarily in re-

[31] *Ibid.*, 283–84.

[32] Although no escorts were provided the traders between 1834 and 1843, troops were sent into the region through which the Trail passed. These soldiers apparently provided indirect protection to Santa Fe traders. *American State Papers: Military Affairs*, V, 632.

sponse to activities by Texans which threatened the safety of the Santa Fe trade.

After declaring independence from Mexico in 1836, the Republic of Texas requested annexation by the United States. Refused by President Jackson, the Texans, under President Mirabeau B. Lamar (elected in 1838), sought recognition of the republic by the world's leading powers. It was hoped that after receiving such recognition, the Texans could force Mexico to acknowledge their independence. Failure to accomplish the desired result led the Lamar administration to attempt an expansion program, intended to extend the Texas boundary to the Pacific. Under this program, the first objective was New Mexico.

Realizing that military conquest would serve only to unite the New Mexicans against the Texans, Lamar sent out a trading caravan, accompanied by a few soldiers, with hopes of gaining control of the province. This group formed the ill-fated Texan–Santa Fe Expedition of 1841. New Mexican Governor Manuel Armijo was warned of the invasion, raised an army, and captured the Texans. The same year President Lamar was replaced by Sam Houston, who had declared his opposition to conquest and his support for annexation by the United States.

Mexico, outraged over the Texan–Santa Fe Expedition, began sending raiding parties into Texas, hoping ultimately to regain the lost province. Texas raised three small forces in retaliation. One, led by Alexander Somervell, crossed the Río Grande and was captured at Mier, Mexico. The second, under Charles A. Warfield, attempted a march on Santa Fe, but it was chased back by New Mexican troops after attacking the village of Mora. The third, met by Captain Cooke in the spring of 1843, was of concern to the Santa Fe traders.[33]

Texas claimed, but did not control, all lands east of the Río

---

[33] The account of Cooke's expedition is in his Journal of the Santa Fe Escort, May 27 to July 21, 1843, published in "A Journal of the Santa Fe Trail" (ed. by William E. Connelley), *Mississippi Valley Historical Review,* Vol. XII (June & September, 1925), 72–98, 227–49 (hereafter cited as Cooke's Journal).

Grande that previously had belonged to Mexico, and maintained that Santa Fe traders were violating her territory without paying customs. Hoping for revenge against the Mexicans for mistreatment of prisoners taken during the Texan–Santa Fe Expedition and later, and hoping as well to confiscate goods being "illegally" transported over Texas soil, the third force mentioned above was formed. It was led by Jacob Snively, former soldier and former acting secretary of war of the Republic of Texas, who had been authorized by President Houston, on February 16, 1843:

> ... to organize and fit out an expedition for the purpose of intercepting and capturing the property of the Mexican traders who may pass through the territory of the republic to and from Santa Fe.[34]

Before the Snively Expedition was outfitted, an incident occurred which indicated to the United States Army that the Texas–Mexican conflict would affect the Santa Fe trade. Early in 1843, Antonio José Chávez, a Mexican trader en route from Santa Fe to Missouri, was robbed and murdered in United States territory by a Missouri-based party of fifteen Texas partisans led by John McDaniel. Colonel Stephen Watts Kearny sent out an expedition to apprehend the raiders. Ten of the party were later captured. McDaniel and his brother David were hanged at St. Louis, and the others were fined and imprisoned.[35] In anticipation of further interference by Texans, Kearny sent Captain Nathan Boone, youngest son of Daniel Boone, and three companies of Dragoons from Fort Gibson to patrol the region south of the Arkansas; this effort was also intended to give some protection to the Santa Fe traders.[36]

The latter purpose arose from two other developments. Warfield's attempted invasion of Santa Fe and the murder of Chávez, plus rumors of another Texan expedition, had caused alarm among traders in New Mexico and Missouri. Fearing further disturbances,

[34] Snively's instructions were copied by Captain Cooke and appear in *ibid.*, 228–29.
[35] Gregg, *Commerce of the Prairies*, 337–38; Henry Inman, *The Old Santa Fe Trail*, 97–100; Young, *The West of Philip St. George Cooke*, 109–10.
[36] "Captain Nathan Boone's Journal" (ed. by W. Julian Fessler), *Chronicles of Oklahoma*, Vol. VII (March, 1929), 58–105.

Soldiers on the Santa Fe Trail

several American traders asked the War Department, on March 15, 1843, to furnish an escort from Missouri to Santa Fe. Two days later the Mexican minister at Washington, General Juan Almonte, requested a military escort for the Mexican merchants then in Missouri for their return trip to New Mexico. Consequently, on March 28 the War Department instructed Colonel Kearny to send an escort with the traders of both nations to the limit of United States territory.[37] At the same time, in New Mexico, Governor Armijo, one of the largest proprietors engaged in the Santa Fe trade, was organizing an escort to meet the traders at the Arkansas River.[38]

For the United States escort, Colonel Kearny selected Captain Cooke, who had been a lieutenant with Riley's expedition in 1829, to lead four companies of the First Dragoons. The total command numbered 190 men and had eleven wagons of baggage and two brass mountain howitzers.[39]

The escort and caravan, which was divided in ownership almost equally between Mexican and American proprietors, left Council Grove on June 6. The following day the soldiers proceeded ahead of the slow-moving traders, but, after encountering a party of approximately one hundred Kansas Indians on June 10, Captain Benjamin D. Moore and his company were sent back to accompany the caravan. Arriving at Walnut Creek on June 13, Captain Cooke made contact with Captain Boone's command, which was camped on the south side of the Arkansas. The two forces remained encamped on opposite sides of the river for several days while waiting for the traders. During this period, it rained almost every day, sending the river and creeks out of their banks and delaying the arrival of the caravan until June 23, one day after Boone's command had moved south.

Meanwhile, Charles Bent and his partner, Céran St. Vrain, arrived from Bent's Fort with a small wagon train, en route to Mis-

[37] 28 Cong., 2 sess., *Sen. Doc. 1,* p. 101.

[38] William Campbell Binkley, "The Last Stage of Texan Military Operations against Mexico, 1843," *Southwestern Historical Quarterly,* Vol. XXII (January, 1919), 268.

[39] Cooke's Journal, 73-74, 78. The four companies were A, C, F, and K.

Military Escorts, 1829-1845

souri. They encamped on Walnut Creek, too, and St. Vrain returned upriver with five wagons to pick up furs which they had attempted unsuccessfully to float down on boats. Bent reported that no Mexican force had reached the Arkansas as he descended, but he had information that Governor Armijo and six hundred men had planned to leave Santa Fe on May 3.

St. Vrain was back at Walnut Creek on June 22 and reported having made contact with the Texas Snively Expedition. After departing from Georgetown, Texas, on April 25, the well-armed Texans had proceeded to a point on the Arkansas sixty miles east of the Cimarron Crossing, where they were joined by Warfield and a remnant of his party who had been defeated following the attack on Mora.[40] St. Vrain met the Texans in this vicinity. He talked with Snively, who informed him that "he intended to remain in the country; and would most assuredly capture the Mexicans and their wagons, wherever they went, whenever they separated from their escort." St. Vrain also reported that the Texans had met an advance guard of the Mexican forces and had defeated them, and that the main body of Armijo's troops had therefore retreated back to New Mexico.[41]

It was later confirmed that on June 20 the Texans had defeated a force of about one hundred Mexican troops sent from Armijo's camp at Cold Spring on the Cimarron River and had killed eighteen and wounded eighteen, with no losses for the Texans. When the survivors reported to Armijo, he took his force of about four hundred men and retreated to Santa Fe. Following that battle, friction developed within Snively's command, and about seventy-five of the party seceded and declared they were returning to Texas. Actually, they moved to another point on the Arkansas to wait for the cara-

---

[40] Jacob Snively's Report to George W. Hill, July 9, 1843, 28 Cong., 2 sess., *Sen. Doc. 1*, p. 99 (hereafter cited as Snively's Report); Binkley, *Southwestern Historical Quarterly*, Vol. XXII (1919), 267-68. For the route followed by the Snively Expedition, see H. Bailey Carroll, "Steward A. Miller and the Snively Expedition of 1843," *Southwestern Historical Quarterly*, Vol. LIV (January, 1951), 261-86.

[41] Cooke's Journal, 90-91.

van. The remainder of Snively's force moved slowly westward along the south bank of the Arkansas.

On June 25 the escort and caravan crossed Walnut Creek and headed toward Cimarron Crossing. Cooke had learned as he was leaving that Bent's party had encountered some of the Texans while coming down the Arkansas, and the party had failed to report that three Texan spies had accompanied the wagon train until within sight of the Dragoons' camp. Cooke was undoubtedly furious, but there was nothing for him to do but proceed and remain constantly alert for the Texan raiders. The soldiers took the Dry Route beyond Pawnee Fork, and on June 29 they camped near the western end of that section of the Trail.

The following morning, as the Dragoons approached the Arkansas, they saw a party of Texans on the north side of the river. Cooke sent a patrol in pursuit, which reported back in about twenty minutes that a large force was encamped on the south side of the river. Advancing his squadron at a trot, Cooke proceeded to the Arkansas, and the Texans raised a white flag. Lieutenant John Love and a trumpeter were sent over to the camp with instructions to meet the commander and determine who the men were and why they were there. Upon reaching the Texans, Lieutenant Love met Snively and, as Cooke had directed, offered him and another officer safe conduct across the river and back. Snively accepted.

In the meantime, Cooke called his officers together to discuss the location of the Texans, and a majority concluded that the Texan camp was in United States territory.[42] That decision made, Cooke inquired if it were not his duty to disarm the force. A majority answered in the affirmative, but some of the men wanted to hear from the Texans before making a final decision. At this point Love returned with Snively, who declared that "he commanded a Texan volunteer force of 107 men; and believed them to

[42] The exact location of the 100th meridian was not known to the soldiers. The Texans were camped fifteen miles below the Caches, Cooke's Journal, 236, which placed them ten miles east of 100 degrees west longitude as later determined, and therefore within United States territory.

be in Texas." Cooke informed him that he and his officers believed that the Texans were camped within United States territory, and he inquired if Snively had a commission. Snively then produced a copy of his commission, cited above, which Cooke read aloud to his officers.

After further questioning of Snively, Cooke asked Lieutenant Daniel Henry Rucker to "entertain" the Texan while he conferred with the other officers. He again posed the question of disarming the Texan force, and the officers voted three to two against such action. Not considering himself bound by the junior officers' advice, Cooke informed Snively that his party was within the United States, that he could not respect the commission authorizing the party to attack the wagon train which his command had been ordered to protect, and demanded that the Texans lay down their arms. He offered the Texans the choice of going to the United States or returning to Texas. Snively protested, but submitted when Cooke threatened to fire upon the Texans' camp with his howitzers and attack them with his troops.

The Dragoons then crossed the river and assumed battle formation near the Texans' camp. Snively's force was ordered to march out of camp and have each man deposit his arms with Captain Burdett A. Terrett's Company A. This accomplished, a detail of soldiers was sent into the camp, where more guns were found. Having completely disarmed the Texans, Cooke allowed ten of them to retrieve their guns for hunting purposes and offered Snively a couple of pistols. In this condition, some of the force requested an escort and protection to Missouri, and this was granted. Others requested to be made prisoners of war, but Cooke wisely declined. The Dragoons then recrossed the river, and Cooke informed the caravan what had happened and advised them that they could proceed safely.

The following day Cooke divided his command and provided an escort, composed of Captain Terrett and sixty Dragoons, for about fifty of the disarmed Texans who chose to go to Missouri. The remainder of the Texans, with five guns among them, preferred returning directly to Texas. They, too, requested an escort, but Cooke refused, telling them to leave the United States territory as soon as possible. As it developed, the men under Snively joined the party that had seceded a few days before and planned to waylay the caravan after it had passed out of Cooke's jurisdiction. However, internal friction delayed them until they were unable to overtake the traders, and they finally dispersed and returned to Texas. Thus the third force of Texans raised to retaliate against Mexico failed. Still, the outlook for Texas was not altogether dark; within two years the republic would be annexed to the United States.

Captain Cooke bore the ill-will of the Texans for the remainder of his life. The Texas government sent protests to the Secretary of State and a court of inquiry was called to investigate Cooke's actions. He was upheld by the court, and high military officials commended his action. But, when sent to serve in Texas later, Cooke found the people so hostile that he was forced to request reassignment outside the state.[43]

With the Texas threat removed, the major part of Cooke's assignment was accomplished. Nevertheless, he escorted the traders as far as Cimarron Crossing. The caravan crossed the Arkansas on July 4. The next day they proceeded toward Santa Fe and the Dragoons started their return march to Fort Leavenworth. They overtook Captain Terrett and the Texans four days later, and that same day the Texans requested a passport through Indian Territory to Texas. Cooke complied, gave them 420 pounds of flour and 25 pounds of coffee, and allowed them 6 guns. At Ash Creek the Texans left the Trail and supposedly headed for Texas.

However, the Dragoons encountered some of them near Cottonwood Creek five days later. While most of the Texans had gone to Missouri, those at Cottonwood Creek evidently had plans to waylay a small wagon train, owned by an Englishman, proceeding west-

---

[43] 28 Cong., 2 sess., *Sen. Doc. 1,* pp. 96–112; Otis E. Young, "Dragoons on the Santa Fe Trail in the Autumn of 1843," *Chronicles of Oklahoma,* Vol. XXXII (Spring, 1954), 44, 45n.; Beers, *New Mexico Historical Review,* Vol. XII (1937), 129–30.

Military Escorts, 1829-1845

ward without protection. Cooke sent a detachment to the Texans' camp and took all their weapons, and when they again requested a passport to Texas, Cooke refused. The small train proceeded unmolested. Cooke continued eastward, meeting several small trains headed for Santa Fe, and arrived at Fort Leavenworth on July 21.

This was the only escort that was required to protect the Trail from non-Indian hostilities. While Cooke's treatment of the Texans might be termed rash and even inhumane, it was clearly effective. Moreover, no Mexican traders were robbed or killed, and the Texans were disarmed without bloodshed. Also, no Indians had dared molest the traders while they were accompanied by the soldiers. The caravan they had escorted reached Santa Fe without difficulty, and the removal of the Texan threat left the Trail open for other traders, whom the soldiers met while returning, to proceed in safety. That Cooke's superior officers were pleased with his operations is evidenced by their selecting him to command a second escort along the Santa Fe Trail the same year, before the court of inquiry to investigate the handling of the Texans had convened.[44]

Anticipating that additional troubles along the Trail might be caused by Texan attempts to disrupt the trade in retaliation for the treatment of the Snively Expedition, Edmund P. Gaines, commanding general of the Department of the West, ordered a second escort for late 1843. Captain Cooke was placed in command of six companies of Dragoons for this duty. In order to give Cooke freedom to operate effectively in the event of unforeseen developments, he was authorized to prepare to spend the winter on the Arkansas River, at Bent's Fort, or in Santa Fe, should it become necessary. It was hoped, however, that Mexico would send an escort to meet the traders at the crossing of the Arkansas.

Cooke and three companies of Dragoons left Fort Leavenworth on August 24, and one week later they met Company A, from Fort

---

[44] The official account of the second 1843 escort is in Captain Cooke's Report of the Santa Fe Escort, August 24 to October 25, 1843, printed in Connelley (ed.), *Mississippi Valley Historical Review*, Vol. XII (1925), 249-55 (hereafter cited as Cooke's Report).

Scott, and the caravan at Council Grove. The train of 140 wagons was entirely owned by Mexican proprietors. Autumn rains delayed the caravan, but Cooke's force went ahead and was joined, on September 10, at the Little Arkansas River by two companies from Fort Gibson. This detachment, fifty-four Dragoons under command of Captain Enoch Steen, was low on provisions, many of the soldiers were sick, and two-thirds of their horses were unfit for service. Cooke selected twenty-five men from the detachment, including two officers, to proceed with his command. After giving them provisions from his supplies, he sent the remainder, which he called the "'Falstaff Company," back to their barracks at Fort Gibson.[45]

A few days later the Dragoons met the American-owned portion of the spring caravan returning from New Mexico. This was the first assurance Cooke had of their reaching Santa Fe safely. He learned that the Texan freebooters had made efforts to resume their "offensive enterprise," but, unsuccessful, had disbanded. This was pleasant news to Cooke, for he did not relish another incident with the Texans. The traders had not heard of any intended Mexican escort coming to meet the autumn caravan, and Cooke, disappointed at this report, resigned himself to marching his force on to Santa Fe.

Cold rains continued to plague the traders; many became sick and several died. The muddy road slowed the progress of the wagons so that they traveled only 126 miles in three weeks. There was a severe frost on September 25, and the command was still twenty-five miles from the Cimarron Crossing on October 1, with the caravan strung out approximately fifteen miles to its rear. Cooke now became concerned that the slow-moving traders might force him to go into camp for the winter on the Arkansas.

Having no desire to spend the winter on the plains or in Santa Fe, Cooke met with the proprietors of the caravan to determine whether or not they desired escort beyond the Arkansas. Although he assured them that the Texans had dispersed, the traders de-

[45] Cooke, *Scenes and Adventures,* 231–51.

manded the escort for 150 miles beyond the Cimarron Crossing and expressed hope that Cooke would go all the way to Santa Fe. Since Cooke's orders instructed him to proceed as far as necessary, he sent a request to Fort Leavenworth for sufficient supplies to provide for his command during the winter.

The problem was resolved on October 3 when Cooke, making camp nine miles below the Cimarron Crossing, was pleasantly surprised to learn that a Mexican escort had arrived at the crossing. The Mexican force had departed from Santa Fe immediately after orders had arrived from Santa Anna in Mexico City. The following morning, leaving their baggage under guard in camp, the remainder of the Dragoons marched to the crossing with the caravan. As they approached, the Mexican troops mounted their horses, but were dismissed when the Dagoons halted on the opposite river bank.

Cooke, recalling the pleasant meeting of several days' duration with the Mexican troops in 1829, sent his adjutant across to invite the Mexican officers to his camp. The invitation was declined, and the Mexican commander informed Cooke that "he had received positive orders not to cross the river, which he would disobey under no circumstances."[46] With some reflection on the past events and the answer he here received, Captain Cooke deduced the following:

> There can be no doubt that the Mexican minister [to the United States], seeing General G.'s [Gaines's] published letter [in *Niles' Weekly Register*, Vol. LXIV (August 19, 1843)], announcing our return and intention, for "free trade" sake, to visit Santa Fe, hastened to inform his government; and that President Santa Anna sent the express with orders to despatch an escort "within the hour" after its arrival in Santa Fe. They were just in time![47]

The Dragoons remained at the crossing until the caravan was safely over and, after firing the howitzer battery in salute, returned to their camp. Captain Cooke, relieved that he could now return to the Missouri River, sent a message to Fort Leavenworth that he was coming in and asked that a supply of corn be sent to him on

[46] Cooke's Report, 252.
[47] Cooke, *Scenes and Adventures*, 272.

Soldiers on the Santa Fe Trail

the Trail. He also sent notice to Bent and St. Vrain that he would not need the provisions which they had contracted to supply. Setting out for their barracks on October 5, the soldiers suffered from the cold and the animals grew weaker from want of forage until the corn sent from Fort Leavenworth reached the command east of Council Grove. As they marched along the Arkansas, the troops occasionally saw Indians, but none came near them. Detachments of three companies left the Trail for Forts Scott and Gibson on October 24, and the other three companies arrived at Fort Leavenworth the following day.

Captain Cooke, having commanded two successful escorts on the Santa Fe Trail during the same year, was ready to leave the Trail for good. Yet Colonel Kearny had other plans for this conscientious officer, who had earned the respect of the Mexicans by disarming the Snively Expedition. Cooke not only proved to be a valuable asset to Kearny during the Mexican War, but also, in the meantime, accompanied Kearny's 1845 South Pass Expedition, which returned over the Santa Fe Trail.

The last American troops to travel the Santa Fe Trail before the Mexican War consisted of five companies of the First Dragoons, under command of Colonel Kearny, during the period from July 29 to August 24, 1845, at the conclusion of the South Pass Expedition. The ostensible purpose of this expedition was to provide protection for emigrants on the Oregon Trail and to reconnoiter the route as far as South Pass in the Rocky Mountain chain. In addition, Kearny was ordered to observe the temper of the Indians in the country through which he passed and to return along the Santa Fe Trail and provide protection for caravans returning from Santa Fe.[48]

There may have been other motives behind the South Pass Expedition. The United States–British dispute over the Oregon Territory was at a high point, and it has been speculated that the War Department may have sent the Dragoons toward the Pacific Northwest in preparation for a possible armed conflict:

[48] Young, *The West of Philip St. George Cooke,* 153.

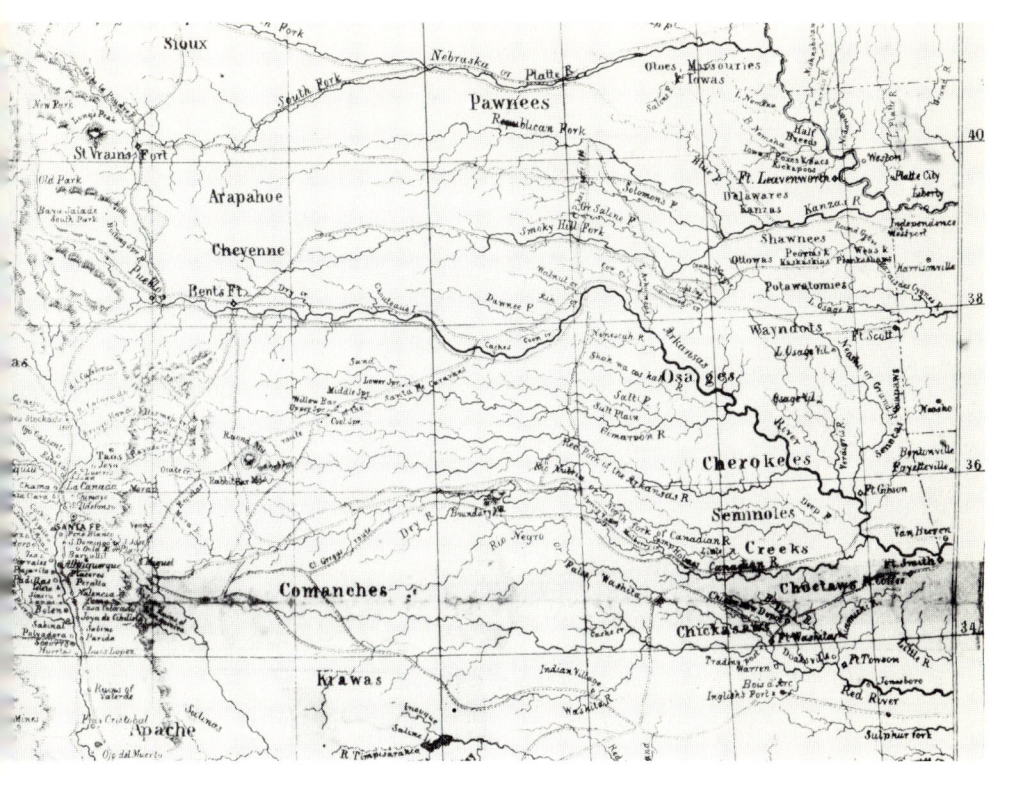

Courtesy Kansas State Historical Society

Map of the Santa Fe Trail and surrounding region, 1847.

Courtesy Kansas State Historical Society

Fort Zarah, 1864.

Courtesy Kansas State Historical Society

Fort Zarah (New Post), 1867–69, painted by Henry Worrall.

Courtesy Kansas State Historical Society

Fort Larned. Sketch published in *Harper's Weekly*, June 8, 1867.

Courtesy Kansas State Historical Society

Company C, Third U.S. Infantry, photographed in front of barracks at Fort Larned, 1867.

Courtesy Kansas State Historical Society

Sod officers' quarters at Fort Dodge, 1868. Sketch published in *Harper's Magazine,* June, 1869.

Courtesy Kansas State Historical Society

Officers' quarters at Fort Dodge in 1879.

Courtesy Kansas State Historical Society

Philip St. George Cooke.

Courtesy Museum of New Mexico

Manuel Armijo.

From Josiah Gregg, Commerce of the Prairies

March of The Caravan.

If located near the center of disturbance, the regiment could either occupy Oregon or else, should the British fight, keep the war going until a proper army was formed and marched overland to the Columbia River Valley. To Department strategists, this posed an ideal solution to the factor of British seapower and the speed with which it could move troops into the disputed region.[49]

Furthermore, Texas had but recently been annexed by the United States. The Dragoons may have been ordered to return along the Santa Fe Trail in case of war with Mexico over annexation, or, if Mexico was contemplating military reprisal, in the belief that such a show of force along her northern border might have a preventive effect. Many troops had already been ordered into Texas, and, in case of war, it would be helpful to have troops on the Santa Fe Trail. If they served no other purpose, they could protect Americans leaving New Mexico. Kearny's biographer declared that the United States government "had deliberately planned this display of force for its effect on Governor Armijo in Santa Fe and the authorities in Mexico City."[50]

Whatever the motives may have been, Kearny was ordered to undertake the expedition in May of 1845. The total command consisted of 280 men, described by Kearny as "well mounted and equipped for any service; each dragoon having his proper arms—a sabre, carbine, and pistol."[51] Departing from Fort Leavenworth on May 18, the Dragoons escorted travelers along the Oregon Trail to South Pass, returned to Fort Laramie, and followed a route along the base of the Rocky Mountains to the Arkansas River, arriving at Bent's Fort on July 29.[52]

Leaving Bent's Fort the next morning, the command moved rapidly along the Santa Fe Trail. At Big Timbers they encountered

---

[49] *Ibid.*, 152.

[50] Dwight L. Clarke, *Stephen Watts Kearny: Soldier of the West*, 97. Kearny implied that such motives existed behind his expedition, although he did not state it directly, in his "Report of a Summer Campaign to the Rocky Mountains," 29 Cong., 1 sess., *Sen. Doc. 1*, pp. 210–13.

[51] *Ibid.*, 210.

[52] *Ibid.*, 210–12; Cooke, *Scenes and Adventures*, 282–417.

Soldiers on the Santa Fe Trail

a large party of Apaches and Kiowas, who had been on an expedition against the Pawnees. Warning them not to disturb travelers using the Trail, as he had been instructed, Kearny continued down the Arkansas River. Cooke recognized the place where he had disarmed the Snively Expedition and had Lieutenant W. B. Franklin of the Topographical Engineers determine the longitude. The place was found, to Cooke's delight, to be within United States territory.

Although Kearny had been ordered to provide protection for returning caravans, he did not find any on the Trail. After meeting several traders going to Santa Fe who reported experiencing no difficulties, he decided that no escort was necessary. Kearny continued without waiting for returning caravans, which might not have come for several weeks. While the Dragoons provided no direct escort, their presence on the Trail probably had some effect upon the Indians of the region, thus giving a certain degree of indirect protection to the traders. The force arrived back at Fort Leavenworth on August 24, after traveling 2,200 miles in ninety-nine days.

This expedition closed the pre–Mexican War military history of the Santa Fe Trail. With the outbreak of the Mexican War, the soldiers who served along the Trail were assigned an additional task. Besides protecting the route, they had to fight a war of conquest and occupation, and, in so doing, they helped to secure for the United States the American Southwest.

3

Effects of the Mexican War, 1846-1848

THE SANTA FE TRAIL served as an essential military road during the Mexican War. The Santa Fe traders had helped to prepare the way for the conquest of New Mexico, and the soldiers who followed the route occupied that territory and marched on into California and Chihuahua. Thus the Trail helped to make possible the acquisition of the American Southwest. As a route of supply to the soldiers operating in New Mexico and beyond, the Trail required increased protection from Indian hostilities during the war.

Since becoming president, James K. Polk had hoped to acquire New Mexico and California by peaceful methods, and the Mexican War presented an opportunity to accomplish by conquest what diplomacy had failed to obtain.[1] When war was officially declared, the War Department immediately began to make preparations to send a volunteer force over the Trail for the purpose of protecting the Santa Fe traders and occupying Santa Fe. These troops, known as the Army of the West, were to prove of importance to the military victory and of value to the territorial outcome of the war.[2]

Preparation for raising this Army began on May 13, 1846, when Adjutant General Roger Jones informed Colonel Kearny, commander at Fort Leavenworth, that fifteen hundred mounted volunteers were being organized to join the companies of First Dragoons stationed at that post for a march to Santa Fe. He also indicated

[1] *Polk: The Diary of a President, 1845–1849* (ed. by Allan Nevins), 19, 66, 90–93 106 (hereafter cited as Polk's *Diary*).
[2] A thorough account of the Army of the West is contained in Ralph P. Bieber's introduction to George R. Gibson, *Journal of a Soldier under Kearny and Doniphan* (Vol. III of *The Southwest Historical Series,* ed. by Ralph P. Bieber), 17–107.

Soldiers on the Santa Fe Trail

that the command of this expedition probably would be assigned to Kearny.[3] At the same time Secretary of War William L. Marcy instructed Missouri Governor John C. Edwards to raise a regiment of mounted volunteers and two companies of volunteer artillery, and to dispatch them to Fort Leavenworth to form an expedition to New Mexico. The governor was told that the commanding officer of the invasion force would have the authority to increase or change the composition of the Missouri volunteers, and they were ordered to follow the commander's requests. Edwards was urged to raise this force immediately, in order that the troops could reach Santa Fe before Mexico could send a large army there.[4]

Colonel Kearny was placed in command of the Army of the West on May 14. He was instructed to send a large supply of provisions to Bent's Fort ahead of the soldiers and to procure items for gifts to the Indians which he might encounter on the Trail.[5] On May 31, General Winfield Scott instructed Kearny to add "as many of the valuable men at and about Bent's Fort to that force as practicable, and as may be needed."[6]

General Scott also intimated to Kearny that the mission of the Army of the West probably would be expanded considerably beyond the original instructions, and the Secretary of War spelled this out on June 3. Marcy informed Kearny that the governor of Missouri had been instructed to raise an additional thousand mounted volunteers and President Polk had directed that Kearny, as soon as his force was in control of New Mexico, was to leave

---

[3] Jones to Kearny, May 13, 1846, Letters Sent, MSS, AGO, AACB, NA.

[4] Marcy to Edwards, May 13, 1846, Secretary of War, Letters Sent, MSS, *ibid*. Governor Edwards was out of the state at the time, but, in anticipation of war with Mexico, he had instructed the adjutant general of Missouri, G. A. Parsons, to fill any federal requisitions for troops that might be made. Edwards arrived in Washington the day after war was declared, and, after a conference with President Polk, he sent an order to Parsons instructing him to supply the volunteers. Parsons had already taken steps to raise the force by the time Edwards' letter arrived on May 24. Missouri House *Journal*, 14 General Assembly, 1 sess., appendix, 182.

[5] Jones to Kearny, May 14, 1846, Letters Sent, MSS, AGO, AACB, NA.

[6] Scott to Kearny, May 31, 1846, 30 Cong., 1 sess., *House Exec. Doc. 60*, p. 241. William Bent and a party of spies were added to the force at Bent's Fort.

a portion of his command at Santa Fe to hold that province, and proceed with the remainder to take possession of Upper California. Marcy stated that a large number of Mormons were on their way to California, and he urged Kearny to maintain friendly relations with them, prevent them from opposing the United States, and secure, if possible, their cooperation in occupying the Mexican provinces. The Mormons, recently driven from their community at Nauvoo, Illinois, were gathered at Council Bluffs, Iowa, preparing to move westward. Kearny was authorized to enlist Mormons and other American emigrants who wished to volunteer for service in the Army of the West, but he was cautioned not to let the number of Mormons exceed one third of his total command.[7]

In the same letter, Marcy instructed Kearny regarding the policies he was to pursue in setting up civil governments in New Mexico and California if the occupation efforts were successful. Kearny had already been directed to assure the Mexicans that their religious institutions would be respected and protected.

When war was declared, there was concern in Washington for the safety of Santa Fe traders en route to New Mexico, as well as for the safety of American citizens already in northern Mexico. Even earlier, Manuel Alvarez, United States consul at Santa Fe, had informed Secretary of State James Buchanan that Americans and their property were threatened. He explained that if news of annexation were to reach Santa Fe before a United States force arrived to protect them, their personal property would be "in very iminent [*sic*] danger."[8]

The War Department evidently had access to this information, because on May 13 Marcy ordered George Thomas Howard, who had accompanied the Texan–Santa Fe Expedition in 1841, to pursue the caravan and warn the traders that war had been declared and the situation in New Mexico might be unfavorable. He was

[7] Marcy to Kearny, June 3, 1846, *ibid.*, 153–55; Polk's *Diary,* 105–109.
[8] Alvarez to Buchanan, February 9, 1846, Consular Reports, Santa Fe, MSS, State Department (Record Group No. 59), Diplomatic, Legal and Fiscal Branch, National Archives.

to persuade the traders to wait until the Army of the West could accompany them to Santa Fe. Howard also was charged with warning the American citizens in New Mexico of the outbreak of hostilities, in order that they might take steps to protect their lives and property.[9]

Howard failed to overtake the traders, who had learned of the outbreak of war and had hurried to Santa Fe, making forced marches, in order to get war prices for their commodities, apparently with no concern for the safety of their property or themselves.[10] Sending some of his party on to Santa Fe and Taos, Howard stayed a safe distance away from the New Mexican settlements. After several narrow escapes from being captured as spies, the men reported to Howard late in June that news of the war had reached Santa Fe, but that the traders and American citizens residing there seemingly were in no danger.[11]

While the War Department was making thorough preparations to assure the conquest of New Mexico and California, Colonel Kearny, an important mission before him, was arranging for the march that would affect much of the present American Southwest. On May 26, he received the letters informing him of the declaration of war, the plan to occupy New Mexico, and his assignment as commander of the expedition. He immediately ordered Captain Benjamin D. Moore, who was at Table Creek on the Missouri River, and Captain William Eustis, stationed at Fort Scott, to proceed to Fort Leavenworth with the major portions of their two companies of Dragoons. With detachments from these two com-

[9] Marcy to Howard, May 13, 1846, Secretary of War, Letters Sent, MSS, AGO, AACB, NA.

[10] The traders, after learning that war existed, made marches of forty-five miles per day in order to reach Santa Fe at the earliest possible date. *The St. Louis Weekly Reveille,* July 6, 1846. James J. Webb, a trader with the caravan, explained: "We thought we would be so far in the interior that there would be no danger of trouble, and as the ports would be blockaded there would be a good demand for our goods and at war prices. So we traveled as expeditiously as we could, with good weather and roads and high hopes of profit to encourage us." Webb, *Adventures in the Santa Fe Trade,* 179–80.

[11] Gibson, *Soldier under Kearny and Doniphan,* 28–29.

Effects of the Mexican War, 1846-1848

panies, plus the three companies stationed at Fort Leavenworth, Kearny was hopeful of having approximately 230 Dragoons for the expedition.[12]

The following day Kearny sent his adjutant, Lieutenant Henry S. Turner, to Jefferson City to meet with the lieutenant governor of Missouri, James Young, and inquire when he could expect the volunteers at Fort Leavenworth. Under the discretionary powers granted him by the War Department, Kearny requested that the State of Missouri raise two companies of volunteer infantry in addition to the forces already requisitioned by Marcy. From Jefferson City, Turner was to proceed to St. Louis and meet with the department quartermaster and commissary officers to obtain the necessary supplies for the volunteers.

A few days later Kearny became concerned that two of his best companies of First Dragoons, led by two of his most capable and conscientious captains (Edwin V. Sumner and Philip St. George Cooke), were not with his command. These two companies (B and K) were stationed at Forts Atkinson and Crawford, respectively. Kearny sent an urgent plea to General George M. Brooke, commanding the Department of the West, requesting that these companies be assigned to his expedition. Although they had been ordered to serve with Zachary Taylor's command, General Brooke obtained permission from the War Department and granted Kearny's request.[13]

In anticipation of Indian difficulties, Kearny appointed Antoine Robidoux, who had spent more than twenty years among the plains and mountain tribes, to serve as interpreter for the expedition. Also, the colonel endeavored to obtain for the campaign

[12] Kearny to Jones, May 28, 1846, Letters Received, MSS, AGO, AACB, NA. On May 31 Kearny countermanded his orders to Captain Eustis and his Company A, and directed this company to proceed to Fort Gibson to be held in readiness for service in Texas. Kearny to Eustis, Kearny to Jones, and Kearny to Brooke, May 31, 1846, Kearny Letter Book, MS, Missouri Historical Society, St. Louis (hereafter cited as KLB).

[13] Kearny to Brooke, May 31, 1846, *ibid.;* Jones to Brooke, June 16, 1846, and Jones to Cooke, June 16, 1846, Letters Sent, MSS, AGO, AACB, NA; Philip St. George Cooke, *Conquest of New Mexico and California*, 3.

the services of about fifty Shawnee and Delaware Indians as a special squadron of six-month volunteers, but no such force was raised.

Kearny, making every effort to assure that his force would be adequately equipped and supplied, made several requisitions upon the federal arsenals at St. Louis and Liberty, Missouri, for muskets, bayonets, carbines and other rifles, pistols, sabers, howitzers, and ammunition. He advertised in the Missouri newspapers for horses, mules, oxen, and wagons to transport the baggage and supplies to New Mexico.

One of Kearny's greatest tasks lay in the quartermaster and commissary departments, for there were many problems involved in obtaining and transporting the supplies required by several thousand troops operating hundreds of miles from their base. As quickly as possible Kearny purchased large quantities of food, hundreds of wagons, and thousands of draft animals in western Missouri. In addition, he hired wagonmasters and teamsters to drive the supply trains over the Trail.

Early in June he began sending small provision trains, consisting of twenty-five to thirty wagons, toward Bent's Fort, and caravans departed from Fort Leavenworth at intervals throughout the summer. When the troops marched, it was found that they sometimes traveled faster than accompanying supply wagons or that the accompanying caravans had insufficient provisions for the entire march. With several trains spread out ahead of the columns of troops, occasionally it was found convenient or necessary to dispatch a rider ahead to stop a train, so the soldiers could secure supplies without having to halt and wait for caravans to come up from the rear.

Proceeding in this manner, although the troops were not always amply supplied, the Army of the West was not detained in its march to New Mexico by the complete absence of basic necessities, one thing that could have brought about the total failure of its mission. Kearny's foresight in this matter, partially a result of his earlier experiences in crossing the plains, demonstrated that a capable and competent soldier had been selected to command the expedition.

Quartermaster General T. S. Jesup revealed the magnitude of the task of supplying the Army of the West and Kearny's preparations for it when he reported in November, 1847, that 516 pack saddles, 1,556 wagons, 459 horses, 3,658 mules, and 14,904 oxen had been furnished for transportation of the Army.[14]

The government and the citizens of Missouri co-operated with the War Department, and the requested companies of volunteers were soon supplied. Although the pay was not outstanding,[15] more recruits volunteered than were needed to fill the companies.

By June 6, three volunteer companies had arrived at Fort Leavenworth, and the last of the thirteen authorized Missouri companies arrived on June 27. As the companies reached the post, they were mustered into the service of the United States by Captain James Allen, First Dragoons, and companies were lettered in order of their arrival at the fort. On June 18, when seven of the mounted companies had arrived, Kearny had them elect regimental field officers. General Thompson Ward, Missouri Militia, conducted the election. Alexander W. Doniphan was elected colonel, Charles R. Ruff was selected as lieutenant colonel, and William Gilpin was chosen major. These officers were placed in command the following day, and the First Regiment of Missouri Mounted Volunteers, con-

[14] Jesup to Marcy, November 24, 1847, 30 Cong., 1 sess., *House Exec. Doc. 8*, p. 545.

[15] The monthly pay for volunteers in the infantry was as follows:

Colonel	$75	Sergeant Major	$17
Lieutenant Colonel	60	First Sergeant	16
Major	50	Sergeant	13
Captain	40	Corporal	9
First Lieutenant	30	Musician	8
Second Lieutenant	25	Private	7

In addition, all received $2.50 per month for clothing, and commanding officers received an extra $10 per month for arms and clothing. The pay for mounted volunteers was the same, except they were allowed an additional forty cents per day for the use of their horses, which they had to furnish. *Missouri Democrat* (Fayette), July 1, 1846.

Soldiers on the Santa Fe Trail

sisting of 856 officers and men when the last mounted company arrived on June 23, was organized.[16]

Although organized, the volunteers were still not soldiers, and many of the Dragoons doubted that this rowdy and undisciplined band of frontiersmen, farmers, artisans, laborers, lawyers, doctors, professors, legislators, and students would ever become soldiers. Kearny, who had a reputation for strict discipline within his command, was forced to endure the insubordination of many of the volunteers. A St. Louis newspaper reported that some of the volunteer companies, especially those from Howard and Jackson counties, cursed the colonel, refused to do the duties assigned them, fought among themselves, and drew knives on their superior officers. While this disturbed Kearny, he had the spirit of tolerance required to overlook some of this misconduct:

> The Colonel has not enough regulars to form a police round the fort; so he takes the annoyances of those boys cooly, but every now and then significantly shakes his head![17]

Getting these raw recruits, described by one of them as mostly "green-horns," to take on the semblance of an army was a difficult task. Until the troops departed from Fort Leavenworth, the officers of the First Dragoons took those already at the post to a nearby field twice a day and drilled them in marching, saber exercises,

---

[16] Kearny to Edwards, June 7, 1846, KLB; General Orders, No. 1, Headquarters Army of the West, June 19, 1846, Letters Received, MSS, AGO, AACB, NA; John T. Hughes, *Doniphan's Expedition*, 25-26. The eight companies of the Missouri Mounted Volunteers, the county where they were organized, and the commanding officer of each were as follows:

Company	County	Commander
A	Jackson	Captain David Waldo
B	Lafayette	Captain William P. Walton
C	Clay	Captain Oliver Perry Moss
D	Saline	Captain John W. Reid
E	Franklin	Captain John D. Stephenson
F	Cole	Captain Monroe M. Parsons
G	Howard	Captain Hancock Jackson
H	Calaway	Captain Charles E. Rodgers

[17] *The St. Louis Weekly Reveille*, June 22, 1846.

charging, rallying, and various cavalry tactics. But the volunteers could see little connection between these monotonous drills and fighting the Mexicans, for which they had enlisted.

Besides the regiment of mounted troops, the other battalions from Missouri were as follows: (1) two companies (A and B) of artillery, respectively commanded by Captains Richard H. Weightman and Woldemar Fischer, with Major Meriwether Lewis Clark as battalion commander, totaling 250 men, all from St. Louis; (2) two companies (A and B) of infantry from Cole and Platte counties, respectively commanded by Captains William Z. Angney and William S. Murphy, with Angney the senior officer and battalion commander, totaling 145 men; and (3) the Laclede Rangers, an independent company of mounted volunteers from St. Louis, commanded by Captain Thomas B. Hudson, totaling 107 men. This last company was attached to the First Dragoons on June 27, and the strength of the regular Dragoons amounted to about 300. The total command under Kearny was 1,658 men, served by 16 pieces of ordnance (12 six-pounders and 4 twelve-pounders). Organization of the Army of the West was completed with the appointment of sutlers, surgeons, quartermaster and commissary officers, and adjutants.

The expedition was accompanied by a small detachment of Topographical Engineers, including Lieutenants William H. Emory, William H. Warner, William G. Peck, and J. W. Abert. Both Emory and Abert kept journals that are valuable sources of information on the campaign.[18]

The First Dragoons were the nucleus of the Army of the West, but their numbers at Fort Leavenworth dwindled while the volunteers were concentrating there. Kearny had to send four detachments, three of them Dragoons, on emergency errands along the Trail. The first, dispatched on May 28, was a small escort for George T. Howard's attempt to overtake the traders' caravan.[19]

From a point on the Trail about seventy miles from Independ-

[18] 30 Cong., 1 sess., *House Exec. Doc. 41*, pp. 7–126, 419–546.
[19] Kearny to Marcy, May 28, 1846, KLB.

Soldiers on the Santa Fe Trail

ence, Howard wrote to Kearny on June 3 that the wagons of Manuel Armijo and Albert Speyer, with the caravan he was pursuing, were believed to contain "a large quantity of Ammunition & Arms," and that two companies of Mexican cavalry were reportedly marching from Santa Fe to escort this contraband to New Mexico. Howard indicated that he expected to overtake the caravan and requested that additional Dragoons be dispatched to prevent the armaments from reaching their destination. Kearny responded the following day, ordering Howard and his escort to detain the wagons when they caught them and stating that he would send two more companies of Dragoons on June 5.[20]

These companies, under the command of Captain Moore, comprised the second detachment that Colonel Kearny ordered out. They carried two twelve-pounders and had orders to halt the wagons of Armijo, Speyer, and all other caravans heading for Santa Fe, until Kearny arrived. The wagons could then proceed to Santa Fe with the Army of the West.[21]

The third detachment, fifty Dragoons under the command of Lieutenant Patrick Noble, was dispatched on June 12 to reinforce Captain Moore's command.[22] The final detachment sent ahead of the main body of troops was comprised of two companies of the First Missouri Mounted Volunteers, under command of Captain David Waldo. This force left Fort Leavenworth on June 22, with orders to report to Captain Moore.[23]

The day after Captain Moore had left Fort Leavenworth, Cap-

---

[20] Kearny to Howard, June 4, 1846, *ibid.;* Kearny to Jones, June 5, 1846, Letters Received, MSS, AGO, AACB, NA. Actually, Speyer was not attempting to supply a large quantity of armaments to the Mexican forces. He was delivering a small shipment of arms and ammunition which had been ordered by the governor of Chihuahua in 1845. See Bieber's introduction to Gibson, *Soldier under Kearny and Doniphan,* 41–42n.

[21] Kearny to Jones, June 5, 1846, Letters Received, MSS, AGO, AACB, NA; Kearny to Moore, June 5, 1846, KLB.

[22] Kearny to Noble, June 12, 1846, *ibid.*

[23] General Orders, No. 1, Headquarters Army of the West, June 22, 1846, Letters Received, MSS, AGO, AACB, NA; Jacob S. Robinson, *A Journal of the Santa Fe Expedition under Colonel Doniphan,* 1, 2n.

Effects of the Mexican War, 1846-1848

tain Waldo, who had formerly been engaged in the Santa Fe trade, and his company of volunteers arrived with additional information regarding the caravan in advance of the troops. Kearny relayed this new intelligence to Moore:

> Captain Waldo ... has just informed me that Gov. Armijo has about $70,000 worth of goods, &c., near the head of the Caravan & that they left Independence about a fortnight since. He is further of the opinion, from his knowledge of the Governor's character, that if we can secure that property, we hold the governor as our friend & ally. He is also of the opinion that no Mexican force will be sent from Santa Fe to meet those goods that your own comp[anie]s cannot easily defeat.[24]

On the basis of this new information, Kearny ordered Moore to select one hundred men and horses from his command and make forced marches until they overtook the caravan:

> It is an object of the *greatest importance* that we get possession of Gov. Armijo's goods.... Tell the Mexicans that we do not intend to deprive them of their property, but to stop its progress for the present.[25]

Kearny's anticipated diplomatic maneuver for winning Armijo's "friendship" failed when Captain Moore was unable to overtake the caravan. Upon reaching the Cimarron Crossing on June 16 and finding that the caravan had crossed and proceeded ahead too far to be overtaken, Moore and his command moved back to Pawnee Fork. He was joined there by the third and fourth detachments sent out, and they all waited at Pawnee Fork for almost a month, stopping all trains coming from the East. Then, on July 11, Captain Moore's command escorted the caravan of about 150 wagons toward Bent's Fort. Ten days later they encamped near the fort and waited for Kearny and the remainder of the Army of the West to arrive.

Although all necessary preparations were being made to ensure

[24] Kearny to Moore, June 6, 1846, KLB.
[25] *Ibid.*

the occupation of New Mexico by force, the Polk administration was hopeful that the Army of the West could take possession of the province without resorting to arms. For a number of years traders and travelers had supplied considerable evidence that Mexico's hold upon New Mexico was weak, and it appeared that this province, a vital doorway to the conquest of California, was ripe for the picking.[26]

The Army of the West, as indicated above, did not depart Fort Leavenworth in one body, but left at intervals between May 28 and July 6, 1846. Because supplies of fuel and water could be obtained only at certain points along the Trail, Kearny prudently decided to conduct the march by separate detachments, each of which was comprised of approximately two or three companies. Kearny designated Bent's Fort as the rendezvous for all troops before going on to Santa Fe, and this famous trading post was chosen to serve as a provision depot for the Army.

In addition to the several special detachments already sent down the Trail, late in June Kearny started the first section of the main body of the Army of the West. The battalions left Fort Leavenworth as follows: June 25, four companies of First Missouri Mounted Volunteers; June 29, two companies of the same regiment, the Laclede Rangers, and the two companies of volunteer artillery, Colonel Kearny, his staff, and a small number of Dragoons who had remained behind to accompany the colonel. On July 6, Sumner's and Cooke's two companies of Dragoons left the post as a combined force under the command of Sumner.[27]

---

[26] See Moorhead, *New Mexico's Royal Road,* 193; Clarke, *Stephen Watts Kearny,* 105–106; Otis A. Singletary, *The Mexican War,* 55–56; W. Eugene Hollon, *The Southwest: Old and New,* 166–67; Gibson, *Soldier under Kearny and Doniphan,* 61–62.

[27] *Ibid.,* 44–45; Charles R. Ruff, "Notes of the Expedition to Santa Fe," MS, Missouri Historical Society, St. Louis (hereafter cited as Ruff's "Notes"); Abraham Robinson Johnston, Journal of the March of the Army of the West from Fort Leavenworth to Santa Fe, New Mexico, Letters Received, MSS, AGO, AACB, NA, printed in Abraham Robinson Johnston, Marcellus Ball Edwards, and Philip Gooch Ferguson, *Marching with the Army of the West* (Vol. IV of *The Southwest Historical Series,* ed. by Ralph P. Bieber), 73 (hereafter cited as Johnston's Journal).

Effects of the Mexican War, 1846-1848

Despite the spaced departure, except for Captain Moore's force the various commands traveled close together on the Trail, some passing the others as they proceeded. Even so, the soldiers were strung out along the Trail for several miles as they marched, and the Army arrived at Bent's Fort in sections during the last week of July. In addition to the 1,658 soldiers, there were numerous teamsters and traders and a few scouts and guides. With soldiers and wagons forming a long thread along the Trail, the Army presented a spectacle to the Indians and animal creatures of the Great Plains, the like of which they had never witnessed.

On July 21, Captain Moore's command encamped about two miles below Bent's Fort. The troops celebrated their arrival, some of them imbibed too freely, there were fights, and one of the Dragoons was killed. Thus dissipation claimed the first casualty of this command.

The Army, more like an armed mob, was still in dire need of discipline. As a result of infractions of the rules, a few days after Moore's command arrived in camp near Bent's Fort a courtmartial found five men guilty of insubordination, and each man was sentenced "to carry forty pounds of sand every two alternate hours during the day." Whether this had a quieting effect on the rowdy volunteers is not known, but it probably affected some of them. While awaiting the arrival of the remainder of the Army of the West, Captain Moore's command was drilled, rested, and drilled some more. If it were possible, he intended to make soldiers out of his men; very little effort was spared in the attempt.

The remainder of the Army, accompanied by additional commissary and quartermaster trains, marched from Fort Leavenworth to the rendezvous in approximately thirty days, much of it the result of the forced marches ordered by Colonel Kearny. The following generalized account of the march to Bent's Fort was taken from a number of the diaries and journals kept by soldiers in the various companies.[28]

[28] *Ibid.*, 74-90; Gibson, *Soldier under Kearny and Doniphan*, 124-65; Hughes, *Doniphan's Expedition*, 31-56; Frank S. Edwards, *A Campaign in New Mexico with*

Soldiers on the Santa Fe Trail

Several of the detachments lost their way in an attempt to reach the Trail from Fort Leavenworth. Some proceeded several miles over the Oregon Trail before a party of Indians directed them to the right road, and others found the Trail but headed toward Westport rather than Santa Fe. As they began the long march, there was much discussion and speculation by the soldiers concerning the fate of the Army of the West. Many believed the war would end before they could reach New Mexico, some were sure they were in for a long, hard fight, and others were confident that the force was so formidable that they would occupy New Mexico without encountering any opposition. Talk came easy, but marching, making camp, taking care of mounts, cooking, breaking camp, and marching again was tiring and monotonous work.

The First Dragoons' previous experiences on the plains had seasoned them for the less-than-glorious adventures encountered on the march, but the inexperienced volunteers were unprepared for the difficulties which they encountered. The soldiers were constantly harassed by numerous problems and tasks. The mounted troops had saddle sores, the infantry had blistered feet, and both suffered aching backs. Sometimes the hot winds burned their skin and caused their lips to crack and bleed. On other days they marched through rain, soaking wet. They suffered from thirst when water was scarce. They were hungry on days when the cooks and their wagons were several miles from the troops they were supposed to feed and missed a hot meal when no firewood could be found or when it had been soaked by rain. There were numerous unpleasant duties, such as building bridges, repairing wagons, fording streams, and handling mules unused to the harness and oxen unused to the yoke. Brackish water, sunburn, exhaustion, sickness, blowing sand and dust, flooded streams, insufficient grass for the animals, flies, gnats, mosquitoes, grasshoppers, rattlesnakes

---

Colonel Doniphan, 24–36; Ruff's "Notes;" Journal of Henry S. Turner, Henry S. Turner Collection, MSS, Missouri Historical Society, St. Louis; Report by Lucian J. Eastin, a private in the Cole County company of infantry, *Missouri Democrat* (Fayette), September 2, 1846.

Effects of the Mexican War, 1846-1848

(even in their blankets!), and numerous other difficulties were faced by all. Was this war? Had they enlisted for this? They often wondered, but remained cheerful, anticipating meeting the enemy.

Many of the discomforts and the monotony of the march were relieved by the sometimes beautiful or unusual scenery—hills, valleys, streams, plains, and great herds of deer, antelope, and buffalo. Other diversions were hunting, bathing in a cool stream after a long day's march, fishing, telling stories, singing, playing cards, reading novels, playing practical jokes, smoking a pipe at at the end of the day, sharing joys and troubles, and a little whisky once in a while. Even the antics of the mules, horses, and oxen, annoying at times, were often funny.

The soldiers were able to overcome the difficulties encountered; the exciting thought of fighting the Mexicans kept their spirits high. The long march was probably of great value for the volunteers. It provided them with training and experience before they encountered the enemy.

It is interesting to note that, in spite of the difficulties of marching (during the first few days some infantrymen had to have their shoes cut off their swollen feet after a march of twenty-five or thirty miles), the infantry passed the mounted forces and were the first to reach Captain Moore's camp near Bent's Fort. This amazing phenomenon was possible because the infantry did not have to groom any horses, did not have to stop and graze, did not have to wait for runaway mounts to be caught before proceeding, and could make and break camp more quickly than soldiers who had the additional duty of caring for their horses.

The mounted volunteers gave their horses the best of care. If one were so unfortunate as to lose his horse by straying, stepping in a hole and breaking a leg, disease, or any other manner, that volunteer ceased to be a mounted soldier and either marched like the infantry or drove a wagon.

On July 17, George T. Howard returned from his mission in New Mexico and reported to Kearny, in camp sixteen miles west of Pawnee Fork, that the "common people" of the province were

... inclined to favor the conditions of peace proposed by Col. Kearny, to wit: that if they would lay down their arms and take the oath of allegiance to the government of the United States they should, to all intents and purposes, become citizens of the same republic, receiving the protection and enjoying the liberties guarantied [sic] to other American citizens.[29]

But the upper, ruling classes were hostile and making preparations to fight. Howard had information that about twenty-three hundred men were already armed for the defense of Santa Fe and that more were being prepared at Taos. John T. Hughes declared: "It was now expected that Col. Kearny's entrance into Santa Fe would be obstinately disputed."[30]

While many soldiers had reservations concerning the fate of the Army of the West during the coming weeks, Kearny was not shaken by this or other similar reports. Instead, he remained extraordinarily confident of success. On August 1 he wrote to Adjutant General Jones from Bent's Fort, assuring the War Department that his troops would be in possession of Santa Fe by August 20. He declared that the force with him was sufficient to overpower any army it might meet, but he still hoped to occupy the region "quietly and peaceably."[31]

With the arrival of Captain Sumner's command at the rendezvous on July 31, the Army of the West was concentrated into a single force for the first time. Kearny decided to rest the men and animals of this last unit for two days in camp near the fort. Last minute preparations were made for the march into Mexican territory, and the sick and disabled soldiers were removed from the command, either for return to Missouri or to remain at Bent's Fort to recover and join the command at a later date.

By August 1, 1846, the Army of the West was poised to strike the fatal blow to Mexican rule in New Mexico, but Kearny had

[29] Hughes, *Doniphan's Expedition*, 56.
[30] *Ibid.*
[31] Kearny to Jones, August 1, 1846, Letters Received, MSS, AGO, AACB, NA.

taken steps to carry out a peaceful occupation of the province in accordance with President Polk's wishes. By spreading propaganda for peace, Kearny attempted to convince the New Mexicans that it would be advantageous for them to submit without fighting.

As mentioned above, Kearny had instructed Howard to inform the New Mexicans that, if they would not take up arms and would take an oath of allegiance to the United States government, they would be guaranteed the same protection and liberties as those enjoyed by other American citizens. The colonel had directed a similar message to the New Mexicans with an express sent by some traders from Independence to Santa Fe on June 20.

When Kearny arrived at Bent's Fort on July 29, he found that the troops had captured three New Mexican spies. The colonel had them escorted through the encampment so they could see the formidable congregation of soldiers and the huge howitzers, and then released them to return to Santa Fe and report what they had seen and heard. It was hoped that the reports of the Army's strength would be exaggerated beyond imagination, and that the New Mexican soldiers would disperse before Kearny reached Santa Fe. The spies gave some indication that the desired result might be obtained, for, while they were looking at the American troops, one of them exclaimed, "My God! What is to become of our republic?"[32]

Kearny also gave the Mexican spies copies of a proclamation to take to Santa Fe. His proclamation, issued on July 31, carried the following announcement to the citizens of the province:

> The undersigned enters New Mexico with a large military force, for the purpose of seeking union with and ameliorating the conditions of its inhabitants. . . . It is enjoined on the citizens of New Mexico to remain quietly at their homes, and to pursue their peaceful vocations. So long as they continue in such pursuits, they will not be interfered with by the American army, but will be respected and protected in their rights, both civil and religious.

[32] Johnston's Journal, 91.

All who take up arms or encourage resistance against the Government of the United States will be regarded as enemies, and will be treated accordingly.

[signed] S. W. KEARNY[33]

Eugene Leitensdorfer, a Santa Fe trader who volunteered to distribute copies of the pronouncement in the Taos area, had his offer accepted and was given an escort of twenty soldiers, under the command of Lieutenant James A. De Courcey. Leitensdorfer also planned to attempt to win the friendship of the Taos Pueblo.

On August 1, one day before departing Bent's Fort, Kearny wrote a letter to Governor Armijo, explaining the purpose and goal of his expedition and appealing to the governor to submit peacefully rather than be destroyed by force.[34] This letter was entrusted to Captain Cooke to be delivered personally to the governor. Cooke was selected for the mission because of his popularity among New Mexicans since the Snively Affair of 1843. He was given a dual assignment, for, in addition to delivering Kearny's letter to the governor, he and twelve other Dragoons were to escort James Wiley Magoffin to Santa Fe.[35]

Magoffin's exact role in the occupation of Santa Fe is not clear.[36] He had been sent by President Polk to precede the Army of the West into New Mexico in an attempt to help Kearny carry out the administration's policy of peaceful occupation.[37] Kearny, who welcomed assistance in this effort, provided the escort for Magoffin and sent Cooke to meet with Armijo.

[33] 30 Cong., 1 sess., *House Exec. Doc. 60,* p. 168.

[34] Kearny to Armijo, August 1, 1846, KLB.

[35] Magoffin had been a Santa Fe trader for about twenty years. In 1825 he became one of the first United States Consuls in northern Mexico when he was appointed to serve at Saltillo. A few years later he moved to Chihuahua and there, in 1830, he married Dona Maria Gertrudes Valdez de Beremende, a member of one of Chihuahua's most prominent families. Mrs. Magoffin's cousin was Manuel Armijo. Howard R. Lamar's foreword to *Down the Santa Fe Trail* (ed. by Drumm), xix-xx.

[36] Magoffin's correspondence on the subject is printed in Ralph Emerson Twitchell, *The Story of the Conquest of Santa Fe, New Mexico, and the Building of Old Fort Marcy, A. D. 1846,* 43-63.

[37] Marcy to Kearny, June 18, 1846, *ibid.,* 42-43.

Effects of the Mexican War, 1846-1848

The two companies of volunteer infantry began the invasion of New Mexico from Bent's Fort on August 1. On the following day, Cooke's detachment, a small party of spies under the direction of William Bent (charged with scouting ahead of the troops), and the remainder of the Army of the West started for Santa Fe.[38]

Crossing the Arkansas, the soldiers moved to Timpas Creek and made their first camp. From there to the Purgatoire River, which they reached on August 5, they covered one of the worst stretches of the Trail. Because of drought, there was an inadequate supply of grass and water over most of this distance, approximately ninety miles. The temperature was excessively hot (reaching 120 degrees), and hard winds and blowing sand irritated the troops. Horses and oxen died from the heat and lack of water. These conditions caused much grumbling among the soldiers; many of the volunteers were ready to call it quits.

Upon reaching the Purgatoire, the troops found sufficient water and grass, and the ascent up Raton Pass was more comfortable, although still quite hot. Because of the rough, rocky, and precipitous trail, it was difficult to get the wagons over the pass, and more draft animals died during the struggle. After descending from the pass and resting for one day, the troops proceeded without difficulty, reaching the first New Mexican settlements near the Río Mora on August 13.

Kearny continued to spread his propaganda for peace at every opportunity. Meanwhile, Cooke and Magoffin had arrived at Las Vegas on August 9. There they visited Don Juan de Dios Maes, the alcalde and Magoffin's friend, and helped to open that town to peaceful occupation by the coming Army. Moving on, they reached Santa Fe on August 12, and Cooke promptly met with Governor Armijo, presented Kearny's letter to the governor, and then took his leave to occupy the quarters which Armijo had provided for him. Several American merchants visited Cooke there, anxious to learn the size and whereabouts of the Army of the West.

Cooke was later called back to the Governor's Palace to present

[38] The traders were to follow a few days later.

his credentials and to engage in a discussion. Armijo "seemed to think that the approach of the army was rather sudden and rapid; and inquired very particularly if its commander, Kearny, was a general or colonel?"[39] After this conversation, Cooke was allowed to walk about Santa Fe, and, taking full advantage of the opportunity, he carefully noted the amount and condition of the Mexican ordnance. Following the evening meal, Magoffin became involved in the discussion. During this long meeting, Cooke and Magoffin attempted to convince the governor that the Americans troops would protect the New Mexicans and give them peace, and that it would be foolish and futile to resist the invasion with force. Armijo would not commit himself. It was agreed that Cooke would leave the following morning to return Armijo's official answer to Kearny, and that he would be accompanied by a commissioner, Dr. Henry Connelly, an American merchant who had resided in Mexico for some time. They departed Santa Fe early the next morning, but Magoffin remained to continue his "negotiations."

Magoffin, because of his influence with the governor, was allowed to spend the next few days entertaining and interviewing the leading military and civilian officers of the province. He learned that Armijo's second in military command, Diego Archuleta, had given notice that he intended to fight the Americans. Apparently he had control over about one thousand New Mexican troops. Realizing that if Archuleta resisted with force Armijo would be obliged to follow suit, Magoffin tried earnestly to dissuade Archuleta from such a course. He pointed out that the United States claimed New Mexico only to the Río Grande, and suggested that if Archuleta accepted this claim he might take command of the territory west of the river for himself. As events later proved, this argument helped to accomplish the desired result.[40]

Neither Cooke nor Magoffin knew whether or not Armijo would

[39] Cooke, *Conquest of New Mexico and California*, 29. Kearny received his commission as brigadier general on August 15, but it was to date from June 30, 1846. 30 Cong., 1 sess., *House Exec. Doc. 41*, p. 27.

[40] Cooke to Magoffin, February 21, 1849, in *Down the Santa Fe Trail* (ed. by Drumm), 264–65; Moorhead, *New Mexico's Royal Road*, 160.

Effects of the Mexican War, 1846–1848

fight, and it is possible that Armijo himself did not yet know. Playing the role expected of the governor and military leader of a territory being invaded, he at least said he would fight. But this may have been only for the sake of appearances. Armijo's reply to Kearny stated that he could not recognize the American claim to any part of New Mexico; that he had sufficient forces to resist the invasion; that the citizens had "risen en masse" to defend their country; and that it was his duty to provide them leadership. But these forthright statements were followed by a request for Kearny to stop at Sapello Creek and negotiate a settlement.[41]

Henry Connelly, after accompanying Cooke to Kearny's headquarters, "returned to Santa Fe with a report on the numbers and equipment of the American army that unnerved many of the New Mexican officials."[42] Although by August 16 Armijo had amassed a substantial New Mexican force at Apache Pass on the Trail fifteen miles from Santa Fe, an apparent loss of confidence caused him to send his volunteers to their homes and order his regular troops to retreat to Chihuahua. Thus it was possible for Kearny's Army to occupy Santa Fe without opposition.

Kearny had moved up to Las Vegas on August 14, and the following morning he addressed the citizens of the town, explaining his peaceful intentions and promising them protection. He also administered an oath of allegiance to the alcalde and two militia officers. Moving on, he delivered a similar speech and administered the oath to local officials at Tecolote and San Miguel. By the evening of August 16 the Army of the West was encamped forty-five miles from Santa Fe.[43]

During the night of August 16, Kearny received the first word of Armijo's flight and the breakup of the New Mexican force. The report was verified the following day, and the troops, somewhat disappointed that they would see no action after their long and diffi-

---

[41] *Ibid.;* Johnston's Journal, 98; Gibson, *Soldier under Kearny and Doniphan,* 71, 74; 30 Cong., 1 sess., *House Exec. Doc. 41,* pp. 25–26.

[42] Moorhead, *New Mexico's Royal Road,* 160.

[43] Johnston's Journal, 98–101.

cult march (but nevertheless relieved that the tension was over), pushed on toward Santa Fe. On August 17 Kearny ordered his men to respect the citizens of New Mexico, not to molest those who would submit peaceably, and warned that anyone violating the order would suffer the consequences.[44] The troops entered the capital city late in the afternoon of August 18.[45]

The first part of the mission of the Army of the West was completed. The story of setting up the new government in New Mexico, establishing control over other parts of the province, the Taos Revolt, and the exploits of the Army while dealing with the Indians of New Mexico, in Chihuahua, and in California are beyond the scope of this study.

Because Kearny and the Polk administration had feared that the the Army of the West was not large enough to accomplish the tasks set before it, provisions were made to send reinforcements as soon as possible. Although these troops arrived in New Mexico too late to be of any assistance in the actual occupation of that province, they did lend valuable support in dealing with the Indians of that region, and some of them proceeded to California behind Kearny, while others went to the battlefront south of New Mexico. Since these forces traveled over the Santa Fe Trail, their marches are briefly considered here.

The total reinforcement was to consist of one mounted regiment from Missouri, one mounted extra battalion from the same state, and one battalion of infantry to be raised among the Mormons. Moreover, in 1847 a force marched to Santa Fe in time to replace those volunteers whose one-year term of service was about to expire. Altogether the reinforcements and replacements numbered approximately 3,950 officers and men.

The first reinforcements obtained were the Second Missouri

[44] General Orders, No. 13, Headquarters Army of the West, August 17, 1846, Letters Received, MSS, AGO, AACB, NA.

[45] Kearny to Jones, August 24, 1846, 30 Cong., 1 sess., *House Exec. Doc. 60*, p. 169; Johnston's Journal, 101–104.

Effects of the Mexican War, 1846-1848

Mounted Volunteers, commanded by Colonel Sterling Price. Price arrived at Fort Leavenworth on July 29, 1846, and the ten companies comprising this regiment were mustered into the serive during the first part of August. The other regimental officers were Lieutenant Colonel David D. Mitchell and Major Benjamin B. Edmonson. A separate battalion of five companies of mounted volunteers, commanded by Major David Willock, was also raised in Missouri and attached to Colonel Price's command. The total strength of these mounted forces was about twelve hundred men.[46]

This cavalry force was assigned several pieces of heavy artillery under the direction of regular army officers. In addition, the command had a large number of wagons for carrying provisions and baggage, many of which were sent ahead on the Trail to insure ready service for marching troops. By August 12 Price's entire command was assembled at Fort Leavenworth, and subsequently they departed that post in small battalions, following the same pattern of travel that Kearny had used earlier. The last battalion left the fort on August 20.[47]

These men encountered the same problems that the Army of the West had faced during its march over the Trail, but they moved more quickly toward Santa Fe. Furthermore, all but two or three companies followed the shorter Cimarron Route, where they passed many trade caravans moving toward New Mexico. The mounted troops arrived at Santa Fe during the second week of October, and the Mormon battalion arrived at about the same time.

Captain James Allen, First Dragoons, had been charged with raising the Mormon battalion on June 19, 1846. Colonel Kearny had ordered him to recruit four or five companies of volunteer infantry at Council Bluffs and march them to Santa Fe, from which point they would follow Kearny to California. The Mormons who enlisted would serve for twelve months and then be discharged in

---

[46] Hughes, *Doniphan's Expedition*, 133; *The St. Louis Weekly Republican*, August 10, 1846; *The St. Louis Weekly Reveille*, August 17, 1846.

[47] Hughes, *Doniphan's Expedition*, 134; *Journal of William H. Richardson*, 6-8.

California. Allen was authorized to inform the Mormons that when discharged they would be allowed to retain as their own private property their guns and accouterments furnished them by the army. Each company was to be allowed to take along four women as laundresses. With these promises, Kearny believed that five hundred "young and efficient men" could easily be raised.[48]

Captain Allen arrived at Council Bluffs on July 1, and five companies of infantry were enlisted by July 16. All the Mormon volunteers were at Fort Leavenworth by August 1. Three companies left the post on August 13, and the remaining companies started down the Trail on August 19. Although originally ordered to proceed via the Mountain Route, the Mormons followed the Cimarron Route in order to save time. They arrived at Santa Fe on October 9 and October 12, having marched approximately eight hundred miles from Fort Leavenworth in less than two months. At Santa Fe the Mormon battalion was transferred to the command of Captain Cooke and marched on to California, reaching there in January, 1847.[49] With the arrival of these troops in New Mexico, approximately thirty-five hundred American soldiers had marched over the Santa Fe Trail during the war. Truly, the Trail had become a military road.

In the spring of 1847, additional volunteers were raised in Missouri and Illinois to replace those whose terms would expire during the summer months. The Third Regiment of Missouri Mounted Volunteers, commanded by Colonel John Ralls; the Missouri Battalion of Volunteer Infantry (five companies), under command of Lieutenant Colonel Alton R. Easton; and the First Regiment of Illinois Infantry Volunteers, led by Colonel E. W. B. Newby, comprised these replacements. They departed from Fort Leavenworth during June and July, 1847, and arrived at Santa Fe be-

---

[48] Kearny to Allen, June 19, 1846, KLB.

[49] For details of the march, see Robert S. Bliss, "Journal of Robert S. Bliss, with the Mormon Battalion," *Utah Historical Quarterly*, Vol. IV (July, October, 1931), 67–96, 110–28; Frank Alfred Golder, Thomas A. Bailey, and J. Lyman Smith, *The March of the Mormon Battalion from Council Bluffs to California, Taken from the Journal of Henry Standage*.

Effects of the Mexican War, 1846-1848

tween August 20 and the first week of October.[50] The details of the march were vividly recorded by Philip Gooch Ferguson.[51]

While marching to New Mexico, many of the detachments were joined by trade caravans and government supply trains seeking protection from the Indians who were harassing travelers on the Trail and plundering wagon trains at almost every opportunity. Because of these Indian hostilities, it became necessary for the army to provide protection for the military supply trains and trade caravans using the route. Before considering the protection of the Trail during this era, it should be noted that those Missouri volunteers whose term of service ended in 1847 marched back to Fort Leavenworth over the Trail. They arrived at the post during August and September and were discharged from the service.[52]

The Indians did not bother Kearny's Army as it marched across the plains in 1846. That overwhelming armed force caused them to maintain a safe distance. While the Indians probably observed and followed the marches of the soldiers, they made no direct attacks upon them. But the supply trains that followed the troops were not so fortunate. The situation was explained by one of the soldiers, John T. Hughes:

> In the spring of 1847, the Indians, principally the Pawnees and Comanches, infested the Santa Fe road, committed repeated depredations on the government trains, . . . killed and drove off great numbers of horses, mules, and oxen, belonging to the government, and in several instances, overpowered, and slew, or captured many of our people. They openly declared that they would cut off all communication between the western States and New Mexico, and capture and enslave every American who might venture to pass the plains.[53]

[50] Annual Report of the Secretary of War, 1847, 30 Cong., 1 sess., *House Exec. Doc. 8*, p. 59; Johnson, Edwards, and Ferguson, *Marching with the Army of the West*, 56-60.
[51] *Ibid.*, 296-318.
[52] James Madison Cutts, *The Conquest of California and New Mexico*, 240; Hughes, *Doniphan's Expedition*, 406.
[53] *Ibid.*, 403.

Soldiers on the Santa Fe Trail

Quartermaster General Jesup declared in his annual report to Secretary of War Marcy, November 24, 1847:

> There is a great difficulty in keeping up the supplies for the troops in New Mexico. The Indians of the plains have committed many depredations on the trains; they have driven off all the cattle of some of them, and have killed many of the drivers. Unless an imposing mounted force be employed against them, and they be severely chastised, it will soon be impossible to send supplies on that route.[54]

Because troops were not available in sufficient numbers to provide continuous escorts for the military and civilian trains, teamsters tried to protect themselves throughout 1846 and much of 1847. This they did by traveling in caravans and taking enough men and arms along to guard their wagons and put up a good fight when the Indians attacked. This was not always effective, but it was the best protection available until troops could be provided to deal directly with the Indians.

During the spring of 1847 the quartermaster department established a small fort a few miles east of Cimarron Crossing near the Caches. This was Fort Mann, the first military post on the Santa Fe Trail.[55] Before this post was erected, Bent's Fort had been the only place along the Trail providing a safe stopping place for wagon trains and containing facilities for repairing wagons between Council Grove, where the quartermaster department established a repair shop in 1846, and Las Vegas, the first place where wagons could be repaired in New Mexico. Caravans following the Cimarron Route did not have access to Bent's Fort.

In an attempt to solve this problem, Captain William McKissack, assistant quartermaster at Santa Fe, suggested to Quarter-

---

[54] 30 Cong., 1 sess., *House Exec. Doc. 8*, p. 545.

[55] There were military posts at each end of the Trail by 1847, Fort Leavenworth at the eastern end, first occupied in 1827, and Fort Marcy in Santa Fe, built in 1846. However, their services to the Trail were only incidental. Fort Leavenworth was the main headquarters and depot for most military activities west of the Missouri River, and Fort Marcy was the headquarters and depot for troops stationed throughout New Mexico.

Effects of the Mexican War, 1846-1848

master General Jesup, February 16, 1847, that a repair station was needed about midway between Fort Leavenworth and Santa Fe. He must have received approval for his idea, because in late March or early April of the same year Captain McKissack sent about forty teamsters, under command of Captain Daniel P. Mann, a master teamster, to construct a post near Cimarron Crossing.[56]

This post, later to become known as Fort Mann, was not intended to serve as a military base of operations or quarters for escort troops; there was not even to be a company of soldiers stationed there. Instead, it was established as a depot where government wagons could be repaired (having a blacksmith shop, wheelwright shop, and rooms to serve for storage purposes), and where teamsters and animals could rest in safety from Indian attacks. In addition to some teamsters, a small force of government employees was to be hired to build, operate, and protect it.

Lewis H. Garrard included a first-hand description of Fort Mann's early history and of the garrison stationed there in his informative *Wah-to-Yah and the Taos Trail*. Garrard had left his home in Cincinnati in 1846, at the age of seventeen to journey to Taos. On his return trip over the Trail a year later, he served as an employee at Fort Mann for about a month. Arriving at the little post on May 15, 1847, while it was still under construction, Garrard stated:

> The fort was simply four log houses, connected by angles of timber framework, in which were cut loopholes for the cannon and small arms. In diameter the fort was about sixty feet. The walls were twenty in hight [sic].[57]

The young adventurer helped complete the construction and learned during his short stay there that the small garrison of about ten men lived in virtually constant fear of Indian attack. While providing some aid to the caravans, the fort was not adequate to

---

[56] Bieber's introduction to Lewis H. Garrard, *Wah-to-Yah and the Taos Trail* (Vol. VI of *The Southwest Historical Series*, ed. by Ralph P. Bieber), 36.
[57] *Ibid.*, 331.

Soldiers on the Santa Fe Trail

protect travelers using the Trail from hostile Indians. In fact Fort Mann was found completely abandoned within one month after Garrard continued his homeward journey.

The Indian threat on the Trail is illustrated by the experience of Lieutenant John Love's command of eighty Dragoons which escorted a paymaster transporting a payroll of $300,000 in specie for the troops at Santa Fe.[58] This force was joined by about thirty traders seeking protection while traveling to New Mexico. Leaving Fort Leavenworth the first part of June, 1847, the party traveled rapidly and reached Pawnee Fork on June 23. There they overtook two large government supply trains heading for Santa Fe, accompanied by more traders who had joined them for protection. These two trains had been encamped on the creek for several days because of high water. On June 22 they had been attacked by a large body of Indians, but had repelled the attack with no losses except for having one man slightly wounded.

Meanwhile, an empty supply train returning from Santa Fe to Fort Leavenworth had arrived and encamped on the west side of Pawnee Fork. After the Indians had retreated from the camp on the east side of the creek, they crossed over and attacked the incoming train, wounded two men, and drove off approximately 150 oxen. This left twenty wagons without means of transportation. They were burned to prevent the Indians from getting them; consequently, additional government property was destroyed because of the Indian threat.

By June 25 the floodwaters had subsided so the wagons were able to cross over, and because of the Indian threat Lieutenant Love directed the master teamsters of each train to travel

---

[58] Information concerning this trip was taken from an unidentified sergeant's report, printed in Cutts, *Conquest of California and New Mexico*, 240–43; and the report of Thomas Fitzpatrick, who had served as a guide for Captain Moore's command on its march to Bent's Fort and the guide for the Army of the West on its march from Bent's Fort to Santa Fe in 1846. He was, in 1847, the Indian agent for the Upper Platte and Arkansas regions. He accompanied Lieutenant Love's command westward on his first official trip among the Indians. 30 Cong., 1 sess., *House Exec. Doc. 8*, appendix, pp. 238–40.

Effects of the Mexican War, 1846-1848

and encamp near his Dragoons during the remainder of the trip. A Mr. Hayden, in charge of one of the supply trains, refused to follow these orders, stating that he had received his instructions from the quartermaster at Fort Leavenworth and would not submit to additional directions. His refusal to comply hampered the effectiveness of the escort, as succeeding events proved.

Crossing the stream required most of the day, and the evening of June 25 found them encamped a few miles beyond Pawnee Fork, about a mile from the Arkansas. Hayden's train had advanced and encamped approximately five hundred yards beyond the Dragoons and the other wagons. This situation created difficulties the following morning. When the oxen from Hayden's train were turned out to graze, a large body of Indians charged and succeeded in driving them off. Lieutenant Love, observing the difficulty, mounted his troops and was ready to move to Hayden's camp when another body of Indians approached the Dragoons' encampment. Fearing that these Indians would attack and rob the other wagons and take the $300,000 in specie if he left them, Love sent twenty soldiers to aid the teamsters of Hayden's train, which had suffered three men wounded and the loss of 160 yoke of oxen.

This detachment of troops moved out to engage the Indians. In the ensuing conflict the Indians did retreat, but they succeeded in taking the oxen with them. The Indians, with an estimated total force of five hundred, had lost twenty-five killed and wounded. The soldiers lost five killed and six wounded.

Following this engagement, the entire party remained in camp for several days until the wounded were able to travel. Determined not to leave the wagons and their cargo on the plains despite the loss of over 300 oxen, Lieutenant Love divided the remaining oxen and placed two or three yoke on each wagon, depending upon the load. In this manner they proceeded, by making short marches of five to eight miles per day, to Fort Mann. This outpost was found abandoned, but Hayden's wagons and teamsters were left there until aid could be sent back from Santa Fe. Encountering no further difficulties, the other supply wagons, traders, paymaster,

Soldiers on the Santa Fe Trail

and Dragoons reached the capital of New Mexico on August 6. Experiences such as this proved the need for a battalion of troops to move out onto the Trail with the sole purpose of protecting it from the Indians, and this type of protection was forthcoming.

On July 24, 1847, the War Department, recognizing the dire situation, requisitioned from Missouri five companies of volunteers, which were soon raised (two mounted companies, A and B; one of foot artillery, C; and two of infantry, D and E). They were ordered to the section of the Trail where most depredations were occurring, "with instructions to chastise the offenders."[59] William Gilpin, who had served as major in the First Missouri Mounted Volunteers, was elected lieutenant colonel of this force, known as the Indian Battalion. Organized and outfitted at Fort Leavenworth, the mounted troops left there late in September, 1847, and the infantry and artillery followed on October 6, all to be employed for one year in protecting the Trail and "overawing" the hostiles. This was the only effective protective force to guard the Trail during the Mexican War.

Gilpin concentrated his entire battalion at Walnut Creek on November 1. As he had proceeded to that point, he had gathered information about the Indian situation from traders, government teamsters, and other travelers returning from New Mexico, in order that he might plan his operations for the ensuing winter. As a result of his inquiries, Gilpin estimated the American losses to Indians during the summer of 1847 at 47 men killed, 330 wagons destroyed, and 6,500 head of stock stolen. Most of these losses had been suffered by the government supply trains. He learned that "no resting places, depots, or points of security" existed between Council Grove and Las Vegas, "a bleak stretch of 600 miles." Fort Mann again had been abandoned.[60]

He was informed that the Pawnees, Comanches, and Kiowas had made their attacks along the Arkansas and Cimarron rivers, while

[59] Annual Report of the Secretary of War, 1847, *ibid.*, 70.
[60] Gilpin to Jones, August 1, 1848, 30 Cong., 2 sess., *House Exec. Doc. 1*, pp. 136–37.

Effects of the Mexican War, 1846–1848

the Apaches had operated primarily along the upper Canadian and westward. In addition, he was told that the Apaches were seeking an alliance with the Cheyennes and Arapahoes, to continue the war against the whites with their united strength during 1848.

On the basis of this information, Gilpin laid his plans for the winter. He stationed the three companies of infantry and artillery at Fort Mann, under command of Captain William Pelzer, for the purpose of repairing and enlarging that post. Then he took the two mounted companies to the upper Arkansas and encamped "in the midst of the winter residences of the Cheyennes and Arapahoes."[61] Wintering on the plains was a difficult task, but Gilpin later explained that the presence of his force produced desired results:

> The Indians were, however, overawed by this immediate contrast of a military force, abandoned all intercourse with the southern tribes, and invited the Kiowas to withdraw from the Camanche [*sic*] alliance; to unite with them (the Arapahoes and Cheyennes) in pacific relations with the Americans. This has accordingly been effected, and the Kiowa Indians, long the scourge of the borders of Mexico, Taos, and this road, have since then been, and are now [August, 1848] awaiting peace, and residing with the Cheyennes upon the upper Arkansas, near Bent's Fort.[62]

Early in March, 1848, Gilpin left his camp on the upper Arkansas and, with two mounted companies and one of infantry, went to Mora, New Mexico. There he purchased provisions and bought mules to mount the infantrymen. This force then proceeded to the Canadian River in a campaign against the Apaches and Comanches. The purpose of this expedition was to attack the Indians in their winter villages before they moved north to harass the Trail. During the remainder of March, April, and the first half of May, the troops moved down the Canadian searching for, but never locating, the Indians.[63]

[61] *Ibid.*, 137.
[62] *Ibid.*
[63] *Santa Fe Republican,* May 13, 1848, reported that Gilpin's command had encountered a large body of Comanches along the Canadian River and had defeated

Soldiers on the Santa Fe Trail

The Comanches and Apaches had been warned of the soldiers' advance by a party of Mexicans, had evacuated their traditional winter quarters, and had dispersed in several directions, some of them going into the Mexican state of Chihuahua. Satisfied that he would not overtake the Indians, Gilpin turned north on May 18 and headed for Fort Mann, arriving there on May 30. The Apaches and Comanches had not been chastised, but the presence of the Indian Battalion had kept them from raiding along the Trail during those months.

At Fort Mann Gilpin found the chiefs of the Kiowas, Cheyennes, and Arapahoes awaiting his return and ready to sign a peace treaty. Gilpin did not have the authority to sign treaties with the Indians, so he sent them back to their camps on the upper Arkansas and asked them to wait there until an Indian agent or commissioner could be sent to negotiate with them. The chiefs complied with his request, but did not secure a negotiator.[64]

The Indian Battalion had been successful in its mission up to this point. However, the Apaches and Comanches returned to the Trail in June. The Apaches committed hostilities along the upper Canadian and near Raton Pass, but were driven off by troops sent out from Santa Fe.[65] The Comanches offered the most serious threat along the Santa Fe Trail during the summer of 1848.

The Comanches usually met with the Osage Indians near the con-

---

them in a hard-fought battle. Apparently this report was based on hearsay. Gilpin did not mention it in his report, and no other evidence has been located to substantiate it.

[64] 30 Cong., 2 sess., *House Exec. Doc. 1*, p. 138. Indian Agent Fitzpatrick confirmed the peaceful behavior of these three tribes, but he left Bent's Fort in the spring of 1848 without concluding a treaty with them. Fitzpatrick to Harvey, October 6, 1848, *ibid.,* 470–73. No explanation for his leaving without negotiating with them has been found; it certainly complicated matters for the army. Gilpin's assurances of a treaty were not carried out, thus the Indians were reluctant to trust the military afterward. It is possible that Fitzpatrick did not have the authority to sign a treaty with these Indians. See LeRoy R. Hafen, "Thomas Fitzpatrick and the First Indian Agency of the Upper Platte and Arkansas," *Mississippi Valley Historical Review,* Vol. XV (December, 1928), 374–84.

[65] *Santa Fe Republican,* June 28, August 1, 1848.

fluence of the Cimarron and Arkansas rivers during the month of May in order to secure arms, powder, lead, knives, and other supplies. After obtaining these items, they ascended the Arkansas and began to attack travelers using the Trail in the vicinity of Walnut or Pawnee creeks. They did not deviate from this pattern in 1848, but that year they were met by the Indian Battalion, which inflicted considerable losses upon them in a series of engagements.

The soldiers first encountered the Comanches in June, 1848. Lieutenant Philip Stremmel, commanding the company of artillery volunteers, led his command from Fort Mann early in June to meet and escort Major Thomas S. Bryant, paymaster, who had left Fort Leavenworth to pay the Indian Battalion. This detachment of sixty-five officers and men, with two six-pound pieces of ordnance, encamped on Pawnee Fork on June 7. There Lieutenant Stremmel met a trader who reported that no hostile Indians had been seen on the Trail that season.

This was soon changed. About dusk, while the soldiers were eating, two Indians were sighted near the camp. The alarm was given, and almost immediately about two hundred Comanches surrounded the encampment and began firing upon the soldiers. In the ensuing conflict, which lasted but ten minutes, the Indians lost five killed and ten wounded, and the soldiers lost twenty mules and two horses, but no troops were wounded or killed. The detachment remained in camp at Pawnee Fork for a week while word was sent to Gilpin at Fort Mann and additional mules were brought from that post. The troops then moved to Walnut Creek, where they at last met Major Bryant, two large government supply trains, 425 head of beef cattle, and their escort of seventy-one recruits on their way to Santa Fe, under command of Lieutenant William B. Royall, First Dragoons.

Lieutenant Royall, senior officer, took command of all troops escorting the paymaster, and they marched west from Walnut Creek. During the next few days they observed Indian scouts following their movements, and Royall proceeded cautiously by having the volunteers and recruits serve as advance and rear guards, alter-

Soldiers on the Santa Fe Trail

nating positions each day. On June 17 they encamped on the Arkansas River near the mouth of Coon Creek, within a few miles of the place where Lieutenant Love's force had been attacked the previous year. Early the following morning over five hundred Comanches surrounded and attacked the camp.

The attack came when the soldiers and teamsters were just about to begin the day's march, so they could be placed in fighting position immediately. They then gave the Indians a "hot reception." The Indians successively charged from one side of the camp and then the other, but, with the two six-pounders operating and the soldiers making optimum use of their carbines, they were repulsed each time. Finally, seeing that their efforts were in vain, the Indians retreated with the few animals they had captured (about twenty-five horses and mules). The Indians had lost nine killed and an undetermined number wounded, while the soldiers suffered no losses. As a final gesture, Lieutenant Royall mounted thirty-eight of the recruits and pursued the Indians who crossed the river and headed into the sandhills.

This detachment, hopeful of overtaking the Indians and recovering the lost animals, pursued a band of about one hundred retreating Indians to a point approximately four miles from the encampment. There, in the sandhills, they found themselves suddenly surrounded by five or six hundred Comanches. Before the Indians could attack them, the soldiers drove through the line of warriors and succeeded in positioning themselves on the crest of a small hill. From this point they sustained repeated charges from the Indians, killing and wounding several during each attack. The Indians lost fourteen more killed, and approximately twice that number wounded; the troops suffered four wounded and none killed.

When the Indians retired to a distance which allowed the detachment to withdraw to their camp, the troops moved back slowly. The Comanches had been effectively checked, losing a total of twenty-three killed, plus about fifty wounded, and obtaining only a few horses and mules. Two days later the soldiers, paymaster,

Effects of the Mexican War, 1846-1848

and supply trains arrived at Fort Mann, having experienced no further difficulties from the Comanches.[66]

Meanwhile, Lieutenant Colonel Gilpin, upon receiving news that Indians were attacking along the Trail, had dispatched several small escorts for caravans moving in both directions. He later reported that these escorts, which operated throughout the summer months, had "defeated the Indians [Pawnees, Comanches, Osages, and Apaches] on many occasions with great slaughter."[67] Gilpin also had sent a detachment, under command of Captain John C. Griffin, to seek out the Comanches' camps and destroy them if possible.[68]

This detachment, consisting of one hundred officers and men who were provided with one six-pounder, left Fort Mann on July 7, headed for the Cimarron, and followed it downstream along the north bank. On July 9 they discovered a deserted Indian camp, and, nearby, met a Mexican boy who was taken prisoner. From him they learned that the Comanches were encamped at a certain point down the Cimarron. Proceeding at once, the command found the camp of about six hundred warriors three hours later. The soldiers attacked immediately (at about noon) and were engaged in fierce battle for three hours before the Indians abandoned their camp. During this conflict the Comanches lost thirty killed and an undetermined number wounded, while the soldiers had none killed and two officers slightly wounded. Exhausted, and lacking the necessary supplies to pursue the Indians, Captain Griffin's force encamped for the night on the battlefield. The following day they proceeded north to Mulberry Creek, as ordered, where they found no Indians. They returned to Fort Mann on July 12.

Lieutenant Colonel Gilpin, believing the Comanches were still encamped at some point near the Cimarron, sent another detachment, under command of Captain Thomas Jones, out from the

[66] Ibid., July 19, 1848; Gilpin to Jones, August 1, 1848, 30 Cong., 2 sess., *House Exec. Doc. 1*, p. 138; Royall to Jones, June 21, 1848; *ibid.*, 141-44; Stremmel to Gilpin, June 23, 1848, *ibid.*, 144-46.
[67] Gilpin to Jones, August 1, 1848, *ibid.*, 138.
[68] *Ibid.*, 136; Griffin to Gilpin, July 12, 1848, *ibid.*, 146-49.

fort on July 15, again with orders to locate and attack the Indians' camp. With 109 officers and men, one six-pounder, and twelve days' provisions, this force marched eastward along the Arkansas for two days, turned south, and reached the Cimarron on July 19. They found fresh Indian signs, but no Indians. It appeared that the Comanches had moved up the Cimarron, and the troops moved in that direction the following day. About ten o'clock in the morning, July 20, they sighted an Indian near a grove of trees by the river. The soldiers promptly investigated the grove, and were there attacked by about fifty Indians, believed to be Pawnees, who had remained concealed. Engaging in hand-to-hand combat, the soldiers killed twenty-one Indians and wounded many more. Captain Jones's command suffered five men injured and none killed.[69]

Having overthrown this attempted ambush, the troops quickly scouted the region for additional Indians. In so doing, they discovered the village of the Comanches, which, according to Captain Jones:

> ... appeared to have been abandoned with the greatest precipitation; lodge poles, saddles, and bags of salt, and provisions being strewn over the ground in great numbers. ... From the visible sign, I estimated the number of lodges and fires to have been from 800 to 1,000; of stock, 1,500 to 2,000 head.[70]

On the same day, the detachment began its return march to Fort Mann. Captain Jones wanted to obtain treatment for his wounded as quickly as possible, moreover, no other Indians had been found in the immediate vicinity. Reaching the fort on July 23, Jones reported that the Comanches had "been effectually driven from the Arkansas, and to have retreated in the direction of the lower Canadian."[71]

The Indian Battalion had succeeded in providing much-needed protection along the Santa Fe Trail, but this had not been easily

[69] Jones to Gilpin, July 23, 1848; *ibid.*, 149–51.
[70] *Ibid.*, 150.
[71] *Ibid.*

accomplished. The operations had been conducted under serious handicaps. The volunteers, in whom the regular army officers apparently had little faith, had been denied proper equipment for their field operations. Lieutenant Colonel Clifton Wharton, First Dragoons, commanding at Fort Leavenworth when the Indian Battalion was mustered into service, had been charged with outfitting the command. Gilpin, whose views were not objective, but who had no reason to give false evidence since his command had been so successful, claimed that Wharton had provided only the poorest equipment available, had refused to issue any books of regulations or instructions, and had overlooked medical supplies almost entirely. Also, the men had not received adequate clothing for wintering on the plains. But, in spite of the difficulties resulting from these factors, Gilpin concluded:

> The active operations of the battalion have nevertheless been constant and successful. The Indians inhabiting the waters of the Arkansas river have . . . been either held in peace or effectually defeated.[72]

The successful operations of the Indian Battalion were commended by the Superintendent of Indian Affairs at St. Louis, Thomas H. Harvey, who stated in October of 1848: "There have been fewer robberies committed by Indians upon our citizens on the route to Santa Fe, during the present year, than the two previous ones."[73] Indian Agent Thomas Fitzpatrick also noted the "cessation of hostilities" along the Trail.[74] Secretary of War Marcy praised the successes of Gilpin's battalion in his annual report.[75]

The soldiers on the Santa Fe Trail during the Mexican War had succeeded in accomplishing all tasks assigned to them. The Army of the West insured the peaceful conquest of New Mexico, and this accomplishment was made permanent by the Treaty of Guadalupe Hidalgo. Although the War Department had been slow in develop-

[72] Gilpin to Jones, August 1, 1848, *ibid.*, 139.
[73] Harvey to Medill, October 4, 1848, *ibid.*, 440.
[74] Fitzpatrick to Harvey, October 6, 1848, *ibid.*, 472.
[75] Annual Report of the Secretary of War, 1848, *ibid.*, 77.

Soldiers on the Santa Fe Trail

ing a policy for protecting the Trail, the Indian Battalion had prevented the Indians from closing the route in 1848. Both the regular army and the volunteers had used the Trail for military conquest and had worked effectively and efficiently to make it a safe road for traders, supply trains, emigrants, and other travelers. The Santa Fe Trail had served as a valuable route for an expansionist America.

With the close of the Mexican War and the expiration of legislation authorizing the raising of volunteer forces, the services of additional volunteers for duty on the Trail could no longer be secured. Continued protection of the Trail would now depend upon the regular army. The accomplishments of the Indian Battalion in 1848 were only temporary, and unless troops were sent out to make the route safe the following year, and unless proper treaties were negotiated with the Indians, all the gains probably would be lost.

Lieutenant Colonel Gilpin realized that his operations were only the beginning of a solution for the problem facing the War Department, so he made several recommendations to the government as the period of service of the Indian Battalion drew to a close. He believed that the establishment of five military posts, the assignment of a large number of troops to garrison them and provide escorts along the Trail, and the negotiation of peace treaties with belligerent Indians would bring an end to hostilities. He recommended purchasing Bent's Fort for one of the military posts and suggested the following sites for the other four: (1) Pawnee Fork, (2) Cimarron Crossing, (3) Upper Crossing, and (4) Upper Canadian River. He thought one thousand mounted troops would be necessary in order to accomplish the desired results.[76] Indian Agent Fitzpatrick made similar recommendations.[77] How well the War Department would heed these recommendations, or how successful they would be if implemented, only time would tell.

[76] Gilpin to Jones, August 1, 1848, *ibid.*, 139–40.
[77] Fitzpatrick to Harvey, October 6, 1848, *ibid.*, 473.

4

Military Protection, 1848-1861

INDIAN ATTACKS on the Santa Fe Trail were not eliminated during the era between the close of the Mexican War and the outbreak of the Civil War. In fact, the Indians increased their hostilities, enticed as they were by additional opportunities such as a greater number of supply trains destined for the military establishments in the Southwest, more emigrants traveling to New Mexico and California, and newly established regular mail and stagecoach service over the Trail. The need for military protection increased proportionately, with special emphasis on the obligation to safeguard the Independence–Santa Fe mail run.

The recommendations of Gilpin and Fitzpatrick, to establish forts, provide large numbers of mounted troops, and negotiate treaties with the Indians, were ignored in the immediate post–Mexican War years, and the War Department was slow in devising a system of protection for the Trail. But steps were taken and a policy did emerge: several patrols were furnished for the protection of travelers and traders, an escort system was put into operation to protect the mail coaches, and four military posts were established along the route and one additional post erected near enough to the Trail to supply protective escorts and serve as a base of operations against hostile Indians.

While these steps were being taken to protect the Trail, the soldiers serving along the route again operated under various obstacles and inadequacies. The military posts were not established rapidly enough, and those occupied were too small and too far apart to be totally effective. The supplies for men and animals and for maintaining quarters and fortifications were sometimes inadequate for optimum year-around operations. Garrison life was extremely lonely at those isolated outposts. The forts were often understaffed for meeting the demands of providing patrols, furnishing escorts, or taking the field to chastise hostile Indians. Nature imposed additional problems; the hot, windy summers and cold, blustery winters made garrison life in the poorly constructed quarters and escort duty along the Trail uncomfortable and difficult, as did the shortage of grass, water, and firewood, timber and other building materials. In the face of such difficulties and handicaps, it is perhaps surprising that the troops accomplished as much as they did.

Fort Mann was abandoned in September, 1848, when the Indian Battalion returned to Fort Leavenworth and was discharged from the service. This left the Trail with no military establishment between Fort Leavenworth and Las Vegas, New Mexico, where a small command had been stationed for protection since late 1846. Fort Mann was used as a safe stopping camp by the emigrants and teamsters traveling the route during the remainder of 1848 and throughout 1849, but it was deserted completely upon the establishment of Fort Atkinson nearby in 1850.[1]

Although no provisions had been made for protecting the Trail when the Indian Battalion's service expired, the increased Indian attacks during 1849 and early 1850 did cause concern within the War Department. Finally, in June, 1850, Adjutant General Jones advised Secretary of War G. W. Crawford:

> It is known that several large Tribes of Indians roam over these prairies, and they will whenever an opportunity offers, attack caravans for the sake of plunder, and sometimes murder our Citizens. These Indians can only be restrained by having among them, or in striking distance of their hunting grounds, a military force able to pursue and punish them whenever they commit aggressions upon travellers. On so long a route through an uninhabited region, it

[1] Averam B. Bender, *The March of Empire: Frontier Defense in the Southwest, 1848–60,* 242n.

doubtless would be well to have one, or more intermediate posts, where the weary traveller, after a tedious journey, could rest *securely*, and be enabled to replenish his exhausted supplies, &c.[2]

Jones recommended the establishment of posts at three positions along the Trail: Council Grove, Pawnee Fork, and the Big Timbers east of Bent's Fort. Shortly thereafter Secretary Crawford authorized the establishment of only one post, which he ordered to be so placed as to provide the most effective protection of the route. Lieutenant Colonel E. V. Sumner, First Dragoons, was designated to select the site and make the necessary arrangements for the construction of the post. However, the fort was to be erected by Company D, Sixth Infantry, then stationed at Fort Leavenworth under the command of Captain William Hoffman.[3]

During July, 1850, a temporary post, Camp Mackay (named for Colonel E. A. Mackay of the quartermaster department) was established near the Cimarron Crossing.[4] The soldiers could protect a section of the Trail from this outpost until Sumner selected a permanent site for the new fort. By the end of August, Sumner had come out to the crossing and had assumed command of the total force of 135 officers and men at Camp Mackay.[5]

Sumner carefully scouted the region between Pawnee Fork and Bent's Fort, seeking the most logical post site. The place he finally chose was located approximately twenty-six miles east of the Cimarron Crossing, a few miles west of the point where the Wet and Dry Routes from Pawnee Fork rejoined, and within one mile of old Fort Mann. This was a location which all travelers using the Trail would pass, since it was above the two alternate routes and below the main crossings of the Arkansas. In addition, the grass appeared to be sufficient for grazing purposes. Sumner directed

[2] Jones to Crawford, June 5, 1850, Letters Sent, MSS, AGO, AACB, NA.
[3] Jones to Scott, June 13, 1850, *ibid.*; General Orders, No. 21, Headquarters Sixth Military Department, June 13, 1850, Orders and Special Orders of the Sixth and Seventh Military Departments, Vol. 247 (1848–50), MSS, *ibid.*
[4] Sumner to Buell, September 10, 1850, Letters Received, MSS, *ibid.*
[5] Camp Mackay, Post Returns August, 1850, MSS, *ibid.*

Soldiers on the Santa Fe Trail

that the buildings be constructed of stone because of the scarcity of timber. In view of the lateness of the season, he did not attempt to erect permanent quarters before winter; instead, the troops were instructed to build temporary quarters of sod to protect them during the coming cold months. After he had decided on the location and established the building plans, Sumner returned to Fort Leavenworth. The troops at Camp Mackay abandoned that temporary post on September 12, 1850, and moved to the new site, which was designated simply as the "New Post" until officially named "'Fort Atkinson" in June, 1851. The troops, however, because of the building materials used, called it "Fort Sod" and "Fort Sodom."[6]

The question of location would seem to have been final when it was approved by the commanding general of the army, Winfield Scott, and during December he ordered that the permanent stone structures be built the following spring.[7] Nevertheless, the commanding officer at Fort Atkinson, Captain Hoffman, decided after completion of the sod quarters that the location was undesirable. He reported:

> To satisfy you of the scarcity of timber in this vicinity, I need only mention the fact, that to construct these temporary quarters, which have sod walls, and are without floors, except in one room, every tree within twenty miles, from which a board twelve feet long could be sawed, has been cut down and brought in, and the lumber thus obtained, mostly cottonwood, is so unfit for use that the roofs which are made of it, have to be daubed with mud, or covered with tarpaulins to make them proof against the rain and snow. In a recent snow storm, the snow was three to five inches deep inside some of the quarters. . . .

---

[6] Sumner to Buell, September 10, 1850, Letters Received, MSS, *ibid.;* Fort Atkinson, Post Returns, September, 1850, and June, 1851, MSS, *ibid.;* Buckner to Jones, February 7, 1852, Departmental Commands, MSS, *ibid.;* Percival G. Lowe, "Kansas as Seen in the Indian Territory," *Kansas Historical Society Transactions,* Vol. IV (1886-90), 363.

[7] General Orders, No. 44, Headquarters of the Army, December 16, 1850, MS, AGO, AACB, NA.

Military Protection, 1848-1861

Stone cannot be found nearer than ten miles and if clay can be found in the vicinity, of a quality to make bricks, there is no wood with which to burn them.[8]

Hoffman recommended that the post be removed to Pawnee Fork, where more timber was available. In addition, he pointed out that this location would be nearer Fort Leavenworth, the source of supplies, and would reduce the cost of transportation. The cogency of his proposal found support, and the following spring orders were issued to move the fort to Pawnee Fork.[9] Yet somehow the move did not take place. The order failed to reach Fort Atkinson for several months, and by that time Captain Hoffman had been relieved of command. It is not clear whether the order was countermanded by department headquarters because of the lateness of the season when it did reach Fort Atkinson, or because the new commander, Captain R. H. Chilton, concluded that the move was not necessary and recommended that the order be rescinded. Whatever the reason, the order was suspended and Fort Atkinson remained on the site selected by Lieutenant Colonel Sumner.[10]

Subsequently, several studies were made of the advisability of relocating the post, but it remained at the original site until abandoned in 1854.[11] Sumner always defended his selection and in 1858 called for its reactivation:

> I would respectfully remark that the best position, and I believe the only one, to protect the Santa Fe road effectually, is the site of old Fort Atkinson. . . . The Indians congregate in large numbers, every summer in that vicinity, and if there are no troops there, travelers have no safety but in the forbearance of the Indians. . . .

---

[8] Hoffman to McDowell, December 10, 1850, Letters Received, MSS, *ibid.*

[9] General Orders, No. 10, Headquarters Sixth Military Department, March 29, 1851, Orders and Special Orders of the Sixth and Seventh Military Departments, Vol. 248 (1851-52), MSS, *ibid.*

[10] Buckner to Jones, February 7, 1852, Departmental Commands, MSS, *ibid.;* Fort Atkinson, Post Returns, June, 1851, MSS, *ibid.*

[11] See Buckner to Jones, February 7, 1852, Departmental Commands, MSS, *ibid.;* Heth to McDowell, March 1, 1853, *ibid.*

Soldiers on the Santa Fe Trail

I would respectfully and earnestly recommend the re-establishment of this post.[12]

The location may have been excellent for protection of the Trail, but the small size of its garrison kept the post ineffective. Captain Hoffman discovered that one company of infantry was not sufficient to protect even that section of the Trail between Walnut Creek and the Cimarron Crossing, where many Indian attacks occurred. He recommended that at least three or four companies be garrisoned at Fort Atkinson and that half of them be mounted. But no reinforcements were sent.

When the post was surrounded by Kiowa and Comanche camps during the spring of 1851, the soldiers lived in constant fear of attack. They were outnumbered so greatly that the Indians could have destroyed them all had they decided to attack. Finally, a call for help was sent out, and Company B, First Dragoons, under the command of Captain Chilton, came to their aid from Fort Leavenworth. Arriving at Fort Atkinson on June 25, this additional company helped to stabilize a serious situation. At this time a large number of recruits were marched over the Trail to New Mexico, and this somewhat intimidated the Indians and removed any immediate threat to the little post. Captain Chilton and the Dragoons then departed, July 6, for their home station, leaving the one company of infantry to protect the Trail for the remainder of the year.[13]

Another problem, of a somewhat amusing nature, faced the soldiers at the post during the summer of 1851. The sod walls of the buildings made ideal shelters for field mice, and they overran the quarters and destroyed provisions at an alarming rate. This difficulty was quickly mitigated when Lieutenant Henry Heth, new commanding officer at the post, requisitioned a dozen cats, and

---

[12] Sumner to Headquarters of the Army, October 5, 1858, Letters Received, MSS, *ibid.*

[13] Fort Atkinson, Post Returns, June, July, 1851, MSS, *ibid.*; Sumner to Jones, October 24, 1851, Departmental Commands, MSS, *ibid.*; Lowe, *Kansas Historical Society Transactions*, Vol. IV (1886–90), 363–64.

Military Protection, 1848-1861

these were sent out from Fort Leavenworth.[14] Unfortunately, no such simple solution existed for the major difficulty—too few troops to deal adequately with the Indians.[15]

Lieutenant Simon B. Buckner, Sixth Infantry, assumed command of the fort on November 6, 1851.[16] He concluded near the end of the following winter that it would be advisable to withdraw the garrison from Fort Atkinson to Fort Leavenworth during the winter months, leaving a small detachment of a dozen men to guard the supplies during that time. Such a move would conserve firewood and curtail expenditures. He found that there was little traffic over the Trail during the winter and that most of the Indians left the region to protect themselves from the cold. With no threat to the Trail, there was no need for a large winter command. On the other hand, he urged that the summer garrison consist of not less than one company of infantry to guard, construct, and supply the post and two companies of cavalry to deal with the Indians.[17]

In connection with this latter request, Buckner pointed out that, if only the company of infantry were stationed at the post, the men would be too busy with other duties during the coming spring and summer to provide any protection to the Trail. The soldiers would be engaged in cultivating a garden, constructing "essential" buildings, cutting and hauling wood at least twelve miles, and gathering hay from points of equal or farther distances.[18] The detachments

---

[14] *Ibid.*, 364.

[15] The commanding officer at the post explained why the garrison was inadequate: "On account of the small number of troops at this Post, it would be impossible to make demonstrations against these Indians; were their numbers such as could warrant any action on my part, it would be highly improper to attempt it, as the entire road would be open to them [while the soldiers pursued the Indians], and I could afford no assistance." Heth to Jones, September 4, 1851, Letters Received, MSS, AGO, AACB, NA.

[16] Fort Atkinson, Post Returns, November, 1851, MSS, *ibid.*

[17] Buckner to Jones, February 7, 1852, Departmental Commands, MSS, *ibid.*

[18] In 1851 the garrison of each frontier post was ordered to engage in farming operations in an attempt to provide some of its own supplies and thus reduce the costs of transportation and storage. General Orders, No. 1, Headquarters of the Army, January 8, 1851, MS, *ibid.* These attempts usually failed because the soldiers were

for each of these duties would be large, for assurance of protection from the Indians. Thus the troops at the post would usually be at the bare minimum to guard it from attack, and no troops would be available for duty along the Trail. He concluded his plea for cavalry reinforcements by stating that he expected several thousand Indians to spend the summer within "a very short distance of the post."[19]

Regardless of the anticipated needs of Fort Atkinson, no reinforcements were sent. By June, 1852, Buckner was simmering because of what he considered to be lack of support from department headquarters. Upon receipt of a communication from the headquarters of the army, stating that the Trail was receiving adequate protection from military patrols, the lieutenant exceeded the boiling point and let off steam in a lengthy and condemnatory reply to the adjutant general.[20] He criticized his superiors' policies, emphasized the ineffectiveness of his force, and again requested—practically demanded—reinforcements. Large encampments of Indians were located nearby, but the seriousness of the situation cannot be determined from the records available.

Within a month of Lieutenant Buckner's outburst—on July 3, 1852—General N. S. Clarke, department commander, ordered Major W. F. Sanderson and his Mounted Riflemen to leave Fort Leavenworth for Fort Atkinson, to help safeguard the situation there. He was to be accompanied by Captain Chilton's company of First Dragoons, which would remain at Fort Atkinson for the duration of the season. Meanwhile, Major Sanderson and the Mounted Riflemen were to proceed to Fort Laramie for the protection of

---

too busy with other duties to devote the necessary time to such pursuits. *Annual Report of the Secretary of War, 1852,* 32 Cong., 2 sess., *Sen. Exec. Doc. 1,* p. 4.

[19] Buckner to McDowell, February 8, 1852, Departmental Commands, MSS, AGO, AACB, NA.

[20] Buckner to Jones, June 9, 1852, *ibid.* Buckner would not know for approximately three more weeks that patrols from Fort Union were operating successfully along the western half of the Trail. See below and Buckner to Jones, July 1, 1852, *ibid.*

Military Protection, 1848-1861

travelers on the Oregon Trail. Captain Chilton was to return to Fort Leavenworth when the grass for his mounts was gone.[21]

These reinforcements did not reach Fort Atkinson until August 1.[22] In the interval, however, the situation at the post had improved. On June 27, Captain James H. Carleton arrived there from Fort Union, New Mexico, with his company of Dragoons which had been sent out to patrol the Trail between those two forts. Lieutenant Buckner detained this force at the post for a time, to help offset the Indian threat by increased strength. Although the Dragoons had been sent back to Fort Union before Major Sanderson arrived, when he reached Fort Atkinson the situation was such that the Mounted Riflemen could proceed immediately to Fort Laramie. Captain Chilton took command of the post and his company remained there until September 27, when they returned to Leavenworth because of the shortage of grass. Thus Fort Atkinson had been effective in restraining the Indians for almost two months, and, in addition, the infantrymen stationed there were able to lay in their supplies for the coming winter.[23]

When the Dragoons left, Lieutenant Heth again assumed command of the garrison, and the company of infantry survived the cold winter at the post without incident. But Heth found cause for alarm by the following spring. In April, 1853, he reported that the Cheyennes were attacking travelers on the Trail, requested reinforcements, and urged that an escort be provided for the May mail train from Independence.[24]

The escort was furnished, and in June Company B, First Dragoons, was sent to serve at Fort Atkinson during the summer months. This meant that on June 25 Captain Chilton again as-

[21] Clarke to Jones, July 3, 1852, McDowell to Sanderson, July 3, 1852, *ibid*.
[22] Fort Atkinson, Post Returns, August, 1852, MSS, *ibid*.
[23] Buckner to Jones, July 1, 1852, Departmental Commands, MSS, *ibid.*, Clarke to Jones, July 3, 1852, *ibid.;* Fort Atkinson, Post Returns, August, September, 1852, MSS, *ibid*.
[24] Heth to McDowell, April 10, 1853, Departmental Commands, MSS, *ibid.;* Fort Atkinson, Post Returns, September, 1852 to April, 1853, MSS, *ibid*.

sumed command of the post, and he and his company remained there until August 6. In the meantime, the garrison provided some protection to the Trail, although the Cheyennes did not cease their hostilities entirely.[25]

One of the important services provided by the garrison at Fort Atkinson was the protection it afforded a mail station for Hall and Company, mail contractor for the route between Independence and Santa Fe. Soon after the fort was established in 1850, the company secured permission to establish a relay station there in order that the trains traveling both east and west could repair their wagons and change mules before completing their journeys.[26] By protecting a mail station nearly equidistant from both ends of the Trail, the post provided valuable assistance to the contractor and the citizens of the Southwest. That the mail station was dependent upon the presence of the military was evidenced by the fact that when the post was abandoned the station was removed.

Early in September, 1853, Fort Atkinson was abandoned. The quarters, having deteriorated, were believed to provide insufficient protection from the coming cold winds and snow. Moreover, neither wood nor forage was available, and it was too difficult and expensive to transport all supplies to the post during the winter months. When the garrison left, the mail station was removed to Walnut Creek, approximately ninety miles east, and the soldiers from Fort Atkinson camped briefly at this station before retiring to Fort Riley.[27]

The effect of the abandonment of Fort Atkinson on the lines of communication to the Southwest was soon felt, and the territorial legislature of New Mexico sent a memorial to Congress, February

[25] Clarke to Fauntleroy, April 18, 1853, Departmental Commands, MSS, *ibid.;* Fort Atkinson, Post Returns, June, July, August, 1853, MSS, *ibid.*

[26] Buckner to Jones, April 20, 1852, Departmental Commands, MSS, *ibid.;* Hall to Sumner, September 26, 1859, Letters Received, MSS, *ibid.*

[27] Johnson to Hancock, May 12, 1853, Departmental Commands, MSS, *ibid.;* Special Orders, No. 44, Headquarters Sixth Military Department, July 29, 1853, Letters Received, MSS, *ibid.;* 33 Cong., 1 sess., *Sen. Exec. Doc. 1,* pp. 95, 116–17; "Early Military Posts, Missions and Camps," *Kansas Historical Society Transactions,* Vols. I and II (1875–78), 265.

Military Protection, 1848–1861

4, 1854, requesting that the post be re-established. The memorial stressed the need for the mail station as being of prime importance. Whether or not the New Mexico plea was the cause, the fort was reoccupied the following May by two companies of Sixth Infantry. They provided protection to the region until the post was abandoned for the last time on October 2, 1854.[28]

Even though it had proved useful, Fort Atkinson had failed to accomplish all that the War Department intended and desired, that is, prevention of hostilities along the Trail. The garrison at the post was never large; the average number of troops stationed there from September, 1850, to August, 1853, was about eighty, except when the company of Dragoons pushed it up to about 145 during August and September, 1852, and June and July, 1853. The average command from May to October, 1854, was approximately 140 men.[29] Except when the company of Dragoons was stationed there, the garrison was unable to pursue and chastise hostile Indians. Beyond occupying and making safe a camp and mail station in the middle of an area of Indian hostilities, the post had produced few results.

It should be noted that stone buildings were never constructed, as Sumner had originally planned, because of insufficient materials and an inadequate number of men with time to perform construction duties. Also, the location proved unsatisfactory because of the distance from the source of supplies and the shortage of wood and forage.

Fort Atkinson was the first of a series of posts established on the Trail during the post–Mexican War era; its relative ineffectiveness exhibited the need for additional forts with larger forces assigned to each one in the future. Its significance was not in what

[28] 33 Cong., 1 sess., *House Mis. Doc. 47;* Fort Atkinson, Post Returns, 1854, MSS, AGO, AACB, NA; General Orders, No. 5, Headquarters of the Army, September 6, 1854, MS, *ibid.*

[29] Fort Atkinson, Post Returns, 1850–54, MSS, *ibid.* These figures are the total number of soldiers stationed at the post, including those sick, in the guard house, and on detached duty. Thus the number on active duty was often less. This qualification also applies to all reports cited on the number of troops garrisoned at other posts.

Soldiers on the Santa Fe Trail

it had accomplished, but in what it was unable to accomplish, for it pointed the way to improvement of military protection for the Santa Fe Trail.

One year after Fort Atkinson was established, a more important post was founded on the Trail in New Mexico. This was Fort Union, occupied until 1891.[30] Fort Union was established for three basic purposes: to serve as a military depot for the forts located in New Mexico, to chastise the hostile Indians and help protect the settlements in northeastern New Mexico, and to aid in protecting travelers on the Santa Fe Trail. Only the last of these purposes will be considered here.

In March, 1851, Major John Munroe, commanding the Ninth Military Department, which embraced New Mexico, sent Captain L. C. Easton, Quartermaster Department, and Lieutenant John G. Parke, Topographical Engineers, to "examine the country in the vicinity of Las Vegas and the Moro [Mora] Creek with a view to selecting a site for the establishment of a depot for supplies coming from the U.S."[31] This examination was conducted and a site selected, but Lieutenant Colonel Sumner replaced Munroe as department commander on July 19, 1851, before a new post was established. However, Sumner immediately continued with the same plans.[32]

---

[30] A somewhat popularized, book-length study of Fort Union, containing much quoted material (some of it poorly documented), is F. Stanley, *Fort Union, New Mexico*. Two brief, scholarly studies of the post are Henry Wood, "Fort Union: End of the Santa Fe Trail," *1949 Brand Book* (Denver, 1950), 205–56 and Robert M. Utley, "Fort Union and the Santa Fe Trail," *New Mexico Historical Review*, Vol. XXXVI (January, 1961), 36–48.

[31] Special Orders, No. 14, Headquarters Ninth Military Department, March 14, 1851, cited in *ibid.*, 37. It is interesting to note that Alexander Barclay and W. B. Doyle constructed an adobe fort at the junction of Mora and Sapello creeks during 1848 and 1849, with hopes of selling it to the army. Transcript of the Alexander Barclay Papers, MSS, State Historical Society of Colorado, Denver. No mention was found in the official military records that Barclay's Fort was ever considered as a military site.

[32] Sumner to Jones, October 24, 1851, Departmental Commands, MSS, AGO, AACB, NA.

Military Protection, 1848–1861

The same day he assumed command of the department, Sumner ordered the principal depot and the headquarters of the department transferred to the Río Mora and a new post established there.[33] One week later, July 26, the post at Las Vegas was abandoned by two companies of First Dragoons and two companies of Third Infantry, and the new post was established on the evening of the same day by these troops, under the command of Captain Edmund B. Alexander. A company of Third Infantry departed Fort Marcy at Santa Fe on July 23 and arrived at this post on July 27, making a total command of 339 officers and men.[34] The new military post was designated "Fort Union" on August 2, 1851.[35] According to F. Stanley, "It became within a few years the largest military post on the western plains."[36]

Fort Union was located approximately five miles from the Río Mora on El Arroyo del Coyote, a few miles from the Turkey Mountains, and about six miles northeast of the confluence of Sapello Creek and the Río Mora, where the Cimarron and Mountain routes of the Santa Fe Trail joined (near present Watrous, New Mexico).[37] This was eighteen miles east of Mora, New Mexico, twenty-six miles from Las Vegas on the Trail, and approximately 100 miles from Santa Fe. The post was located on the Mora Land Grant, and the government paid rent to the proprietors of this grant until the post was abandoned in 1891. In addition to serving the three purposes mentioned above, the post was located to cut down on the expenditures of the army by removing the troops from Santa Fe

---

[33] General Orders, No. 17, Headquarters Ninth Military Department, July 19, 1851, Ninth Military Department Orders, Vol. 36, MSS, United States Army Commands (Record Group No. 98), Army and Air Corps Branch, National Archives (hereafter cited as USAC, AACB, NA).

[34] Fort Union, Post Returns, July, 1851, MSS, AGO, AACB, NA.

[35] General Orders, No. 21, Headquarters Ninth Military Department, August 2, 1851, Ninth Military Department Orders, Vol. 36, MSS, USAC, AACB, NA.

[36] Stanley, *Fort Union*, 56.

[37] The exact geographic location was 35° 54' 21" north latitude and 104° 57' 15" west longitude. Fort Union, Medical History, Army Post Records, MSS, AGO, AACB, NA.

Soldiers on the Santa Fe Trail

and Las Vegas and placing the soldiers away from the "demoralizing" life in these two towns.[38]

Consonant with the purpose of providing additional protection to the Trail, on August 2, 1851, Sumner ordered Captain Carleton and his company of First Dragoons to begin patrolling the route between Forts Union and Atkinson, along the Cimarron Route.[39] Here was an experiment with a new method of protecting the Trail. The purpose of this command was not to escort caravans, nor was it to locate the Indians' camps and chastise the hostiles. Rather, it was hoped the presence of troops just marching along the Trail in the region would restrain the Indians and thus safeguard traders and travelers using the route. In addition, this force would provide assistance, when necessary, to those experiencing Indian attacks. Thus patrols were added to the methods of protection already in operation—escorts, fortifications, and expeditions against hostile bands of Indians.

The 1851 patrol made one trip to Fort Atkinson, a distance of 319 miles as measured by a viameter attached to the wheel of a wagon, and returned to Fort Union. Lieutenant Colonel Sumner believed that it was successful in preventing the Kiowas, Comanches, and Apaches from committing hostilities upon the freight caravans, travelers, and mail trains using that section of the Trail.[40] The following summer this same company made two trips between Fort Atkinson and Fort Union, and again the results were gratify-

[38] Sumner to Jones, October 24, 1851, Departmental Commands, MSS, *ibid.* Sumner had been ordered by Secretary of War Conrad to make the system of defense in this department more effective by revising the method of operations, reducing expenditures, removing the troops from the towns, and organizing expeditions against the hostile Indians to make them feel the power of the United States Army. Conrad to Sumner, April 1, 1851, 32 Cong., 1 sess., *Sen. Exec. Doc. 1*, pp. 125–26. For a description of Sumner's economy drive, of which Fort Union was a part, see Aurora Hunt, *Major General James Henry Carleton, 1814–1873: Western Frontier Dragoon*, 130–31.

[39] General Orders, No. 21, Headquarters Ninth Military Department, August 2, 1851, Ninth Military Department Orders, Vol. 36, MSS, USAC, AACB, NA.

[40] Sumner to Jones, October 24, 1851, Departmental Commands, MSS, AGO, AACB, NA; Hunt, *James H. Carleton*, 113.

Military Protection, 1848-1861

ing. In addition to protecting the route, the patrol had provided valuable assistance to the little garrison at Fort Atkinson in late June and early July, as noted above.

Besides the patrols, the garrison at Fort Union provided at least one special escort along the Trail in 1852. In May, twenty-one Dragoons were detailed to accompany New Mexican Territorial Governor James S. Calhoun on his way to Missouri. Calhoun was very ill at the time of departure and was confined to bed at Fort Union several days before resuming his journey. He intended to go to Washington on business, but he must have known he could not make it that far. He had the carpenters at Fort Union build his coffin, and he carried it with him along the Trail. The detachment escorted the governor at least as far as Fort Atkinson, possibly to Pawnee Fork, and then returned to Fort Union. Although the soldiers had safely conducted Calhoun through the region of threatened Indian hostilities, he succumbed to his disease shortly before reaching Independence on July 2.[41]

William Carr Lane was appointed by President Millard Fillmore to succeed Calhoun, and he left immediately for New Mexico. Taking the stage from Independence, he arrived at Fort Atkinson in July, 1852, where Captain Carleton and his patrol had been detained by Lieutenant Buckner. The Dragoons were ready to march back to Fort Union, so Lane left the stage and traveled with Carleton. They arrived at Fort Union on August 2, and the new governor (who was sixty-three years old) remained for a few days at the home of Captain and Mrs. Carleton to recuperate from the arduous journey. After his rest, the governor rode to Santa Fe in an army ambulance, escorted by Carleton and his company of Dragoons.

The experiment with patrols had apparently proven successful so far as results were concerned. Nevertheless, patrols were no longer provided after 1852. The exact reason is not clear from avail-

---

[41] Special Orders, No. 31, Headquarters Ninth Military Department, Vol. 37, MSS, USAC, AACB, NA; Outline Description of Fort Union, MS, AGO, AACB, NA; Hunt, *James H. Carleton*, 118.

Soldiers on the Santa Fe Trail

able records. Whatever the reason, the patrols were discontinued and a system of escorts for the Independence-Santa Fe mail trains was inaugurated.

The mail escorts were not sent on a regular basis, but beginning in 1853 they were provided whenever the Post Office Department, officials of the mail contracting company, or the commanding officer of Fort Union considered the danger sufficient to require military protection. In February, 1856, the commanding officer at Fort Union, Lieutenant W. T. Magruder, recommended that the escorts be discontinued because there was no apparent threat from the Indians.[42] His recommendation was rejected, and, as a matter of fact, during the latter part of 1857 the commander of Fort Union, by order of the Secretary of War, began sending regular escorts with all mail trains.[43]

The size, methods, and problems of the mail escorts have been succinctly described by Robert M. Utley:

> The escort usually consisted of an officer and 20 to 40 men, later of a sergeant and 15 to 20 men, who accompanied the stages to the Arkansas and returned to Fort Union with the next westbound mail. The soldiers, infantry or dismounted horsemen, rode in wagons. This method had been adopted by Col. John Garland, Department Commander, because it afforded better defense in the event of attack and because of the scarcity of grass, especially in winter, along the road between the Canadian and the Arkansas. Even so, the mules drawing the escort wagons frequently broke down and always had trouble keeping up with the mail coaches. The stage company had relay stations with fresh animals on the Mora and the Arkansas, but the army mules travelled over 600 miles from Fort Union to the Arkansas and back, without relief. So troublesome did this problem become that Colonel Garland in March 1858 requested the Adjutant General of the Army to have instructions issued to the mail company to keep pace with the slower moving escort.[44]

---

[42] Magruder to Nichols, February 10, 1856, Fort Union, Letters Sent, MSS, USAC, AACB, NA.

[43] Utley, *New Mexico Historical Review,* Vol. XXXVI (1961), 41.

[44] *Ibid.,* 41-42. Also, see Fauntleroy to Nichols, December 10, 1854, Fort Union,

Military Protection, 1848–1861

The success of these mail escorts is evidenced by Colonel Garland's report in January, 1858, which boasted "that no mail has been lost since my administration of this Military Department—four years and a half—and that I have never failed to furnish escorts whenever in my judgment they were deemed necessary."[45] However, because of the absence of Indian hostilities along the western half of the Trail, Garland discontinued the mail escorts in May of 1858. Colonel Thomas Turner Fauntleroy replaced Garland as department commander in October of that year, and he authorized regular mail escorts again. This was fortunate, because a band of Kiowas attacked the mail coach and its escort at Cold Spring on December 4, 1858. After a battle of several hours, the Indians retreated, having wounded one soldier.[46]

Beginning in 1858 the Kiowas and Comanches became a more serious and constant threat to the Trail, and this continued until

---

Letters Sent, MSS, USAC, AACB, NA; McFerran to Loring, March 9, 1858, Loring to Easton, March 10, 1858, Departmental Commands, MSS, AGO, AACB, NA. One of the orders for the mail escort is copied here to show the stipulations laid down for them:

HEADQUARTERS FORT UNION, N.M.
OCTOBER 14, 1857

Wm. B. Lane
Lieut., Mtd. Riflemen
SIR:

I am directed by the colonel commanding, to instruct you to take command of the escort of 2 non-commissioned officers and 23 privates detailed from the Mounted Riflemen as an escort for the United States Mail which leaves this post on or about the 3rd inst. You will accompany the mail giving it and the party with it protection against Indians as far as the Arkansas, if upon arriving there you should discover that the mail party may be menaced beyond that point, you will accompany it two or three days farther, taking every precaution to guard against Surprise either going or returning.

Your marches will not be farther than 30 miles a day or as far as in your judgement your horses can possible go.

By order of COL. W. W. LORING

Fort Union, Letters Sent, MSS, USAC, AACB, NA.

[45] Garland to Cooper, January 30, 1858, Letters Received, MSS, AGO, AACB, NA.

[46] Utley, *New Mexico Historical Review,* Vol. XXXVI (1961), 42–43.

the Civil War. In December, 1860, Colonel Fauntleroy directed Lieutenant Colonel George B. Crittenden, commanding officer at Fort Union, to chastise the Kiowas and Comanches at every opportunity. Upon receipt of information that these Indians were plundering along the Mountain Route about seventy miles north of Fort Union, Crittenden and a detachment of eighty-eight Mounted Riflemen moved into the field to locate and punish the offenders. Meanwhile the Indians moved from the Mountain Route to attack travelers on the Cimarron. Crittenden pursued them, and by making forced marches surprised an encampment of approximately 175 lodges of Comanches and Kiowas about ten miles north of Cold Spring on January 2, 1861. The Indians were driven from their camp, suffered at least ten killed, and lost an unknown number wounded. Three Mounted Riflemen were injured, none was killed. The troops destroyed the encampment and the supplies the Indians had left behind, and returned to Fort Union with forty horses they had captured during the engagement.[47]

The troops stationed at Fort Union had provided protection for the western half of the Santa Fe Trail after its establishment in 1851. Unlike that at Fort Atkinson, the garrison at Fort Union was large enough that detachments could be detailed specifically for duty along the Trail. Another advantage came from the fact that permanent quarters of adobe were constructed at Fort Union, and it was one of the most comfortable posts established on the Santa Fe Trail. This post continued to provide valuable service during and after the Civil War, and its importance in those eras will be considered below.

Fort Riley, although not located on the Santa Fe Trail, deserves brief mention at this point, with further notice later, because it was situated near enough to the Trail to furnish escorts and serve as a base of operations against the Indians who roamed the region. In July, 1852, Colonel Fauntleroy recommended to the quarter-

[47] Crittenden to Mauny, January 9, 1861, Departmental Commands, MSS, AGO, AACB, NA; Fauntleroy to Thomas, January 12, 1861, Letters Received, MSS, *ibid.*

Military Protection, 1848-1861

master general that a military post be established for protecting the frontier, "at or near a point on the Kansas River where the Republican fork unites with it."[48]

Secretary of War C. M. Conrad soon acted upon this recommendation, directing General Clarke, Sixth Military Department, to appoint a board of officers to select a site for the new post. On September 21, 1852, Clarke appointed several officers, consisting of two captains of the Quartermaster Department, E. A. Ogden and L. C. Easton, Captain Charles S. Lovell, Sixth Infantry, and Lieutenant J. C. Woodruff, Topographical Engineers, to investigate the region where the Smoky Hill and Republican rivers joined to form the Kansas. Escorted by Captain Chilton and his company of First Dragoons, the board established a camp at the present site of Fort Riley and designated it Camp Center because it was believed to be near the geographic center of the United States. The report of the board, dated November 10, 1852, was approved by the secretary of war on January 7, 1853, and the following March Congress appropriated $65,000 for construction of the post.[49]

Three companies of Sixth Infantry, under command of Captain Lovell, occupied Camp Center in May, 1853, and began the construction of temporary quarters. A little more than a month later the post was given the name "Fort Riley" in honor of Major General Bennet Riley, who had led the first military escort on the Trail in 1829.[50] The fort was made a cavalry post by act of Congress in 1855, and construction of permanent buildings was begun that same year.

When Fort Atkinson was abandoned in 1853, as mentioned above, the company of infantry stationed there was sent to Fort Riley. This pushed up the strength of the garrison to four com-

[48] Fauntleroy to Jesup, July 31, 1852, cited in W. F. Pride, *The History of Fort Riley*, 60-61.
[49] *Ibid.*, 61.
[50] General Orders, No. 9, Headquarters Sixth Military Department, March 31, 1853, General Orders, No. 17, Headquarters of the Army, June 17, 1853, cited in *ibid.*

Soldiers on the Santa Fe Trail

panies of Sixth Infantry, according to the October, 1853, returns, making an aggregate of 244 officers and men, 211 on active duty.[51]

Fort Riley was nearer the scenes of Indian hostilities along the Trail than Fort Leavenworth, and so from the first its garrison provided occasional escorts to mail trains and spent the summer months in the field protecting the routes of travel across the plains.[52] Because of the increased hostilities of the Kiowas and Comanches along the Cimarron and Arkansas rivers in 1859 and 1860, troops from Fort Riley were actively engaged in protecting the Trail from these Indians.

The Kiowas and Comanches had caused troubles for travelers on the Trail since the 1820's. Indian Agent Fitzpatrick had negotiated the first treaty with these Indians in 1853, the terms of which pledged the Indians to remain peaceful. The treaty granted the government the right to build military posts and construct roads through lands claimed by the Indians, and provided for an annual payment of $18,000 in commodities to the Indians. The treaty was to last for ten years, and could be extended for five more years if both parties agreed. The Indians had promised not to commit hostilities against the whites; if they did, their annuities could be withheld.[53]

The Kiowas and Comanches had found it difficult to keep the promises made in the treaty. In August, 1858, the Indian agent for the upper Arkansas region, Robert Miller, reported that he found the Kiowas and Comanches quite hostile, and that they had made an attack, "in sight of my camp, while preparing to distribute presents [annuities] to them, upon two Mexican trains which they robbed of all their provisions."[54] His recommendation, with regard

[51] 33 Cong., 1 sess., *Sen. Exec. Doc. 1*, pp. 116–17.

[52] Percival G. Lowe, "Recollections of Fort Riley," *Kansas Historical Collections*, Vol. VII (1901–1902), 102–103.

[53] *Indian Affairs, Laws and Treaties* (ed. by Charles J. Kappler), II, 600–602; LeRoy R. Hafen and W. J. Ghent, *Broken Hand, the Life Story of Thomas Fitzpatrick, Chief of the Mountain Men*, 251–55; *Relations with the Indians of the Plains, 1857–1861: A Documentary Account* (ed. by LeRoy R. Hafen and Ann W. Hafen), 191.

[54] Miller to Robinson, August 17, 1858, 35 Cong., 2 sess., *Sen. Exec. Doc. 1*,

Military Protection, 1848-1861

to the Plains Indians, was that "Nothing short of a thorough chastisement, which they so richly deserve, will bring these people to their proper senses."[55]

Indian Agent William Bent, who replaced Miller in 1859, reported in October of that year:

> The Kiowa and Comanche Indians have, for two years, appeared in full numbers and for long periods upon the Arkansas....
>
> These I encountered, on my return [to St. Louis] at the mouth of Walnut Creek, on September 16, to the number of 2,500 warriors. They signified to me their desire for peace, which up to that time they have continued to preserve in the presence of the United States troops.
>
> So soon, however, as the latter withdrew to Fort Riley, the Comanches assumed a threatening attitude, which resembles the prelude of predatory attacks upon the unprotected whites, now at all seasons passing and repassing by the Santa Fe roads in great numbers.... A smothered passion for revenge agitates these Indians, perpetually fomented by the failure of food, the encircling encroachments of the white population, and exasperating sense of decay and impending extinction with which they are surrounded.[56]

Bent recommended the establishment of a military post at Pawnee Fork and another near the Big Timbers, and stressed that "To control them, it is essential to have among them the perpetual presence of the controlling military force."[57] During the following year, his recommendations were put into effect with the establishment of Forts Larned and Wise and a military campaign against the Kiowas and Comanches.

With the hostile activities of the Kiowas and Comanches along the Trail and the gold rush to Colorado increasing the traffic over the route in 1859, additional military protection was needed. The War Department recognized the danger of the situation and took

p. 450, reprinted in *Relations with the Indians of the Plains* (ed. by Hafen and Hafen), 166.

[55] *Ibid.*, 163.

[56] William W. Bent's Report, October 5, 1859, in *ibid.*, 185-86.

[57] *Ibid.*, 186.

Soldiers on the Santa Fe Trail

appropriate action. Three companies of First Cavalry, under the command of Captain W. D. DeSaussure, left Fort Riley on June 10, 1859, to establish a summer camp near old Fort Atkinson and protect that section of the Trail. This force was later joined by Captain W. T. Walker and his company of First Cavalry. The entire command was supplied by wagon trains operating out of Fort Riley.[58] During the summer one company of this detachment was sent to Pawnee Fork to establish a camp which later became Fort Larned. Since the activities of DeSaussure's command and the establishment of Fort Larned were interconnected, they are here considered together.

Pawnee Fork, as indicated above, had been suggested several times during the 1850's as a possible site for a military post, but no positive action had been taken. The camp located there in 1859 was established to provide protection for Hall and Company's new mail station. Jacob Hall, mail contractor, had attempted to establish a mail station at Pawnee Fork in the spring of 1859, but the effort had been countered by the Comanches and Kiowas, whose chiefs declared they would allow no relay station west of Walnut Creek. They threatened to burn any buildings constructed and kill any men sent to build or occupy them. In the face of this opposition, plans for a station at Pawnee Fork had been temporarily abandoned.[59]

Hall then applied to Postmaster General Joseph Holt for aid in removing the Indian threat, and Holt took up his cause. He explained the situation to Secretary of Interior Jacob Thompson, and resquested that his department, in charge of Indian affairs, take appropriate action to persuade the Indians to allow the mail station at Pawnee Fork. But Holt did not rely entirely on the efforts of the Department of Interior and its powers of persuasion. He re-

---

[58] General Orders, No. 2, Headquarters of the Army, May 16, 1859, MS, AGO, AACB, NA; Special Orders, No. 40, Headquarters Department of the West, May 21, 1859, Departmental Commands, MSS, *ibid.*

[59] Holt to Thompson, August 1, 1859, Letters Received, MSS, *ibid.*

Military Protection, 1848-1861

quested that the War Department provide a display of military force, and it was this appeal that brought results.[60]

Acting Secretary of War William R. Drinkard immediately directed Colonel Sumner, commanding the Department of the West, to send a company of cavalry to Pawnee Fork. Sumner accordingly ordered Captain DeSaussure to dispatch one of his companies of First Cavalry to encamp at that place until his command returned to Fort Riley in the autumn. Sumner also directed DeSaussure to make it clear to the chiefs of the Kiowas and Comanches "that if a mail station is established there, they must not molest it, or they will bring down upon themselves severe chastisement."[61]

On September 1, DeSaussure sent Captain Edward W. B. Newby and his company of cavalry to Pawnee Fork. With this assurance of military protection, on September 22 Jacob Hall sent a train of seven wagons of supplies and a number of employees, under direction of William Butze, from Independence to Pawnee Fork, with instructions to cut hay and construct permanent buildings and corrals.[62]

The mail contractor feared that the new station would be the object of Indian attacks as soon as the company stationed there withdrew in the early autumn, and he appealed to Sumner to leave the company of cavalry there until the middle of November. By that time he hoped to have the buildings and corrals up, hay cured, and enough men on hand to protect the station. In view of this request and the incidents that occurred along the Trail, described below, Sumner ordered that a company of cavalry replace the one already withdrawn from Pawnee Fork, for the protection of the mail party and passage of the mails until the threat from the Kiowas and Comanches subsided.[63]

Captain DeSaussure, near old Fort Atkinson, broke camp on

[60] Holt to Drinkard, August 4, 1859, *ibid.*
[61] Sumner to Cooper, August 10, 1859, *ibid.*
[62] DeSaussure to Jones, September 26, 1859, Hall to Sumner, September 26, 1859, *ibid.*
[63] *Ibid.;* Sumner to Cooper, October 4, 1859, *ibid.*

Soldiers on the Santa Fe Trail

September 14, 1859, and began the return march to Fort Riley. He arrived at Pawnee Fork on September 17, picked up Captain Newby's company, and continued to Walnut Creek, where he was scheduled to meet with the chiefs of the Kiowas and Comanches. Two days later he held a conference with one Comanche and several Kiowa chiefs, informed them that the army would protect the mail station at Pawnee Fork, and warned them not to molest the mail party there. The Indians professed to be friendly and assured the captain that the relay station would be left alone.[64]

DeSaussure's command then marched to Cow Creek where they encamped on September 20. There they met Major J. L. Donaldson, Quartermaster Department, in command of a small train of wagons heading for New Mexico, accompanied by a paymaster with $50,000. Major Donaldson proceeded to Walnut Creek the following day and discovered that two Kiowa sub-chiefs, Pawnee and Satank, intoxicated with liquor secured from a Mexican caravan, had attempted to murder the proprietors of Allison's Ranch, a small trading post located at Walnut Creek.[65] The two Indians had been driven off after a fight, but Donaldson feared that the Kiowas would return in force the following day and destroy the ranch. Consequently, he sent an express to Captain DeSaussure requesting that a detachment of sufficient size to restrain the Indians be rushed to that point.[66]

Captain W. T. Walker, with two companies of cavalry, was sent to examine the difficulty at Allison's Ranch. Arriving early on the morning of September 22, after a night march, the soldiers discovered that Pawnee, one of the perpetrators of the difficulties there, had returned. The Indian attempted to leave, but Walker took him prisoner in order to prevent him from warning his tribe

---

[64] DeSaussure to Jones, September 26, 1859, *ibid*.

[65] A few years previously, Bill Allison had erected a stockade near the site of present Great Bend, Kansas, from which he traded with the Indians. *Relations with the Indians of the Plains* (ed. by Hafen and Hafen), 103n.

[66] DeSaussure to Jones, September 26, 1859, Donaldson to DeSaussure, September 21, 1859, Walker to DeSaussure, September 23, 1859, Letters Received, MSS, AGO, AACB, NA.

that the troops had arrived. Captain Walker intended to take Pawnee with him to visit the chiefs of the Kiowas, make an investigation into the affair of the previous day, and "require such satisfaction as I thought the circumstances justified."[67]

Pawnee, now completely sober, made an attempt to escape, and Lieutenant George D. Bayard, adjutant of the detachment, was directed to place a guard over him. Before the guard could be set up, Pawnee jumped on a horse and took flight. Lieutenant Bayard quickly mounted and pursued him and, after several attempts to get him to stop, began firing over the Indian's head. Pawnee rode on, and Bayard, having exhausted all peaceable means of halting the Kiowa, shot him to prevent his escape. Pawnee died within ten minutes.

Captain Walker, realizing that the Kiowas probably would attempt to revenge the death of one of their sub-chiefs, sent an express to DeSaussure informing him of developments and then encamped near Allison's Ranch to protect it. Captain DeSaussure, leaving the dismounted men in charge of the quartermaster and commissary trains, rushed to Walnut Creek with the remaining mounted soldiers, arriving there the same evening, September 22. The following morning DeSaussure led a detachment in search of the Kiowas, failed to locate them, and returned in the evening and encamped at Walnut Creek. The mail from Independence arrived there during the night, and the conductor of the party requested an escort as far as Pawnee Creek. Lieutenant Elmer Otis and thirty men were provided for this duty, and the mail proceeded the following morning, September 24.[68]

The mail party reached Pawnee Fork about one o'clock that same afternoon, and grazed the animals and rested there for several hours. The escort, under orders to go only as far as Pawnee Fork, refused a request to advance farther, so the mail coach continued unguarded with its crew of three men—Conductor Michael Smith,

[67] *Ibid.*
[68] DeSaussure to Jones, September 26, 1859, Sworn Affidavit of William H. Cole, October 8, 1859, *ibid.*

Soldiers on the Santa Fe Trail

his brother, Lawrence, and William H. Cole. They traveled only about five or six miles before they were overtaken by a party of fifteen Kiowas, whose actions were later described by Cole:

> They at first appeared very friendly, and asked for sugar and crackers, which we gave them as was our custom. They insisted on more which was given them. This did not satisfy them, and they became very insolent, and one seized me by the breast, desiring me to get on behind an Indian. I broke loss [sic] from him, and as I did so, was shot in the back of the head & arm . . . at the same instant a ball pierced the heart of Lawrence Smith, who was sitting with lines in hand in the drivers seat, and the next instant, ten or twelve guns were simultaneously discharged, but neither the Conductor, nor myself was hit by this volley.[69]

Cole succeeded in dragging Lawrence Smith's body back into the wagon, and he grabbed the reins and headed the mules back toward Pawnee Fork. The conductor was astride one of the mules, "whipping up the team." The Indians' swift ponies soon overtook the wagon, and Michael Smith was shot and killed. With his two companions dead, Cole kept the mules going, until one of the Indians rode in front and attempted to stop them. Cole shot the Indian, who fell between the lead mules, causing one of them to rear up and entangle the team. Unable to proceed farther in the wagon, Cole jumped out and hid in the tall grass while the Indians stopped to examine their dead companion. The Indians then took those mules which had not been shot severely and left, after failing to locate the surviving member of the mail party. Remaining hidden during the night, Cole managed to make it back to the troops at Pawnee Fork early the following morning.

Lieutenant Otis and his detachment went out to investigate the scene of the attack; they buried the Smith brothers and recovered the mail. Meanwhile, the surgeon treated Cole's wounds, and later the entire party marched to Lost Spring where Captain DeSaussure and the remainder of his command were encamped.[70]

[69] *Ibid.*
[70] *Ibid.;* Butze to Hall, September 30, 1859, *ibid.*

Military Protection, 1848–1861

It was these events, plus the direct request from Jacob Hall, that caused Colonel Sumner on October 4, 1859, to order a company of First Cavalry to return and occupy a position near the mail station and to escort the mail coaches through the region of danger.[71] Unfortunately, even before the troops could carry out this assignment, the Kiowas committed additional hostilities. The eastbound mail from Santa Fe, which left that place without escort on September 19, had traveled without difficulty as far as Big Coon Creek, about thirty miles west of Pawnee Fork. There they met a westbound Mexican caravan which informed them of the Indian attack upon the westbound mail and the death of the Smith brothers. Afraid to proceed without escort, the mail party turned around and accompanied the Mexican train for eighteen miles. Then they met a train of the Majors and Russell Company returning from New Mexico and joined it until out of danger five days later. This party had found three returning Pikes Peak emigrants murdered in the road a few miles west of where the Kiowas had attacked the westbound mail.[72]

Company K, First Cavalry (seventy-five men in all), under the command of Captain George N. Steuart, was sent from Fort Riley to establish the post at Pawnee Fork, and the company arrived there October 22, 1859. Encamping about half a mile from the place of Captain Newby's summer camp, Steuart selected the site that would become Fort Larned.[73]

The post was designated as "Camp on Pawnee Creek" until February 12, 1860, when it was named "Camp Alert" because the soldiers had to remain constantly alert for Indian attacks. On May 6, 1860, its commanding officer, Captain H. W. Wessells, requested Adjutant General Samuel Cooper to change the name of the post to "Fort Larned," in honor of the paymaster general, Colonel Benjamin Franklin Larned. This request was approved by the secretary

---

[71] Sumner to Cooper, October 4, 1859, *ibid*.
[72] Hall to Sumner, October 9, 1859, *ibid*.
[73] Steuart to Jones, October 30, 1859, *ibid*.; Fort Larned, Medical History, Army Post Records, MSS, *ibid*.; Compiled Data on Fort Larned, MS, *ibid*.

of war on May 28, and the order changing the name was issued the following day.[74]

The exact geographical location of Fort Larned, occupied until July 13, 1878, was latitude 38° 10′ 10″ north, longitude 98° 57′ west. It was situated on the south bank of Pawnee Fork, about eight miles from its confluence with the Arkansas River, and approximately 280 miles from Fort Leavenworth.[75] It provided valuable protective service to the Trail immediately before, during, and after the Civil War.

Captain Steuart, first commanding officer at Camp on Pawnee Fork, reported on October 30, 1859, that the mail station had been made safe and the escorts were keeping the mail coaches running on time. The presence of the troops made that section of the Trail secure. However, the Kiowas had moved to a point about eighty miles west of Cimarron Crossing and were continuing their attacks upon emigrants returning from the Colorado gold fields. Steuart estimated from information he had received that at least nine "Pike's Peakers" had been murdered in recent weeks.[76]

Steuart explained that, in order to provide the necessary escorts for the mail trains, one half of the garrison of the post was constantly on the road. The escorts were forced to leave their horses at the camp and ride in wagons because the grass was drying up. The remainder of the garrison was kept busy taking care of the horses, performing guard duty, building corrals, cutting hay, and constructing temporary quarters of sod for the coming winter.[77]

On November 11, 1859, Colonel Sumner ordered part of the garrison at Camp on Pawnee Fork to return to Fort Riley for the winter, leaving a small command to guard the post and provide escorts for the mail during the winter months. Accordingly, Captain

[74] *Ibid.;* Fort Larned, Medical History, Army Post Records, MSS, *ibid.;* Wessells to Cooper, May 6, 1860, Letters Received, MSS, *ibid.;* General Orders, No. 14, Adjutant General's Office, May 29, 1860, AGO General Order Book, Vol. 14, MSS, *ibid.*
[75] Fort Larned, Medical History, Army Post Records, MSS, *ibid.*
[76] Steuart to Jones, October 30, 1859, Letters Received, MSS, *ibid.*
[77] *Ibid.;* Bell to Jones, November 25, 1859, *ibid.*

Military Protection, 1848-1861

Steuart and a portion of his company departed Pawnee Fork on November 26, leaving Lieutenant David Bell in command of thirty non-commissioned officers and privates.[78]

The mail escort had continued successfully, but there remained a problem in arranging a working plan with the garrison at Fort Union in order that the escorts from both posts could provide continuous protection for every mail party. That escorts were needed is indicated by the experience of the eastbound mail that arrived at Camp on Pawnee Fork on November 24. It had left Fort Union in company with Captain J. N. Macomb's party of Topographical Engineers, but was not under charge of an escort. Upon reaching the Cimarron River Captain Macomb stopped for several days in order to perform duties previously assigned to him. The mail had continued in company with a few citizens from New Mexico. After traveling without difficulty for three days, the mail party was attacked by Indians during the night, but no losses were suffered. Following this experience, the party quickly returned and rejoined Captain Macomb, and stayed with his detachment until they arrived at Pawnee Fork.[79]

Lieutenant Bell had only a small garrison at the fort, but he had worked out a plan for escorting the mails, which he described:

> I will escort the mails from this point eastward to Big Cow Creek, 52 miles, and westward to the crossing of the Arkansas river—a total distance of 140 miles. The escort to the crossing will remain as long as 4 days awaiting the arrival of the mails from New Mexico. It will be absent 10 days and as I am unwilling either to send a party on the road so weak that it could be placed at a disadvantage by Indians, or leave this point without proper guard, I will not send an escort for the mails from the East until the arrival of the escort from the West. I will therefore not be able to furnish an escort over the whole distance oftener than once in two weeks, but this will be done without fail.[80]

[78] *Ibid.;* Fort Larned, Post Returns, November, 1859, MSS, *ibid.*
[79] Bell to Jones, November 25, 1859, Letters Received, MSS, *ibid.*
[80] *Ibid.*

Soldiers on the Santa Fe Trail

The mail had been placed on a weekly schedule in 1859, but Sumner requested that it be reduced to bi-weekly until the situation was improved along the Trail. Apparently Sumner's request was adopted.[81]

On November 25, Bell was able to report that the condition of his command was good, a corral for the animals was almost completed, a sufficient supply of hay had been secured for the winter, and the troops had moved into "comfortable" sod quarters. Yet he expressed concern over the smallness of his force and requested reinforcements:

> With an increase of 20 footmen and one or two teams I could escort a weekly mail. With my present numbers, I cannot do it safely or properly. The services of another officer would not be required.[82]

The request was granted. Sumner sent Lieutenant J. D. O'Connell, Second Infantry, with twenty-three men. This detachment, accompanied by a surgeon, Dr. A. L. Beysacher from St. Louis, arrived at Pawnee Fork on December 22. The bi-weekly escorts had been completely successful. On January 4, 1860, Bell reported that every mail from the East had been accompanied by escort from Cow Creek, and that he had sent escorts from Camp on Pawnee Fork with the westbound mail on November 28, and December 12 and 26. The first of these had arrived at Cimarron Crossing two days after the detachment from Fort Union had started its return, but the mail train was able to overtake the soldiers at a point sixty miles beyond the crossing. About eighty miles farther down the Trail it was attacked by Kiowas, but the troops forced them to retreat and no losses were suffered.[83]

The second escort remained at the crossing four days and returned with the eastbound mail, which had accompanied a large caravan from New Mexico. No escort from Fort Union was there to accompany the westbound mail beyond the Arkansas. As a re-

---

[81] Sumner to Cooper, November 15, 1859, *ibid.*; Bell to Jones, January 4, 1860, *ibid.*

[82] Bell to Jones, November 25, 1859, *ibid.*

[83] Bell to Jones, January 4, 1860, *ibid.*

Military Protection, 1848-1861

sult, the escort dispatched from Pawnee Fork on December 26, consisting of two non-commissioned officers and eighteen privates, was provided with rations for twenty days and ordered to accompany the mail all the way to Fort Union if no escort had been sent out from the west. Lieutenant Bell wanted to establish a permanent system of escorts in co-operation with Fort Union, but this was not accomplished on a regular basis before the Civil War.[84]

Fort Larned continued providing escorts until the time of the Civil War. The garrison at the post was maintained at approximately fifty men from December, 1859, to May, 1860, when it was increased to about 160 with the arrival of two companies of infantry for the summer months. During that time several adobe buildings were constructed—stone buildings were not erected until after the Civil War. In September, 1860, two companies of Second Dragoons arrived, increasing the garrison to an aggregate of 270 officers and men. However, with the approach of winter in November, the garrison was reduced to approximately sixty, and it remained at that level until the second year of the Civil War.[85]

Forts Union and Larned had helped make the passage of the mails over the Trail safe by 1860, but the Indians continued their attacks upon other travelers using both this route and other pathways across the plains. Because of this continued threat, the War Department directed that an active campaign be conducted against the Kiowas and Comanches "as early in the Spring [1860] as the grass will permit."[86] Accordingly, four companies of First Cavalry from Fort Riley, joined by two companies of Second Dragoons from Fort Kearny, were sent into the field to operate against the marauding Indians.[87]

[84] *Ibid.;* Wessells to Jones, October 4, 1860, *ibid.*

[85] Fort Larned, Post Returns, 1859-1862, MSS, *ibid.;* Fort Larned, Medical History, Army Post Records, MSS, *ibid.;* General Orders, No. 8, Headquarters of the Army, June 30, 1860, MS, *ibid.;* Special Orders, No. 34, Headquarters Department of the West, April 3, 1860, MS, USAC, AACB, NA.

[86] Scott to Sumner, March 10, 1860, Letters Received, MSS, AGO, AACB, NA.

[87] Special Orders, No. 34, Headquarters Department of the West, April 3, 1860, MS, USAC, AACB, NA, printed in *Relations with the Indians of the Plains* (ed. by Hafen and Hafen), 195.

Departing from their respective posts in May, 1860, the two detachments of the campaign force concentrated at Pawnee Fork under command of Major John Sedgwick, First Cavalry, in preparation for their operations along the upper Arkansas and in surrounding regions.[88] Leaving that place on June 1, the expedition marched along the Wet Route and crossed the Arkansas at the Lower Crossing. Since the Kiowa Range extended to the Canadian River, the troops intended to scour that entire region. Proceeding south from the Arkansas, they marched to the North Canadian River, arriving near the point where Wolf Creek joined the river. They followed up Wolf Creek for several miles, returned to the North Canadian, and followed it upstream to a point almost due south of Bent's New Fort on the Arkansas.[89] Then they moved north to the Cimarron and proceeded to the Arkansas, rejoining that stream just above Chouteau's Island. They reached the Arkansas on June 28, after marching approximately five hundred miles from Pawnee Fork, and in all this time they had seen no Kiowas or Comanches.[90]

Men, animals, and supplies were exhausted after this long march, and the command encamped on the Arkansas until provisions were brought out from Fort Larned. Sedgwick received information from Captain Wessells, commanding Fort Larned, that the Kiowas were reported to be near Denver, Colorado. This was later found to be untrue, but on the basis of this information the command resumed its march on July 6, moving up the Arkansas toward Bent's New Fort. Upon camping three miles below that fort on July 9, the force learned that a small party of Kiowas supposedly was located about twenty-five miles to the north. Captain William

---

[88] J. E. B. Stuart's Official Journal, *ibid.*, 217–22. For Colonel Sumner's instrucetions to Sedgwick for the campaign, see Sumner to Sedgwick, May 9, 1860, *ibid.*, 197–98.

[89] William Bent had abandoned his original trading fort, which was built in 1833, and, in 1853, had constructed Bent's New Fort about thirty-five miles downstream from the old fort. Bent's New Fort was on the north bank of the Arkansas River approximately ten miles west of present Lamar, Colorado. *Ibid.*, 232n.

[90] Stuart's Journal, *ibid.*, 222–30; Sedgwick to Jones, July 2, 1860, *ibid.*, 202–204.

Military Protection, 1848-1861

Steele, Second Dragoons, and eighty-six men were dispatched to verify the report. On July 11, the remainder of the force moved up the river beyond Bent's New Fort, and as they passed the fort they learned that a small party of Kiowas, believed to include Chief Satank, had been seen earlier that morning and had gone off in a northerly direction. Lieutenant J. E. B. Stuart, First Cavalry, and twenty men were sent in pursuit. After following the Indians for twenty-six miles, Stuart's command was joined by Steele's detachment, which had been unsuccessful in its efforts to locate a Kiowa camp. The two forces united and attacked the party Stuart had been trailing, killing two warriors, and capturing sixteen women and children. Satank was not with the party. The soldiers suffered three men wounded and none killed.[91]

The Kiowa prisoners were left in charge of Indian Agent Bent, and the campaign force moved several miles above Bent's New Fort and encamped. A detachment under command of Captain DeSaussure was sent approximately thirty miles up the Purgatoire; it then returned down that stream, crossed to Bent's Old Fort, and came down the north bank of the Arkansas to the main camp. No Indians were sighted by this detachment.[92]

Sedgwick's force then moved down the Arkansas to a point about forty miles east of Chouteau's Island, proceeded north to the Smoky Hill River, followed that stream down to the point where they had crossed it while traveling from Fort Riley to Pawnee Fork in May, and returned to Fort Larned, arriving there between August 8 and 11, 1860.[93] Major Sedgwick concluded that the two tribes he had been sent to punish had broken up:

> My opinion is that the Kiowas and Comanches have scattered; a few roving about in small bands, the others, with women and

[91] General Orders, No. 11, Headquarters of the Army, November 23, 1860; Sedgwick to Jones, July 24, 1860; Steele to Thompson, July 14, 1860; Stuart to Thompson, July 12, 1860; Stuart's Journal; *ibid.,* 205-206, 208-12, 231-33.

[92] *Ibid.,* 233-35; Sedgwick to Jones, July 24, 1860, *ibid.,* 208-209.

[93] Stuart's Journal, *ibid.,* 235-43; Sedgwick to his sister, August 8, 1860, *ibid.,* 260.

Soldiers on the Santa Fe Trail

children, being mixed with the Cheyennes, Arrapahoes, and Apaches.[94]

This seemed a logical conclusion after failing to locate the tribes while traveling over twelve hundred miles. However, another expedition against the Kiowas and Comanches, six companies of First Cavalry from Forts Arbuckle, Cobb, and Washita in Indian Territory under the command of Captain Samuel Davis Sturgis, on August 6, 1860, had succeeded in overtaking an encampment of approximately seven hundred of those Indians on the Republican River about sixty miles south of Fort Kearny. In the ensuing battle, the soldiers killed twenty-nine Indians, wounded an undetermined number, and suffered two Indian guides killed, one sergeant and two privates wounded, and one private missing.[95] In addition, a detachment of Mounted Riflemen from Fort Union, as indicated above, attacked an encampment of about 175 Comanche and Kiowa lodges north of Cold Spring on January 2, 1861, killing ten Indians, and destroying their winter camp.

Although Sedgwick's command had failed to locate and punish the Indians as ordered, the presence of his force helped to ease the Indian threat to the Santa Fe Trail during the summer of 1860. An additional measure was taken by the War Department to protect the Trail during that year. Soon after the campaign force had begun its expedition, a military post was ordered established in the region of the Big Timbers on the upper Arkansas. This order awaited Major Sedgwick when he returned to Fort Larned, and he left on August 18 to establish Fort Wise.[96]

The order directing the establishment of Fort Wise, named for Governor Henry A. Wise of Virginia,[97] stated that four companies of First Cavalry and two companies of Tenth Infantry were to

[94] Sedgwick to Jones, August 11, 1860, *ibid.*, 213–14.

[95] For documents relating this campaign, see *ibid.*, 245–54.

[96] General Orders, No. 8, Headquarters of the Army, June 30, 1860, *ibid.*, 259; Sedgwick to Jones, August 11, 1860, *ibid.*, 214; Stuart's Journal, *ibid.*, 243–44.

[97] On June 25, 1862, the name was changed because Governor Wise was a Confederate, and the post was named "Fort Lyon" in honor of Brigadier General Nathan-

Military Protection, 1848-1861

comprise the garrison. Also, buildings were to be erected by the soldiers before the winter season. Colonel Sumner, in additional instructions, left the selection of the exact location to Major Sedgwick, but suggested that several good sites could be found just above Bent's New Fort.[98]

Sedgwick and his men were "disgusted" at being sent immediately to establish a new post after having just marched over twelve hundred miles on an unsuccessful campaign. In a letter to his sister, the major declared: "I am so disgusted that I cannot write anything pleasant."[99] Lieutenant Stuart wrote: "Everybody is blue and disgusted."[100] These troops had left Fort Riley in May, with intentions of returning to that point at the close of the summer campaign, and they were justifiably unhappy. However, the frontier armies were not operated for the desires and comfort of the troops, and the orders had to be obeyed.

Major Sedgwick and his four companies of First Cavalry left Fort Larned on August 18, and, after a pleasant march of 237 miles, they went into camp near Bent's New Fort on August 29.[101] The site for the new post, about half a mile west of Bent's New Fort, was selected on September 1, and construction was begun immediately.[102] The large garrison helped speed the erection of necessary buildings.[103] Sedgwick was able to report on October 22, 1860:

iel Lyon, killed at the battle of Wilson's Creek on August 10, 1861. General Orders, No. 11, Department of Kansas, June 25, 1862, Departmental Commands, MSS, AGO, AACB, NA.

[98] Sumner to Sedgwick, July 6, 1860, *Relations with the Indians of the Plains* (ed. by Hafen and Hafen), 257-58.

[99] Sedgwick to his sister, August 8, 1860, *ibid.*, 260-61.

[100] *Ibid.*, 243n.

[101] Stuart's Journal, *ibid.*, 244; Sedgwick to his sister, September 12, 1860, *ibid.*, 268.

[102] Sedgwick to Assistant Adjutant General, Dept. of the West, October 22, 1860, *ibid.*, 271; Fort Lyon, Medical History, Army Post Records, MSS, AGO, AACB, NA; Fort Wise, Post Returns, August, 1860, MSS, *ibid.*

[103] The total number of officers and men stationed at Fort Wise at the close of each of the first three months of occupation was as follows: August, 268; September, 417; October, 480. Fort Wise, Post Returns, August, September, October, 1860, *ibid.*

Soldiers on the Santa Fe Trail

> Up to this day, the following work has been accomplished;—four ample and comfortable stables, with stone walls, and good roofs of timber and hay,—two sets of company quarters, whilst three more sets will be ready for occupation by the end of this week. The stone corral for Quartermaster's animals, similar to the Cavalry stables will be completed in four or five days, as will also a proper guard-house, of the same material as that used in the quarters. A Hospital is in the process of construction, which will accomodate comfortably at least twenty-six patients, and the ground has been broken today for the quarters of "H" Company, 10th Infantry, which arrived at this Post two days since. The officer commanding confidently expects to put the company under shelter by the 20th of November. A stone bake-house, with oven of the same material, is nearly completed, which will be ample for the supply of the Post. The windows, etc., for the above mentioned buildings have not yet arrived, but are expected daily. They can be set after the quarters are occupied.[104]

Sedgwick concluded this report with a brief statement regarding the Indian situation:

> Small parties of emigrants are, and have been constantly on the road between the Post, Denver City, and Fort Larned, since our arrival here, and, as yet, no depredations have been committed by Indians, nor has it been reported that any *hostile* [Indians] have been seen.[105]

These peaceful conditions allowed the garrison to devote full time to construction duties. By November 17 all buildings except officers' quarters had been completed, and Sedgwick estimated that those would be ready for occupancy within two more weeks. Although he had expected numerous difficulties in establishing a new post and was intensely displeased when informed that he had been selected for the duty, Sedgwick was in better humor and delighted with the results of his command's efforts by mid-November:

[104] Sedgwick to Assistant Adjutant General, Dept. of the West, October 22, 1860, *Relations with the Indians of the Plains* (ed. by Hafen and Hafen), 272.
[105] *Ibid.*, 273-74.

Military Protection, 1848-1861

... [I] am now at ease in regard to the comfort of the men for the winter. The last mail brought a complimentary letter from the Secretary of War, extolling our energy and perseverance.[106]

Captain W. T. Walker, First Cavalry, explained the importance of the position of Fort Wise in a lengthy report to the quartermaster general on January 15, 1861.[107] He based his remarks on what he considered to be the two most important factors in evaluating a frontier military site: strategy and economics. Concerning the strategical importance of Fort Wise, Walker declared that the post was in the heart of Indian country, being in the region inhabited by the Cheyennes, Arapahoes, and Kiowas. In addition, the Pawnees, Comanches, and Apaches often frequented the vicinity, and the post was within striking distance of the Navahos and Utes. The post was, he concluded, ideally situated to control the Indians, and he recommended that the fort be retained with a large cavalry garrison.

From the viewpoint of economics, Walker stated that the post was situated in a fertile valley that could supply the garrison with corn, fresh vegetables, and hay. He pointed out that one farmer about eighty miles up the Arkansas had raised five thousand bushels of corn during the past season and that William Bent had over fifteen hundred head of cattle twenty miles above the post, "kept in good condition on the winter grass."

The garrison at Fort Wise was not called upon to deal with hostile Indians before the outbreak of the Civil War, but an important treaty with the Arapahoes and Cheyennes was concluded there on February 18, 1861, by which the Indians ceded their claim to much of the land over which they roamed and agreed to occupy a reservation in southeastern Colorado.[108] The Indians later violated the treaty and had to be subjugated by the soliders, but, for

[106] Sedgwick to his sister, November 17, 1860, *ibid.*, 276.
[107] Walker to Quartermaster General of the Army, January 15, 1861, Consolidated Correspondence File, MSS, Quartermaster General's Office (Record Group No. 92), Army and Air Corps Branch, National Archives (Hereafter cited as CCF, MSS, QMGO, AACB, NA).
[108] *Relations with the Indians of the Plains* (ed. by Hafen and Hafen), 283-99.

the time being, it was an important step in making the routes of travel safe. Fort Wise (Lyon), occupied until November 15, 1889, although moved to a new site in 1867, provided valuable protective service during and after the Civil War, as did both Fort Union and Fort Larned.

By the eve of the Civil War, with the establishment of forts and the institution of escorts to guard the mails, the protection of the Trail was much improved over what it had been in the immediate post–Mexican War years. The Indian threat had not been eliminated—that would not occur until after the Civil War. But the Trail had been protected, and the Indians still demonstrated a healthy respect for the soldiers. This would soon change, for the era of the Civil War brought Indian hostilities more severe than those encountered in any previous period in the history of the Trail. In addition, soldiers on the Santa Fe Trail were to become involved in the military conflict that erupted between the North and the South in 1861.

5

Effects of the Civil War, 1861-1865

THE AMERICAN CIVIL WAR, which broke out in April of 1861, was fought mostly in the region east of the Mississippi River. Nevertheless, the war was not confined entirely to that area, and several important conflicts occurred in the Southwest. The Confederate effort there was one of conquest, whereas in the East it was primarily a defensive war for independence. Two Civil War battles were fought on the Santa Fe Trail as a result of Confederate attempts to conquer the western territories, and one of these engagements has been compared in significance to Gettysburg because it was the turning point of the war in the Far West.

In addition to these two battles, the soldiers serving on the Santa Fe Trail during the war, including companies or regiments of volunteer troops from New Mexico, Colorado, Kansas, and other states, met increased Indian hostilities. The Indians made a determined effort to close the Trail and drive the whites from the region, but were prevented from accomplishing their goals by the operations of the troops protecting it.

In their drive to expand westward to the Pacific, Confederate troops from Texas invaded New Mexico during the summer of 1861.[1] On March 11, 1862, they took possession of Santa Fe. Led by General Henry Hopkins Sibley, they were planning a move

[1] Because the story of the Confederate invasion of New Mexico and the Confederate–Union fighting in that territory has been told many times and the author found no new material in the military records of these events, the treatment of them here is only a brief account. Two recent studies offering detailed accounts of these activities are Ray C. Colton, *The Civil War in the Western Territories,* and Martin Hardwick Hall, *Sibley's New Mexico Campaign.*

against Fort Union in an attempt to obtain the supplies stored at the depot there and to secure their position in the territory. Meanwhile, Fort Union's defensive position had been improved, under the orders of Lieutenant Colonel Edward Richard Sprigg Canby, commanding the Department of New Mexico, by moving the post from its original location, which was dominated by a nearby mesa, and rebuilding it about a mile out in the valley. The new Fort Union was a square-bastioned fortification with earthen breastworks extending outward from the square to form the shape of an eight-pointed star. Also, the First Regiment of Colorado Volunteers, consisting of ten companies and led by Colonel John P. Slough, Lieutenant Colonel Samuel F. Tappan, and Major John M. Chivington, had marched from Colorado to Fort Union to assist in repelling the Texan invaders. Colonel Slough and his command, numbering 1,342 men, marched from Fort Union toward Santa Fe on March 22, 1862.[2] A small garrison, under command of Colonel G. R. Paul, was left to guard the post.[3]

Confederate Major Charles L. Pyron, in command at Santa Fe with a force of between 250 and 300 men, apparently received word of the Union advance from Fort Union. With his troops and two six-pound howitzers, he marched from Santa Fe on March 25 and encamped that night at Johnson's Ranch near Apache Canyon, the western entrance to Glorieta Pass. Meanwhile, Slough's com-

[2] The following units made up the column: First Regiment of Colorado Volunteers, 916 men; Captain W. H. Lewis's battalion, Fifth United States Infantry, and Captain James H. Ford's Colorado company, 191 men; Captain George W. Howland's detachment, First and Third United States Cavalry, 150 men; Captain John F. Ritter's regular battery of two twelve-pounders and two six-pounders, 53 men; and Lieutenant Ira W. Claflin's regular battery of four twelve-pound howitzers, 32 men. U. S. War Department, *The War of the Rebellion: A Compilation of the Official Records of the Union and Confederate Armies*, Series 1, IX, 534 (hereafter cited as *OR*, Ser. 1, IX, 534).

[3] *Ibid.*, 534, 645–46. For histories of the Colorado Regiment, see Ovando J. Hollister, *Boldly They Rode: A History of the First Colorado Regiment of Volunteers*, and William Clarke Whitford, *Colorado Volunteers in the Civil War: The New Mexico Campaign in 1862*.

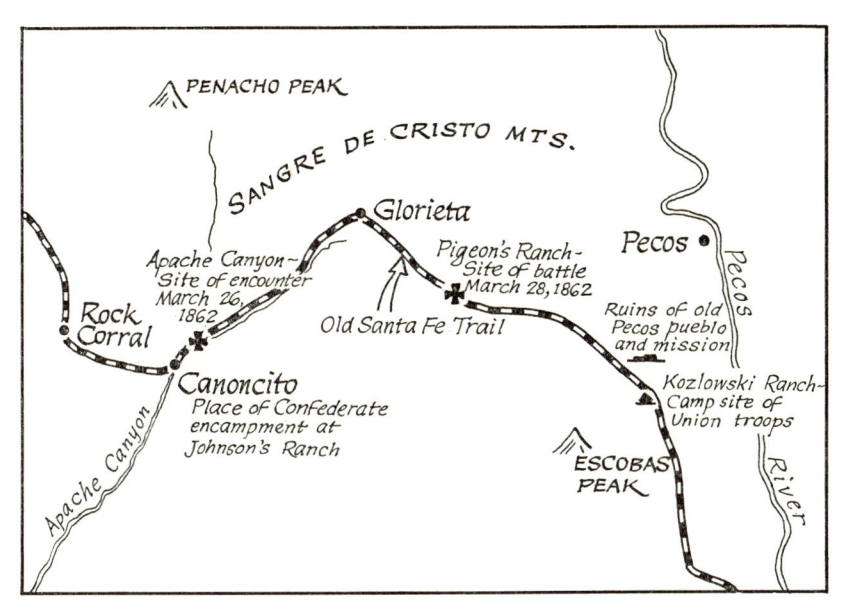

Map of battle area of Glorieta Pass, March 26, 28, 1862. From Chris Emmett, *Fort Union and the Winning of the Southwest*.

mand moved down the Trail, passed through Las Vegas, and, on March 25, set up temporary camp at Bernal Springs. During the afternoon of the same day, Major Chivington and 418 men were sent ahead with instructions to march to Santa Fe, surprise the small enemy force reported to be there, and drive them from the New Mexican capital.[4]

Chivington reached Kozlowski's Ranch about midnight and learned that Confederate pickets were in the neighborhood. He sent out a detachment in an attempt to capture one of the enemy's scouts, and the mission was accomplished when four Confederates were captured without firing a shot. It was learned from them that a sizable body of Sibley's advance forces was near the western

[4] *Ibid.*, 82; *OR*, Ser. 1, IX, 530–31, 534.

Soldiers on the Santa Fe Trail

end of the pass and was expected to head for Fort Union the following day.[5] Chivington decided to advance and engage the enemy.

Departing Kozlowski's Ranch the following morning, Chivington's force marched into Glorieta Pass and reached the summit of the divide about two o'clock in the afternoon. As they descended the slope and entered Apache Canyon proper, they sighted the Rebel force four or five hundred yards ahead. The Confederates had begun their march from Johnson's Ranch about two hours earlier. They were completely surprised by the Federals, since Chivington had captured their advance guard. Although caught entirely off guard, Major Pyron immediately formed his troops into a skirmish line, planted his artillery in the road, and began throwing grapeshot and shell at the Union troops. Chivington had no artillery with him, although he enjoyed the advantage of superior numbers.

In the three-hour battle which followed, the Texans were driven from the field, but Chivington did not pursue them because the sun was going down and he feared that Confederate reinforcements might be near. Instead, he retired to Pigeon's Ranch at the eastern entrance to Glorieta Pass and encamped.[6] During the evening following the battle, Major Pyron requested, and was granted, a cessation of hostilities until eight o'clock the following morning to allow for burying the dead and treating the wounded.[7] The Battle of Apache Canyon was the first repulse suffered by the Confederate invaders since entering New Mexico and probably had a demoralizing effect upon the Texan troops despite the small number involved (the total number of Confederate soldiers in

---

[5] *Ibid.*, 530; Hollister, *Boldly They Rode*, 59; Whitford, *Colorado Volunteers*, 82, 84.

[6] *OR*, Ser. 1, IX, 530–32.

[7] It is impossible to determine the exact number of casualties because of the varying accounts. Chivington reported Union losses as 5 killed and 14 wounded, and Confederate casualties as 32 killed, 43 wounded, and 71 taken prisoners. *Ibid.*, 531. Hollister, *Boldly They Rode*, 67, listed Confederate losses at 16 killed, 30 or 40 wounded, and 75 prisoners. Ralph Emerson Twitchell, *The Leading Facts of New Mexican History*, II, 382, gave the following figures: Confederates, 35 killed, 43 wounded, 71 prisoners; Union, same as Chivington.

Effects of the Civil War, 1861-1865

New Mexico was about 3,500). At the same time, the Colorado Volunteers had proved themselves in battle and surely had acquired a new feeling of confidence.

The Union force set up a hospital at Pigeon's Ranch, and Chivington sent a dispatch to Colonel Slough at Bernal Springs relating the events of the day and urging that the remainder of the command move up immediately. The water supply at Pigeon's Ranch was insufficient for all the men and animals, therefore, after burying the dead, all except the wounded moved back to Kozlowski's Ranch on March 27. A detachment of First Cavalry then escorted the captured Texans to Fort Union.

During the engagement at Apache Canyon, Major Pyron had dispatched a messenger to Colonel William R. Scurry at Galisteo, about sixteen miles away, reporting that he had met an enemy superior in numbers and requesting immediate assistance. Scurry's force, consisting of parts of the Fourth and Seventh Regiments of Texas Cavalry, left Galisteo immediately, and, marching late into the night, they arrived at Johnson's Ranch about three o'clock in the morning. Scurry assumed command of all Confederate troops located there, and, informed by Pyron that Chivington had agreed to a truce until eight o'clock, the colonel had formed his command into a battle line around the ranch and in Apache Canyon to protect his position by that time.[8]

The Union force was expected to return and attack at any moment, but twenty-four hours later the Confederates were in the same position, and no enemy had appeared. Not satisfied to sit it out any longer, Scurry decided to move forward and attack. Leaving a small force and one piece of artillery to guard the supply train, Scurry, with approximately seven hundred men and three pieces of artillery, moved down the Trail through Apache Canyon to engage the Federals. After marching about six miles, his advance pickets informed him that the enemy was immediately ahead, located at Pigeon's Ranch. The Confederate troops went into battle formation and unlimbered the artillery.[9]

[8] *OR*, Ser. 1, IX, 542-43.   [9] *Ibid.*, 543.

Soldiers on the Santa Fe Trail

Upon receipt of Chivington's dispatch relating the battle of Apache Canyon, Colonel Slough decided to advance with the main body of his troops to Kozlowski's Ranch, where they arrived about two o'clock in the morning, March 28. After conferring with Chivington and learning from spies that the enemy at Johnson's Ranch had been reinforced, Slough planned a daring two-column offensive movement. Chivington, with about 430 infantrymen, was to move a few miles on the road toward Galisteo, then follow a trail across the mountains to the principal heights overlooking Apache Canyon and Johnson's Ranch. He was to occupy these heights, reconnoiter the Confederates, and harass them from the rear while Slough and the remaining nine hundred men moved directly through the pass along the Santa Fe Trail toward Johnson's Ranch. Both columns would then be in position to converge upon the Texans.[10]

The Federal troops left Kozlowski's Ranch between eight and eight-thirty o'clock on the morning of March 28. At about nine-thirty Chivington's column headed toward Galisteo, and Slough continued to Pigeon's Ranch where all his command had arrived by ten-thirty. The colonel sent his cavalry ahead to reconnoiter the enemy while the remaining troops rested and visited the wounded. They were totally unaware that the enemy had approached to a point approximately a mile away. The Union cavalry that had been sent forward had advanced only a few hundred yards when the pickets rushed back and reported a large body of Confederates just ahead. This information was then communicated to Slough at the ranch, and the startled troops were rushed forward to form a battle line. Before the Federals were in position, however, the Confederate artillery opened fire, which was soon returned by the Union batteries. Scurry had surprised the Union force, and throughout the battle Colonel Slough was forced to use defensive tactics.[11]

The fighting started between ten-thirty and eleven o'clock and

[10] *Ibid.,* 533–34.
[11] *Ibid.,* 533–34, 536.

Effects of the Civil War, 1861-1865

lasted more than six hours. The two opposing forces at Glorieta Pass were about evenly matched in numbers. Colonel Slough, after he had detached details for guarding the supply wagons from his total force of nine hundred men, held the regular cavalry troops in reserve so that they did not participate in the battle, and he, also, entered the engagement with approximately seven hundred men. The advantages, if there were any, lay with the Confederates, since they had surprised the Federals and held the offensive.

According to Slough, the rough, rocky, and timbered terrain made "the engagement of the bushwacking kind."[12] Mounted troops could not be used, and all the Confederate cavalry and the mounted company of Colorado Volunteers fought as infantry. Because both sides had artillery (the Confederates had three howitzers and the Federals had eight), the battle was primarily an attempt by each to capture or disable the other's cannons so a charge could be made down the road. Thus both commanding officers deployed skirmishers upon the mountainsides and kept supporting units around their batteries. The rugged topography, however, reduced the effectiveness of the howitzers, except on the roadway and floor of the canyon, and determined that small arms would actually decide the outcome. It was a hard-fought, bloody engagement for both forces.[13]

The Texans slowly advanced during the day, despite the determined efforts of the Federals to turn them back. The Union batteries retreated and took up new positions twice during the battle before abandoning the field soon after five o'clock in the afternoon. At about that hour Colonel Slough ordered his forces to begin a retreat back to their camp at Kozlowski's Ranch. His men were exhausted, there was not a suitable position for making another stand, and he did not want to risk the capture of his artillery. The supply wagons followed the artillery from the field, and when these had safely escaped, the remaining troops withdrew.

The Confederates attempted to pursue them, but, according

[12] *Ibid.*, 533.
[13] *Ibid.*, 533-38, 540-45.

Soldiers on the Santa Fe Trail

to Colonel Scurry, were "forced to halt from the extreme exhaustion of the men."[14] Perhaps another reason the pursuit was abandoned was Colonel Scurry's receipt of information that his supply train at Johnson's Ranch had been destroyed during the afternoon. Both sides had suffered heavy losses, but the Confederates could claim victory in the battle, having driven the enemy from the field.[15] Nevertheless, as Martin Hall accurately pointed out, "though they had won the battle of Glorieta Pass, they had lost the victory at Johnson's Ranch."[16] While Slough was fighting a losing battle, Chivington's force had succeeded in delivering the decisive blow to the Confederate invasion of New Mexico.

After leaving the main column that morning, Chivington's command, with Lieutenant Colonel Manuel Chavez of the New Mexico Volunteers and Indian Agent James L. Collins as guides, followed the road toward Galisteo for about eight miles, then proceeded through the mountains approximately the same distance, and reached the heights overlooking Johnson's Ranch in the early afternoon. A Confederate sentinel stationed there as lookout was captured before he could sound the alarm. Thus, with the enemy unaware of his presence, Chivington spent approximately an hour observing the situation below and deciding upon a plan of attack to destroy the supply train of some seventy wagons.[17]

When the plan was ready, the Federals descended the mountainside, captured and destroyed the cannon which Scurry had left behind, and burned the Confederate supply wagons containing ammunition, clothing, baggage, forage, medical supplies, and other items. In addition to destroying the supply train, the infantrymen

[14] *Ibid.*, 544.

[15] It is impossible to determine accurately the losses of either side because of the varying reports. It appears that the commanding officers underestimated their own losses and overestimated those of the enemy. Colonel Slough estimated Union losses at 28 killed, 40 wounded, and 15 prisoners, and Confederate casualties of at least 100 killed, 150 wounded, and several prisoners. Colonel Scurry reported 36 killed and 60 wounded in his own command and stated that Union killed must have exceeded 100. *Ibid.*, 535, 546.

[16] Hall, *Sibley's New Mexican Campaign*, 160.

[17] *OR*, Ser. 1, IX, 539; Whitford, *Colorado Volunteers*, 116, 118.

Effects of the Civil War, 1861-1865

killed three Texans, wounded several others, and took seventeen prisoners. Then they climbed back up the mountain and returned to Kozlowski's Ranch, arriving about ten o'clock in the evening.[18]

Colonel Scurry, his entire supply train destroyed, was unable to follow up his success at Glorieta Pass. Ovando J. Hollister, referring to Chivington's successful destructive efforts, declared: "This was the irreparable blow that compelled the Texans to evacuate the Territory."[19] Afterward, Scurry's men suffered intensely from want of food, blankets, and medical supplies.

The Battle of Glorieta Pass (or Pigeon's Ranch as it was sometimes called), including the affair at Johnson's Ranch, was the last Civil War battle between the Union and Confederate troops on the Santa Fe Trail. It was the turning point of the Civil War in the Far West; Ray C. Colton called it the "Gettysburg of the West."[20] Following this engagement, Colonel Slough's command returned to Fort Union, as ordered by Lieutenant Colonel Canby, and Scurry took his men to Santa Fe. General Sibley was forced to abandon his planned attack on Fort Union, and his brigade was driven from New Mexico during the late spring and early summer of 1862.

Because of the Confederate threat to the American Southwest during 1861 and 1862 and the uprising of the Apache and Navaho Indians in New Mexico during the remainder of the Civil War, the need to keep supplies flowing to Union forces in that region made the Santa Fe Trail, as in previous times, an extremely important route. It was the only reliable direct route between New Mexico and the "States" after Texas joined the Confederacy. All this additional importance made it imperative that the Trail be kept free from Indian attacks. But during the war, military restraints upon the Plains Indians were loosened when some of the soldiers were called out of the West to fight in the East, and many of the remaining Federal troops and volunteers in Kansas, Colorado, and

---

[18] *Ibid.*, 118-22; *OR*, Ser. 1, IX, 539.
[19] Hollister, *Boldly They Rode*, 72.
[20] Colton, *Civil War in Western Territories*, Chap. IV.

New Mexico were engaged in fighting, or making preparations to fight, the Confederates. The result was an increase in Indian hostilities, especially during 1864.

Instances of any direct connection between the Confederates and the "wild tribes" apparently were few, but the fact remains that the Indians had some idea of what the Confederates were attempting to do.[21] Furthermore, it appeared to be a good time to attempt to drive the whites, who were taking over the Indians' hunting grounds and slaughtering the buffalo, from the Redman's territories. This was another reason behind the increased Indian activities along the Trail.

After the Confederate defeat in New Mexico, the major task of the soldiers serving along the Trail was to deal with Indian threats. The Indians became less cautious in meeting the soldiers as they became more determined in their efforts to drive them from the region, with the result that the protecting forces found more demanded of them than of those who had served in any previous era along the Trail. The Indian threat, as stated above, was not eliminated by 1865, but the route was kept open through continued and expanded use of escorts, patrols, campaigns, and establishment of additional military posts.

Early in the conflict, Lieutenant Colonel Canby recognized the importance of keeping the Trail open and assuring the arrival of supply trains. Before the Confederate invasion of New Mexico was launched, on June 19, 1861, he directed the commanding officer at Fort Union, Major William Chapman, to make any arrangements necessary to protect the trains between his post and the Arkansas crossing, from Texans as well as Indians.[22] Realizing that the garrison at Fort Union might not be sufficient to provide adequate forces for such duty, Canby requested Governor Abraham Rencher to raise three companies of New Mexico volunteers for

[21] Marvin Garfield, "Defense of the Kansas Frontier, 1864–1865," *Kansas Historical Quarterly*, Vol. I (February, 1932), 140.
[22] Canby to Chapman, June 19, 1861, *OR*, Ser. 1, IV, 40.

Effects of the Civil War, 1861-1865

service along the Cimarron Route, then believed to be threatened by Comanches.[23]

Major Chapman was instructed to organize a command of at least one hundred mounted regulars and two companies of New Mexican volunteers under Captain Thomas Duncan, and to take rations for thirty days and patrol the road between Fort Union and the Middle Crossing. Believing the Mountain Route to be the safer one, Canby requested the commanding officer of Fort Larned, Captain Julius Hayden, to advise all trains passing his post to follow it.[24] In August, Canby sent a squadron of Mounted Riflemen to Fort Wise to strengthen the post and provide protection for trains using that branch of the Trail.[25] During the same month, he ordered Colonel Céran St. Vrain, First Regiment New Mexico Volunteers, to dispatch Lieutenant Colonel Christopher "Kit" Carson and four companies of the regiment to protect supply trains coming to Fort Union via the Cimarron.[26] These actions demonstrate Canby's recognition that the arms, ammunition, and supplies coming from the East were essential to the continued operation of the Federal forces in New Mexico.

Perhaps Canby was overly cautious. Carson and the four companies of volunteers left Fort Union on August 22 and marched to Cold Spring. In all that distance they sighted no signs of Indians. Finding everything quiet and learning that the expected supply trains had taken the Mountain Route, they returned to Fort Union.[27]

While the soldiers were securing the western half of the Trail, the Arapahoes began looting trains near Fort Larned. Their acts were apparently motivated by a desire for supplies rather than a

[23] Canby to Rencher, June 20, 1861, *ibid.*, 42.
[24] Canby to Chapman, June 30, 1861, *ibid.*, 49.
[25] Canby to Chapman, August 15, 1861, Fort Union, Letters Received, MSS, USAC, AACB, NA.
[26] Canby to St. Vrain, August 18, 1861, *ibid.*
[27] Chapman to Anderson, August 22, 1861, Fort Union, Letters Sent, MSS, *ibid.;* Carson to Chapman, September 5, 1861, Fort Union, Letters Received, MSS, *ibid.*

Soldiers on the Santa Fe Trail

determination to stop the continual flow of wagons. Nevertheless, they were a nuisance and were stealing much property.[28] Captain Hayden declared that a mounted force placed at his disposal could secure the road between Cow Creek and the crossing, but that his small infantry command was unable to furnish escorts to wagon trains or send scouting parties to watch the Indians. Beyond the small escorts for mail coaches, he was helpless to counteract the hostilities. And mounted troops were not readily available because of the war.

Not all Plains Indians were a threat to the Trail in 1861. The Kiowas, traditional enemies of the Texans, were serving as spies for Captain Elmer Otis, commanding at Fort Wise. While most of the Kiowas were encamped near that post, a party of about seventy-five warriors kept the soldiers informed of the whereabouts of the Texans moving into New Mexico.[29]

Finding the Kiowas and their allies, the Comanches, disposed to be friendly when he arrived at Fort Wise in September, 1861, Indian Agent A. G. Boone succeeded in signing an agreement with them to suspend all hostilities for one year. They further agreed to negotiate a permanent treaty of friendship at the end of that year. The Indians promised not to molest mail coaches, wagon trains, settlements, travelers using the overland routes, or any white citizen of the United States, and agreed to conduct their hunting expeditions in buffalo country, away from the routes of travel. In return, the government was to issue annuities, the amount to be determined in the permanent treaty.[30] Although this agreement was later violated, it was an encouraging accomplishment during the first year of the war.

---

[28] Captain Hayden listed the following losses to the Arapahoes by a train attacked near Coon Creek on August 30, 1861: 3 oxen, 16 sacks sugar, 1 sack coffee, 18 sacks flour, 3 barrels whisky, 20 gallons brandy, 1 basket champagne, 3 boxes smoking tobacco, 1 rifle, 1 powder flask, 3 wagon covers, and 11 blankets. Hayden to Kellin, September 2, 1861, Fort Larned, Letters Sent, MSS, *ibid.*

[29] Otis to Canby, August 22, 1861, *OR*, Ser. 1, IV, 67.

[30] Agreement between A. G. Boone and Chiefs of Kiowas and Comanches, September 6, 1861, Fort Union, Letters Received, MSS, USAC, AACB, NA.

Effects of the Civil War, 1861-1865

The soldiers on the Trail, by the escorts and patrols they provided, apparently succeeded in giving mail coaches and supply trains adequate protection during 1861 and early 1862.[31] In May of the latter year, however, Captain Hayden at Fort Larned reported that the Kiowas, Apaches, and Arapahoes were infesting the Trail between Walnut and Cow creeks and commiting depredations which his garrison was unable to prevent. He urged the commander of the Department of Kansas, Brigadier General James G. Blunt, to take "prompt action" to make the route safe and to avert a possible Indian war. He also explained the reasons for the Indians' actions:

> ... [It is] an inevitable consequence of the license of plunder and immunity from the consequences which results from the absence of mounted troops from the plains. Evil-disposed white men are driving a brisk trade in whisky with the tribes above mentioned; this, and this alone, is the reason of their continued presence upon the road, and none but mounted men continually patrolling the road between the Little Arkansas and Walnut Creek can break up the business.[32]

Hayden had received information that the Kansas Indians served as "go-betweens" in the liquor traffic, and he requested that they be confined to their reservation. He suggested that the large force then being organized at Fort Riley for service in New Mexico be marched along that section of the Trail where the Indian hostilities were occurring. The mere presence of such a large column, he declared, might have the desired effect of causing the Indians to leave. In addition, he recommended that a mounted company be sent to patrol the Trail between Cow Creek and Fort Larned, with full authority to keep the Indians away from the road and prevent the liquor transactions. If the Indians were prevented from obtaining supplies from passing trains and the trading-post ranches, Hayden believed they would soon leave in search of food.

While Hayden's many suggestions were not implemented, reinforcements were sent to Fort Larned. During June, 1862, with the

[31] Utley, *New Mexico Historical Review*, Vol. XXXVI (1961), 45.
[32] Hayden to AAAG, Dept. of Kansas, May 14, 1862, *OR*, Ser. 1, XIII, 382.

Soldiers on the Santa Fe Trail

arrival of two companies of Kansas volunteers, the aggregate garrison was increased from 63 to 292.[33] This made possible the detachment of patrols, and the Indians removed from the Walnut Creek area, apparently to the Cimarron River.[34]

During July the garrison at Fort Lyon (formerly Fort Wise) was increased by four companies of the Second Regiment Colorado Volunteer Cavalry, under command of Colonel J. H. Leavenworth.[35] These troops were specifically ordered to help keep the Trail open between Forts Larned and Union. To provide additional protection, five companies of the Ninth Kansas Volunteer Cavalry were sent out from Fort Riley to increase the garrisons at both Larned and Lyon and to guard the vicinity of the Big Bend of the Arkansas.[36]

The mails, wagon trains, and travelers had plenty of protection, but the Indians did not cease their hostile activities. For this reason, early in August, S. G. Colley, Indian agent for the Upper Arkansas, was sent to Fort Larned to meet with the Indians encamped nearby. Following a council with the principal chiefs of his agency, Colley persuaded the Indians to go to their hunting grounds and return about October 1 for the distribution of their annuities. The Indians apparently had been encamped along the Trail awaiting the annual distribution. According to Colonel Leavenworth, writing from Fort Larned:

> The late trouble with the Indians near here was occasioned by interested parties residing in the neighborhood and on the Indian lands, hoping if the Indians received their goods they would be able to purchase for little or nothing whatever the Indians received from the Government.[37]

As soon as the Indians had left the region surrounding Fort Larned, its garrison was reduced. The Kansas volunteers who had

[33] Fort Larned, Post Returns, May, June, 1862, MSS, AGO, AACB, NA.
[34] West to Moonlight, June 25, 1862, *OR,* Ser. 1, XIII, 448–49.
[35] The aggregate command at Fort Lyon was increased from 79 to 323 during the month. Fort Lyon, Post Returns, June, July, 1862, MSS, AGO, AACB, NA.
[36] Blunt to Canby, June 26, 1862, *OR,* Ser. 1, XIII, 450–51.
[37] Leavenworth to Moonlight, August 13, 1862, *ibid.,* 566.

Effects of the Civil War, 1861-1865

been sent out earlier in the summer were returned to Fort Riley. Fort Larned did not have quarters for these men, while Fort Riley did, and the cost of supplying them would be reduced by moving back to the latter post. The Indian hostilities near Fort Larned had ceased for the time being.

But the scene of their aggressions only shifted farther west. A train in northeastern New Mexico, on its way to Fort Union, was robbed of 115 mules during the latter part of August.[38] While measures had been taken earlier that month to secure the Trail between Forts Union and Lyon,[39] troops were not available to patrol the Cimarron Route. Major H. D. Wallen, commanding at Fort Union, reported on August 31 that Indian hostilities were becoming quite frequent near his post, and the following day he declared that the Indians were in such large force that he urgently needed two or more mounted companies.[40] There is a gap in the records at this point, and it cannot be determined whether or not these Indian activities were suppressed immediately. On the basis of the numerous measures already initiated, it seems reasonable to assume that adequate steps were taken also to protect the Cimarron Branch.

Brigadier General James H. Carleton replaced Canby as Commander of the Department of New Mexico on September 18, 1862, and Canby went east to other duties.[41] Carleton, who had commanded patrols on the Trail in 1851 and 1852, also recognized the

[38] Wallen to Chapin, August 30, 1862, Fort Union, Letters Sent, MSS, USAC, AACB, NA.

[39] A mounted company from Fort Union was sent out to patrol the road between that post and Fort Lyon early in August, 1862. During the same month a system of patrols was set up between the two forts, with Raton Pass as the point where each post's detail turned around. In addition, a battalion of the First Colorado Volunteers was sent to establish a camp at the crossing of the Huerfano, to assist in protection of the mails and trains using the route. Chapin to Commanding Officer Fort Union, August 3, 9, 1862, Fort Union, Letters Received, MSS, *ibid.;* Chapin to Leavenworth, August 7, 1862, *ibid.*

[40] Wallen to Chapin, August 31, September 1, 1862, Fort Union, Letters Sent, MSS, *ibid.*

[41] Carleton to Thomas, September 30, 1862, 39 Cong., 2 sess., *Sen. Report 156,* appendix, p. 98.

145

importance of the Santa Fe Trail and was familiar with the problems involved in protecting it. Seemingly he took the same care in providing that protection as did his predecessor.

The Indians remained quiet during the winter of 1862-1863, or at least no evidence of hostilities has been located. But, as was their usual practice, the Plains Indians began to assemble along the Trail during the spring months. Their pursuit of the buffalo naturally brought them to the region, but they also congregated along the route in anticipation of receiving annuities. With their return, depredations were renewed. Traders and travelers crossing the plains during April, 1863, stated that the Indians showed evidence of hostile intentions. Some of the traders had been warned by an Indian agent, name unknown, to be prepared for a general uprising among these Indians unless measures were taken to prevent it.

General Carleton, upon receiving this information, communicated it to Adjutant General Lorenzo Thomas and proposed a plan for making the Trail safe. Carleton believed that the only sure way to protect the route was to station a sufficient number of troops at strategic points. He recommended placing a regiment of cavalry at old Fort Atkinson, four companies of mounted troops at the Lower Spring on the Cimarron, the same amount at Cold Spring, and maintaining garrisons at Forts Larned and Lyon "in good strength."[42] Placing that many companies of cavalry along the route surely would have produced desired results, but the plan called for reinforcements which were not available and therefore it was not adopted. Carleton attempted a similar plan on a much smaller scale the following year, when the expected Indian uprising became a reality.

In anticipation of increased Indian attacks during 1863, on June 8 Colonel J. H. Leavenworth, commanding at Fort Larned, was placed in command of all troops serving along the Santa Fe Trail within the District of Kansas. This was done so that he could co-

[42] Carleton to Thomas, May 10, 1863, *ibid.*, 109-10.

ordinate military operations.[43] The Plains Indians assembled near Fort Larned during the late spring. By June 11, 1863, a large number of Comanches, Cheyennes, Arapahoes, Kiowas, Apaches, and Caddoes,[44] according to Leavenworth:

> ... fill this part of Kansas full to repletion with Indians, and, if anything should occur to arouse their passions, nothing could save us from certain destruction, and unless some more troops are sent promptly on to this Santa Fe route, I cannot vouch for its safety one day.[45]

Clearly, Leavenworth was alarmed. He had met several Mexican trains carrying large amounts of whisky, "enough in one train I met," he declared, "to intoxicate every Indian on the plains." Expressing fear of what might happen should some of this fall into the hands of the Indians, he requested that someone check all trains farther east and remove any whisky. Indian Agent Colley concurred.[46] No evidence has been found to show that such action was taken.

The Indians, however, became a nuisance without whisky. The wagonmaster of a government commissary train which arrived at Fort Larned from the East on June 27 reported that the Kiowas and Comanches had harassed his train from Cow Creek to Walnut Creek, and that in his eighteen years on the plains he had never seen the Indians "so impudent and insulting as now."[47] Colonel Leavenworth sent for the chiefs of the tribes involved and warned them that if they could not keep their younger braves from robbing the trains, the soldiers would. But, with several large encampments surrounding the post, there was little the small garrison could do. Indian warriors apparently outnumbered the soldiers by at least ten

---

[43] General Orders, No. 1, Headquarters of Troops on Santa Fe Road, Fort Larned, June 8, 1863, *OR*, Ser. 1, XXII, pt. 2, 313.

[44] The Caddoes, numbering about five hundred, had left Texas because of ill-treatment by the Confederates. Anthony to [?], September 24, 1863, *ibid.*, 572.

[45] Leavenworth to Curtis, June 11, 1863, *ibid.*, 316.

[46] *Ibid.*

[47] Leavenworth to Williams, June 27, 1863, *ibid.*, 339.

Soldiers on the Santa Fe Trail

to one. It was an explosive situation. If someone lighted the fuse, the soldiers could be annihilated.

Leavenworth feared the explosion was imminent on July 9 when, at about one o'clock in the morning, a sentinel at the fort shot and killed an Indian. Leavenworth later explained that the post had been surrounded by Apache, Kiowa, and Arapaho Indians,

> ... and not knowing to which tribe he [dead Indian] belonged, our position was rather unpleasant, owing to not having many troops here; and, as the Indians had been troublesome on the Santa Fe road, I had out on scout some 50 of our small garrison, to protect trains above and below on the river. As soon as this Indian was killed, I sent runners out for all the scouts to return to this post, and called a council of all the chiefs. By 8 a.m. all the chiefs (principal chiefs) were here.... Upon examination of the dead Indian by the chiefs, it was found to be a Cheyenne; they happened to be in small numbers, and we happily escaped a collision for the moment.[48]

The Indians soon began to drift away from the post, and Fort Larned was not seriously endangered during the remainder of the year. Throughout the summer, however, the Indians, especially the Kiowas and Comanches, continued to harass the wagon trains using the Trail. By late August they were operating near the Cimarron Crossing. Their objective was still supplies and provisions, and no loss of life was reported. Nevertheless, some men and women were taken prisoners.[49] Major Scott J. Anthony, commanding at Fort Lyon, upon learning of the difficulties in the vicinity of the crossing, sent a detachment of seventy men to establish a camp there. He then investigated the situation between his post and Fort Larned. Leavenworth set up patrols to cover the route from Walnut Creek to old Fort Atkinson. Soon afterward, Anthony reported that the Indians had stopped their depredations.[50]

The presence of troops was still sufficient to control the Indians. The Comanches and Kiowas agreed to leave the vicinity of the Trail

---

[48] Leavenworth to Williams, July 15, 1863, *ibid.*, 400–401.
[49] Anthony to Stilwell, September 2, 1863, *ibid.*, 507.
[50] Anthony to Stilwell, September 14, 1863, *ibid.*, 532.

Courtesy Kansas State Historical Society

Sutler's store, Fort Dodge. Sketch published in *Harper's Weekly*, May 25, 1867.

Courtesy Kansas State Historical Society

Fort Union, late 1850's.

Courtesy National Archives

Fort Union hospital, said to be the best-equipped along the Trail. U.S. Signal Corps Photo.

Courtesy National Archives

Edwin V. Sumner. U.S. Signal Corps Photo (Brady Collection).

Courtesy Kansas State Historical Society

Bennet Riley.

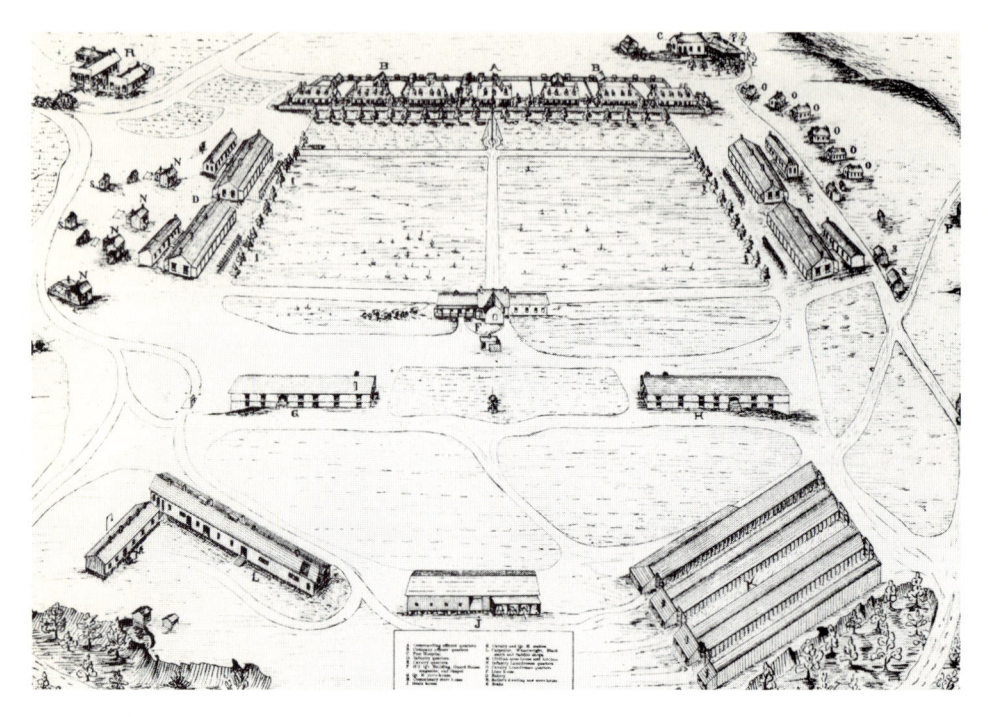

Courtesy Kansas State Historical Society

Fort Lyon (New Post), 1875
A. commanding officers' quarters; B. company officers' quarters; C. post hospital; D. infantry quarters; E. cavalry quarters; F. headquarters building, guardhouse, magazine, and chapel; G. Quartermaster storehouse; H. commissary storehouse; J. grain house; K. cavalry and Quartermaster stables; L. carpenter, wheelwright, blacksmith and saddler shops; M. civilian mess house and kitchen; N. infantry laundresses quarters; O. cavalry laundresses quarters; L. lime house; Q. bakery; R. sutler's dwelling and storehouse; S. sinks.

Courtesy of Library, State Historical Society of Colorado

John M. Chivington.

Courtesy Kansas State Historical Society

Winfield S. Hancock.

Effects of the Civil War, 1861-1865

in late September.[51] A drought had plagued the plains during 1863, making it difficult for the Indians to obtain food and other provisions. Anthony believed their raiding activities were motivated basically by need. Early in the autumn he declared that the government would either have to support them during the coming months or allow them to starve. And the latter, Anthony suggested, "would probably be much the easiest way of disposing of them."[52] After the annuities were issued during the early fall, the Indian threat to the Trail subsided for the remainder of the year. Indians had been active along the Trail from 1861 to 1863, but their hostilities had not been seriously damaging.

The routine nature of protecting the Trail would be shattered the following year, and Anthony gave an indication of what might come in September, 1863:

> I will give you the statements of Yellow Buffalo, chief of the Kiowas, Little Raven, chief of the Arapahoes, and other Indians, who report the same thing, and let you take it for what it is worth; I don't believe it. They state that runners have been down among the Indian tribes on the Arkansas from the Sioux and Cheyennes, of the Platte, trying to get the Indians of the plains all united for a general attack upon both the Platte and Arkansas routes, the attack to be made this fall, and that all the tribes, except the Cheyennes, refused; that the Cheyennes have agreed with the Sioux to commence war upon the Platte route very soon, and that we may look for trouble up there, but not here.[53]

It is not clear whether Anthony discounted the reports or did not believe that the attacks would be confined to the Platte. If his

---

[51] Anthony to [?], September 24, 1863, *ibid.*, 571.

[52] *Ibid.*, 572.

[53] Anthony to Stilwell, September 14, 1863, *ibid.*, 533. Robert North, who had been living with the Arapahoes, made the following statement to Governor John Evans, Colorado Territory, in November of 1863: "The Comanches, Apaches, Kiowas, the northern band of Arapahoes, and all the Cheyennes, with the Sioux, have pledged one another to go to war with the whites as soon as they can procure ammunition in the spring. I heard them discuss the matter often and the few of them who opposed it were forced to be quiet and were really in danger of the loss of their lives." Evans to Dole, November 10, 1863, *ibid.*, XXXIV, pt. 4, 100.

Soldiers on the Santa Fe Trail

opinion was the latter, he was correct, for the spring of 1864 saw a disastrous Indian uprising along both routes and across the country lying between.

Military and civil authorities wondered throughout the winter of 1863–64 if the portended Indian outbreak would occur. No overt action had occurred by mid-March 1864, and Indian Agent Colley reported that he had found the Indians along the Santa Fe route "all quiet." There was, however, the prospect of a war between the Kiowas and Arapahoes. Colley feared that open conflict between the two tribes would involve all the Plains Indians, and he recommended strengthening the garrisons of the posts along the Trail because, "If the Indians go to war among themselves, I fear that it will extend much farther."[54]

An internecine conflict, however, was not the precipitating factor of the Indian uprising. The Cheyennes opened the warfare between Indians and whites in Colorado Territory during April, 1864. They attacked ranches along the Platte River and stole stock. Troops were dispatched after them, and a series of skirmishes ensued.[55] Following the surprise attack and destruction of a large Cheyenne encampment on May 3, 1864, by a squadron of the First Colorado Cavalry commanded by Major Jacob Downing, other tribes joined the conflict.[56] By late spring the Indians throughout the plains were out of control, attacking settlements and routes of travel in a bloody campaign to drive out the whites.

The first report of hostilities along the Santa Fe Trail in 1864 came from Fort Larned on April 20. Lieutenant W. D. Crocker, commanding, reported that the Kiowas were attacking trains and stealing stock. The Kiowas usually committed some hostile actions upon their arrival near the post, but this time the frequency of attacks and openness of their operations were causing much alarm among those traveling the route. Crocker, who had served at the

---

[54] Colley to Evans, March 12, 1864, *ibid.*, XXXIV, pt. 2, 633–34.
[55] See correspondence in *ibid.*, XXXIV, pt. 3, 149–50, 166–67, 218–19, 242, 303–304.
[56] Curtis to Halleck, May 5, 1864, *ibid.*, 465.

Effects of the Civil War, 1861-1865

post for two years, declared that he had "never known the Indians to be so insolent as they are at present." He requested cavalry reinforcements, fearing there would soon be "serious difficulty."[57] No mounted troops were immediately available.

Depredations continued to increase near Fort Larned as other tribes joined in the attacks. The situation did indeed become serious, and the new commanding officer at the post, Captain J. W. Parmetar, declared on May 17 that "unless there is a cavalry force sent here, travel across the plains will have to be entirely suspended."[58] The captain was unable to provide escorts because of the small garrison and lack of animals for mounting those troops present. The following day he received information that the stage station thirty-two miles east of the fort had been attacked by Cheyennes and all the mules driven away.[59] The Indians almost succeeded in closing the Trail because the number of troops available was inadequate to counteract them. Nevertheless, a company of cavalry was soon sent from Fort Riley, and the mails and trains were only held up temporarily.[60]

Before the cavalry left Fort Riley, the ranchkeepers at most of the stage stations on the Trail between Fort Larned and Council Grove, and between Fort Larned and Salina on the Fort Larned–Fort Riley road, had been driven back to the settlements. A herder for the Kansas Stage Company at Cow Creek was killed. Other employees had forced the Indians back, killing two and wounding another, and then abandoned the station. News of these attacks brought the troops from Fort Riley. There was fear that the eastbound mail coach might have been attacked, but it had been detained at Fort Larned where a detachment of Colorado troops arriving on May 19, following an engagement with the Cheyennes, had reported the danger.[61]

---

[57] Crocker to AAG, Dist. of South Kansas, April 20, 1864, *ibid.*, 241.
[58] Parmetar to AAG, Dist. of South Kansas, May 17, 1864, *ibid.*, 643.
[59] Parmetar to AAG, Dist. of South Kansas, May 18, 1864, *ibid.*, 661.
[60] Hampton to Parmetar, May 25, 1864, *ibid.*, XXXIV, pt. 4, 39.
[61] Jones to Osburn, May 31, 1864, *ibid.*, 149-50. Chivington had sent Lieutenant George S. Eayre and a detachment of eighty men, First Colorado Cavalry, in pursuit

Soldiers on the Santa Fe Trail

On May 25 Captain Parmetar took eighty men and went into the field to find the Kiowas believed to have attacked the mail stations, but failed in his mission. He then called a council of the Arapahoes, Kiowas, and Comanches near the post and ordered them off the Trail and the Arkansas River, directing them to move south. The Indians professed to be peaceful and agreed to remove themselves, but even while they were talking other members of their tribes were busy robbing trains between Forts Larned and Lyon.[62]

The entire route was becoming perilous just at the time assistance was on the way. Chivington dispatched ten companies of Colorado volunteers to the Trail, some to reinforce the garrison at Fort Lyon and others to set up Camp Wynkoop about sixty miles east of Lyon. Regular mail escorts were again put into operation, and although they had frequent skirmishes with the Indians, the mails did go through. A company of troops was stationed at Council Grove and another at Salina to aid in keeping the routes open east of Fort Larned.[63] Yet the Indians did not let up in their efforts to close the Trail; in fact, they became more brazen.

On July 17 the Kiowas made a direct attack on Fort Larned and took 172 army animals. They were pursued but were not overtaken. The attacks continued upon trains between Forts Larned and Lyon. Major General Samuel R. Curtis, commander of the Department of Kansas, decided that the Indian threat was so serious that he would lead a battalion of Kansas militia and United States

---

of the Cheyennes following the outbreak of hostilities along the Platte. On April 18 they found a small group of Cheyennes who abandoned their camp, five lodges, and it was burned. Eayre continued on the trail of a larger band which he engaged about forty-five miles north of Fort Larned on May 17, killing twenty-five Indians and losing four of his command. Afterward they marched to Fort Larned, arriving there May 19. Eayre to Chivington, April 18, 1864, *ibid.,* XXXIV, pt. 3, 218–19; Fort Larned, Post Returns, May, 1864, MSS, AGO, AACB, NA.

[62] *Ibid.;* Jones to Osburn, May 31, 1864, *OR,* Ser. 1, XXXIV, pt. 4, 150; Wynkoop to Maynard, June 8, 1864, *ibid.,* 273–74.

[63] Chivington to Curtis, June 8, 1864, *ibid.,* 273; Curtis to Commanding Officers Fort Riley and Fort Larned, June 3, 1864, *ibid.,* 205; McKenny to Charlot, June 15, 1864, *ibid.,* 404; Fort Larned, Post Returns, June, 1864, MSS, AGO, AACB, NA.

Effects of the Civil War, 1861-1865

volunteers from Fort Riley to punish the hostiles. Before leaving that post, he created the District of the Upper Arkansas, which included Forts Riley, Larned, and Lyon, and placed the entire region under command of Brigadier General James Blunt.[64] Apparently, operations had been hampered by the fact that a portion of the Trail had been placed under two military districts, South Kansas and Colorado.

General Curtis, with four hundred men and two pieces of artillery, arrived at the crossing of Walnut Creek on July 28 and established Fort Zarah there, in a location utilized for military camps from time to time since 1853. He reported that upon his approach the Indians scattered, and a wagon train that had been besieged at Cow Creek was safe thereafter, although it had already lost two men and about three hundred head of stock. The following day he proceeded to Fort Larned, arriving just as four companies of the First Colorado Cavalry marched in from Fort Lyon. Upon learning that the last train from the West had been attacked and two men killed at Cimarron Crossing, Curtis sent a force of Coloradans back to guard the crossing.[65]

At Fort Larned Curtis split his command into three detachments.

---

[64] Chivington to Charlot, July 5, 1864, *OR,* Ser. 1, XLI, pt. 2, 55; Curtis to Halleck, Curtis to Charlot, July 23, 1864, *ibid.,* 368-69; General Orders, No. 41, Headquarters Department of Kansas, July 25, 1864, *ibid.,* 396; Fort Larned, Post Returns, July, 1864, MSS, AGO, AACB, NA.

[65] *Ibid.;* Curtis to Halleck, Curtis to Carney, July 28, 1864, *OR,* Ser. 1, XLI, pt. 2, 445-46; Curtis to Chivington, July 30, 1864, *ibid.,* 483-84. Fort Zarah, located approximately two miles from the Arkansas River, was occupied until December, 1869. Until June 30, 1868, it was not classified as a separate fort, but was under the commanding officer of Fort Larned and made its reports to that officer. Quarters were constructed, but it was never of major significance as a military post, being overshadowed by the larger garrison at Fort Larned, approximately thirty miles west. The major purpose of the garrison, which fluctuated between 52 and 641, aggregate, was to provide escorts. From that standpoint it was valuable, providing twenty-one escorts during a typical month, January, 1865. Its command, along with those of the other posts along the Trail, helped to subdue the Indians after the Civil War. Fort Zarah, Post Returns, 1864-69, MSS, AGO, AACB, NA; Outline Summary of Fort Zarah, MS., *ibid.;* Special Orders, No. 92, Headquarters District of the Upper Arkansas, June 30, 1868, MS, *ibid.;* Curtis to Blunt, August 9, *OR,* Ser. 1, XLI, pt. 2, 630.

Soldiers on the Santa Fe Trail

He sent one north of the Arkansas to scout for Indians and punish them if located. Another was ordered westward along the Trail to provide additional protection for trains on that section of the route. The third he himself commanded in a march south of the Arkansas. None of these detachments overtook any Indians, but Curtis later reported that they had succeeded in frightening the Indians away from the Trail and that stages and trains were again moving regularly. He then discharged the Kansas militia and returned to his headquarters at Fort Leavenworth.[66] Unfortunately, the Indians immediately returned to the Trail and attacked the trains not protected by troops.

When Fort Larned was reinforced and Curtis made his brief thrust into that region, the Indians moved farther west and continued their attacks.[67] On August 7, a band of Kiowas and Comanches struck at a train seven miles below Fort Lyon.[68] Four days later a party of fifteen Indians pursued a sergeant who was searching for a stray horse north of Fort Lyon until they were withing sight of the post. Two squadrons of fifteen men each were immediately sent in pursuit, and additional troops were dispatched the following day. Except for a small skirmish near Sand Creek, in which no losses were suffered by either side, the pursuit was a failure.[69]

Upon reaching Fort Larned on August 13 after a march from Fort Lyon, Major Scott J. Anthony reported that the Indians had "recently stolen a large quantity of Government and citizens' stock."[70] During the second week of August, the Comanches killed five men near Lower Cimarron Springs and stampeded all the

---

[66] Curtis to Chivington, July 30, 1864, *ibid.*, 484; Curtis to Halleck, August 8, 1864, *ibid.*, 610.

[67] Colley to Evans, August 12, 1864, *ibid.*, 673.

[68] Wynkoop to Maynard, August 9, 1864, *ibid.*, XLI, pt. 1, 231.

[69] Wynkoop to Maynard, August 13, 1864, Cramer to Wynkoop, August 12, 1864, Baldwin to Denison, August 12, 1864, Quinby to Wynkoop, August 12, 1864, *ibid.*, 237–40.

[70] Anthony to Loring, August 13, 1864, *ibid.*, XLI, pt. 2, 692.

Effects of the Civil War, 1861-1865

cattle from a train.[71] On August 19, Indians attacked and burned a train near Cimarron Springs, killing ten men, and taking all the stock. Two days later, four government trains and one trader's caravan were attacked while encamped near old Fort Atkinson. The wagonmaster of one train was killed, all the stock was taken from one train, and about one hundred head of stock was captured from the others.[72] Troops were dispatched after the offenders, but none of the guilty parties was overtaken.

During August, Brigadier General Carleton, commanding the Department of New Mexico, sent troops from his department to help protect the route. He ordered Captain Nicholas S. Davis, with one hundred men and two howitzers, to Cimarron Crossing; Major Joseph Updegraff, with the same number of troops, to Lower Cimarron Springs; and Captain E. H. Bergmann, with eighty cavalry and infantry, to Upper Cimarron Springs. All were rationed for sixty days. In addition, Carleton ordered one company of New Mexico volunteers to Fort Lyon to aid the garrison in fighting Indians, and he stationed another company at Gray's Ranch on the Purgatoire River to provide escorts for the mails between Fort Lyon and Lucien Maxwell's Ranch. These commands, also, were to remain at their duties for sixty days.[73] It might appear that a number of troops adequate to prevent hostilities was already serving on the Trail, but it was impossible to provide every train with an escort and attacks continued at an alarming rate.

Colonel J. C. McFerran reported the seriousness of the situation along the Trail on August 28, after traveling from Kansas City to Santa Fe:

Both life and property on this route is almost at the mercy of

[71] Carleton to Carson, August 15, 1864, *ibid.*, 723; Davis to Commanding Officer Fort Union, August 23, 1864, *ibid.*, 828–29.

[72] *Ibid.;* Anthony to Loring, August 23, 1864, *ibid.*, 827.

[73] Carleton to McMullen, August 1, 1864, *ibid.*, 512; Cutler to Davis, August 23, 1864, *ibid.*, 811; Special Orders, No. 34, Headquarters Department of New Mexico, August 28, 1864, *ibid.*, 915.

Soldiers on the Santa Fe Trail

the Indians. Every tribe that frequents the plains is engaged in daily depredations on trains, and immense losses to the Government and individuals have occurred, and many lives have already been lost. Several persons were killed and large numbers of animals run off during my trip of fourteen days from Kansas City to this place. Many contractors and private trains are now corralled and unable to move from their camps for fear of Indians, and other trains have had their entire stock run off, and cannot move until other animals can be had.[74]

Major Anthony reported on August 29 that no hostilities had been committed near Fort Larned during the past week.[75] Nevertheless, McFerren declared:

This evil is on the increase, and the number of troops on the route is so small that they are unable to securely protect the public property at their respective stations. They have in several instances lost a large number of public horses and other animals, run off by these Indians, within a few hundred yards of their posts. Soldiers and citizens have been killed within sight of a large number of troops. You cannot imagine a worse state of things than exists now on this route. Women and children have been taken prisoners to suffer treatment worse than death.[76]

Colonel McFerran predicted that, unless immediate action were taken to chastise the Indians, the situation would only grow worse. He recommended that a large force of twenty-five hundred or three thousand troops be sent against the hostiles with orders not to stop the campaign until the Indians were exterminated or until the most effective chastisement possible had been inflicted. Other officers had reached similar conclusions. Chivington suggested that killing the Indians appeared the "most feasible" solution to the problem.[77] General Curtis declared in September, when it was learned that some of the Indians were making peace overtures

[74] McFerren to Carleton, August 28, 1864, *ibid.*, 927.
[75] Anthony to Tappan, August 29, 1864, *ibid.*, 926.
[76] McFerran to Carleton, August 28, 1864, *ibid.*, 927.
[77] Chivington to Curtis, August 11, 1864, *ibid.*, 660.

Effects of the Civil War, 1861-1865

(presumably because of the approaching winter season): "I want no peace till the Indians suffer more.... No peace must be made without my direction."[78]

Early in September a large number of Cheyenne and Arapaho Indians sent a letter to Indian Agent Colley at Fort Lyon, offering to make peace, in return for which they would bring back the white prisoners they held. Major E. W. Wynkoop took 130 troops and marched to the Indians' camp and demanded the prisoners. Four prisoners were released to Wynkoop after he agreed to take the chiefs to Denver for a meeting with Governor John Evans.[79] Governor Evans met with seven chiefs of the two tribes on September 28 and reported the following day: "I have declined to make peace with them, lest it might embarrass the military operations against the hostile Indians of the plains.... [They] must make peace with the military authorities."[80] There the matter stood for the time being.

While peace was being discussed in Colorado Territory, Brigadier General Blunt took command of troops at Fort Larned and moved westward looking for Indians. He followed their trail from Cimarron Crossing to the west branch of Pawnee Fork, about seventy-five miles above Larned, where he overtook a large encampment of three or four thousand Kiowas, Arapahoes, and Cheyennes on September 25. He routed and pursued them for several days, killing nine Indians and wounding an undetermined number and losing two soldiers killed and seven wounded. The Indians finally escaped, and the troops returned to Fort Larned.[81]

Following that engagement, things quieted down along the Trail, but hostilities became worse in Colorado and along the Platte route.

[78] Curtis to Chivington, September 28, 1864, *ibid.*, XLI, pt. 3, 462. Chivington was operating under these directions when he led the attack upon the Indians encamped at Sand Creek two months later; see below.

[79] Colley to Evans, September 4, 1864, *ibid.*, 195-96; Wynkoop to Tappan, September 18, 1864, *ibid.*, 242-43.

[80] Evans to Colley, September 29, 1864, 39 Cong., 2 sess., *Sen. Report 156*, appendix, p. 82.

[81] Curtis to Chivington, October 7, 1864, *OR*, Ser. 1, XLI, pt. 3, 696; Fort Larned, Post Returns, September, 1864, MSS, AGO, AACB, NA.

157

By order of General Blunt, Major Wynkoop, who had allowed those Indians claiming to desire peace to encamp near Fort Lyon and draw rations from the post, was replaced as commander of the fort by Major Anthony on November 2. Anthony was ordered to

> ... investigate and report upon the official rumors that reach headquarters that certain officers have issued stores, goods, or supplies to hostile Indians, in direct violation of orders from the general commanding the department.[82]

Anthony found the rumors to be true and that Major Wynkoop had issued the order to supply the Indians from the commissary department. There were 113 lodges of Arapahoes encamped near the fort and drawing rations at the time Anthony assumed command. He disarmed the Indians and allowed them to remain in camp as prisoners until he could receive orders from Blunt:

> They pretend that they want peace, and I think they do now, as they cannot fight during the winter. ... I do not think it is policy to make peace with them now until all perpetrators of depredations are surrendered up, to be dealt with as we may propose.[83]

A band of about two hundred Cheyennes, under Chief Black Kettle, requested a council with Major Anthony during the second week of November. They declared their peaceful intentions and were directed to encamp at Sand Creek, about twenty-five miles northeast of Fort Lyon, until "the pleasure of the commanding officer of the district could be learned."[84] The major also sent the Arapahoes encamped near the post into the same region. Both groups were dissatisfied because Anthony would not make peace, but he declared it was his intention "to let matters remain dormant until troops can be sent out to take the field against all the tribes."[85] These bands of Arapahoes and Cheyennes did encamp on Sand

---

[82] General Orders, No. 4, Headquarters District of the Upper Arkansas, October 17, 1864, *OR,* Ser. 1, XLI, pt. 4, 62.

[83] Anthony to AAAG, District of the Upper Arkansas, November 6, 1864, *ibid.,* XLI, pt. 1, 913.

[84] Anthony to Helliwell, November 16, 1864, *ibid.,* 914.

Effects of the Civil War, 1861-1865

Creek, and they were attacked there on November 29 by the Chivington-led expedition.

Before Chivington moved his force against these Indians, Colonel Carson was sent from New Mexico to attack the home country of the Kiowas. This expedition was organized by General Carleton to punish the Kiowas for their attacks along the Trail during the past summer.[86] Leading 334 officers and men, plus 75 Utes and Jicarilla Apaches, on November 25 Carson attacked a large camp (150 lodges) of Kiowas near the ruins of Adobe Fort, William Bent's old trading post on the Canadian River. The Indians abandoned their camp and made a stand at Adobe Fort, but the troops succeeded in driving them out and occupying the position. The Kiowas were then joined by the Comanches, and a bitter fight followed. Carson's force had a hard time of it, but the howitzers finally repulsed the Indians, and a detachment of troops returned to the abandoned village and destroyed it. Upon seeing their village burning, the Indians retreated. Carson then returned to New Mexico.[87] This was a serious blow to the Kiowas because of the approaching winter.

The destruction of the Kiowa camp was soon followed by the Sand Creek Affair. On the evening of November 28 Colonel Chivington led an expedition of about seven hundred men from Fort Lyon. His force consisted of the Third Regiment Colorado Cavalry, raised for one hundred days of service and under the command of Colonel George L. Shoup, and two battalions of First Cavalry, one commanded by Major Anthony and the other by Lieutenant Luther Wilson. After marching all night, the next morning Chiv-

---

[85] *Ibid.*

[86] General Orders, No. 32, Headquarters Department of New Mexico, October 22, 1864, *ibid.,* XLI, pt. 4, 198–99.

[87] Carson to Cutler, December 4, 1864, ibid., XLI, pt. 1, 939–42. According to Carson's report, this was quite a battle. It lasted from about eight-thirty in the morning of November 25, 1864, until sunset. The fighting was severe during most of that time. Carson lost 2 soldiers killed and 10 wounded, 1 Indian killed and 5 wounded, and "a large number of horses wounded." He estimated the Indians' losses as at least 60 killed and wounded.

Soldiers on the Santa Fe Trail

ington's troops attacked the Arapahoes and Cheyennes encamped on Sand Creek. A fierce battle, which is still the subject of controversy, ensued, and the village was destroyed. The soldiers lost ten men killed and forty wounded, and the reports of the Indian losses vary from about seventy to between five and six hundred killed.[88]

The Indians were beginning to suffer as General Curtis had directed, yet Sand Creek did not bring an end to hostilities. William H. Leckie states that ". . . The immediate result of Sand Creek was an Indian War of unprecedented scope and violence. The survivors . . . obtained aid from the Northern Cheyennes and Arapahoes and from the Comanches and Kiowas. . . . slew scores of whites and fought off all troops sent against them."[89] Along the Santa Fe Trail, however, the period immediately preceding the Sand Creek Affair was the most violent, making 1864, without doubt, the year of the most serious Indian hostilities throughout its history, and afterward Indian attacks were less severe.

Some military protection had been provided for the Trail during 1864, even though the number of troops was inadequate for the task at hand. While the Trail had not been closed, neither had the Indians been subdued. They had wreaked much destruction along the route during that year. At best, the soldiers serving along, and in the region of, the Santa Fe Trail had brought the situation to a stalemate. Much money, time, and bloodshed would be required before the soldiers could claim a definitive victory, but some progress toward peace would be made during 1865.

During the winter of 1864-65 there was a lull in the fighting along the Santa Fe Trail. With most of the Indians in their winter camps and traffic along the Trail greatly reduced, the only hostilities were occasional raids by small bands of Indians. A series of scouts were kept up along the route throughout the winter season, and most of them returned to their respective posts and re-

---

[88] *Ibid.,* 948–72; 39 Cong., 2 sess., *Sen. Exec. Doc. 26;* 39 Cong., 2 sess., *Sen. Report 156,* appendix, pp. 26–98.
[89] William H. Leckie, *The Military Conquest of the Southern Plains,* 24.

Effects of the Civil War, 1861-1865

ported no Indians sighted.[90] About forty-five Cheyennes and Arapahoes attacked a sutler's train west of Fort Larned on January 17, but the escort drove the Indians away, killing three and wounding three.[91] On February 1, fifteen Indians charged a fatigue party of eight soldiers chopping wood near Fort Zarah and killed one man.[92] Such incidents were few and far between, and, compared to the previous summer, it was indeed quiet along the Trail.

It was expected, however, that there would be a general uprising of all the Plains Indians during the coming spring.[93] In anticipation of renewed hostilities, several steps were taken by department commanders and the federal government to make the protection of the Trail more effective. A new system of escorting trains was put into operation, three additional military posts were established, preparations were made to launch a campaign against the hostile tribes, and efforts to negotiate a peace settlement were continued. The result was a safer Santa Fe Trail during 1865.

General Carleton decided in February to send an escort from Fort Union to Fort Larned on the first and fifteenth day of every month, beginning March 1. These escorts would alternate between Cimarron and Mountain routes, and all merchants were invited to assemble their trains near Fort Union, preparatory for departure on these dates if they desired protection.[94] Upon reaching Fort Larned, the escorts were sent back to Fort Union with the trains that had collected at the former post. In addition to the escorts, all trains planning to move west from Fort Riley and Council Grove were to be halted at those points until a large caravan could be organized and a captain selected to take charge, a plan similar to the pre-Mexican War method of organization. All persons with the train were to be armed, and no citizens' caravan would be allowed to proceed until at least one hundred men were present.

[90] *OR*, Ser. 1, XLVIII, pt. 1, 25, 47-48, 74, 99, 111, 117.
[91] Wynkoop to Taber, February 4, 1865, *ibid.*, 57-58.
[92] Ford to Charlot, February 9, 1865, *ibid.*, 74; Greene to Tappan, February 1, 1865, *ibid.*, 75.
[93] Ford to Charlot, January 3, 1865, *ibid.*, 407.
[94] Cutler to the People, February 8, 1865, *ibid.*, 782-83.

All government trains were to be provided with escorts at the above-named places, and citizens could join them. The commanding officer in charge of the escort would be in complete command of the caravan in such instances. All mail coaches were to be assigned an escort, and all mail stations located in the region of Indian difficulties were to be within protecting distance of a military post, or have a detachment of troops stationed to guard them.[95]

The system of periodic escorts was extended eastward from Fort Larned to Council Grove on May 1. Troops were to leave each point on the first and fifteenth of each month, and no trains were allowed to leave between those dates.[96] With the exception of several trains moving between Forts Union and Larned, every stagecoach and caravan was accompanied by troops throughout the summer of 1865. This had the effect of reducing the number of Indian attacks considerably from the previous year, and those attacks which occurred were much less destructive.

The additional military posts established along the Trail had a similar effect. Fort Dodge was founded in April, just west of where the Wet and Dry routes rejoined, Camp Nichols was occupied near Cold Spring on the Cimarron Route during late May, and Fort Aubrey was established approximately sixty miles east of Fort Lyon in September.

The first of these posts was proposed on March 18, when Major General Grenville M. Dodge, commanding the Department of Missouri, directed Colonel James H. Ford, commanding the District of the Upper Arkansas, to establish a post near old Fort Atkinson "as soon as practicable."[97] The section of the Trail between Forts Larned and Lyon, a distance of about 230 miles, had been the scene of a large number of Indian hostilities the preceding year. This stretch of road was known as the "Long Route" because of

[95] Special Orders, No. 41 and 42, Headquarters Department of Missouri, February 10, 11, 1865, *ibid.*, 807–808, 817.

[96] Ford to Tappan, April 17, 1865, *ibid.*, XLVIII, pt. 2, 114; General Orders, No. 11, District of the Upper Arkansas, April 20, 1865, *ibid.*, 147–48.

[97] Dodge to Ford, March 18, 1865, *ibid.*, XLVIII, pt. 1, 1211.

Effects of the Civil War, 1861–1865

the great distance caravans and stagecoaches had to travel without benefit of a protected camping place.

Colonel Ford ordered Captain Henry Pierce, with his company of Eleventh Kansas Cavalry and a company of the Second United States Volunteer Infantry, to move from Fort Larned and establish Fort Dodge, named for General G. M. Dodge.[98] Captain Pierce located the new post on the site of Adkin's Ranch, a stage station erected in 1863 and burned by Indians the following year. About nine miles east of old Fort Atkinson, Fort Dodge was occupied on April 10 and was garrisoned until October 2, 1882.[99] The troops at this fort were quartered in tents and dugouts in the banks of the Arkansas River until 1867, when stone barracks were constructed. Rating along with Larned, Lyon, and Union, this post was one of the most important along the Trail during the post-Civil War era.

For the second post, General Carleton ordered Colonel Carson to establish Camp Nichols during May, believing there was a definite need for a military establishment on the Cimarron Route between Forts Union and Larned. The post was designed to be occupied temporarily; the orders stated until November 1, when the peak travel season on the Trail would be completed.[100] Colonel Carson led three companies of New Mexico and California volunteers from Fort Union on May 20 and occupied a position near Cold Spring. The garrison assisted with escort duty along the Trail and provided a safe stopping place until the time appointed for its return to Fort Union. In late June or early July, Carson was called to Santa Fe to testify before a joint congressional committee in-

[98] Roe to Pierce, March 30, 31, 1865, District of the Upper Arkansas, Letters Sent, MSS, AGO, AACB, NA.

[99] Janes to Tappan, April 11, 1865, *OR,* Ser. 1, XLVIII, pt. 2, 74–75; General Orders, No. 1, Headquarters Fort Dodge, April 10, 1865, Fort Dodge Document File, MSS, USAC, AACB, NA; Fort Dodge, Medical History, Army Post Records, MSS, AGO, AACB, NA. For a history of the post, see the author's "Fortification on the Plains: Fort Dodge, Kansas, 1864–1882," *1960 Brand Book* (Denver, 1961), 137–79.

[100] Carleton to Carson, May 4, 1865, *OR,* Ser. 1, XLVIII, pt. 2, 317; Special Orders, No. 15, Headquarters Department of New Mexico, May 7, 1865, *ibid.,* 344–45.

163

vestigating Indian affairs, but Major Albert H. Pfeiffer was left in command of the camp.

Although Camp Nichols was intended to be a temporary post, Carson erected a breastwork of stone and earth, enclosing a space two hundred feet square, and built six sets of stone officers' quarters and a stone warehouse for quartermaster and commissary stores. The troops lived in tents set up inside the defenses. Wood, water, and building stone were abundant, making it an ideal location for a permanent post from that standpoint.[101] The camp was abandoned in November as originally planned, and it was found in ruins the following summer, apparently destroyed by Indians.

Another temporary post, Fort Aubrey, the last military establishment founded on the Trail, was occupied in September. It was located about sixty miles east of Fort Lyon at the site of old Camp Wynkoop, in what is now Hamilton County, Kansas. The garrison occupying the post averaged about 220 men until it was abandoned on April 20, 1866. During those few months the soldiers assisted the command at Fort Lyon with escort duty.[102]

After all these measures had been taken, the troops on the Santa Fe Trail were better prepared to cope with the Indian problem during 1865 than they were the previous year. And the Indians, for what exact reason is not clear, were much less hostile. It can be assumed that more effective protection of the Trail was a contributing factor to the decline of hostilities. A few attacks were made during April and May, and more during June and July; but the threat of a military campaign against them, plus the efforts of the congressional committee investigating Indian affairs and Indian Agent J. H. Leavenworth, kept many Indians peaceable.[103]

[101] Carson to Cutler, June 19, 1865, *ibid.*, 941.

[102] Special Field Orders, No. 20, Headquarters District of Kansas, September 15, 1865, Departmental Commands, MSS, AGO, AACB, NA; Outline Summary of Fort Aubrey, MS, *ibid.;* Special Orders, No. 45, Headquarters District of Kansas, March 26, 1866, Departmental Commands, MSS, *ibid.;* Fort Aubrey, Post Returns, 1865–66, MSS, *ibid.;* General Orders, No. 23, Headquarters Fort Aubrey, April 20, 1866, Departmental Commands, MSS, *ibid.*

[103] Information for this and following paragraphs is found in numerous items of correspondence located in *OR,* Ser. 1, XLVIII, pts. 1 & 2.

Effects of the Civil War, 1861-1865

Colonel Ford organized a unit of about four hundred men during March and April and equipped them for an expedition against all hostile tribes along the Arkansas. The campaign was held back by General Dodge, as directed by the president and chief of staff because of growing public indignation over what had come to be called the "Sand Creek Massacre," demands for a more humane solution to the Indian problem, and the fact that peace negotiations were being attempted with the Indians along the Arkansas River. Nevertheless, the campaign force was kept in readiness at Fort Riley, and moved to Forts Zarah and Larned several times during the summer when it appeared that the peace efforts were failing.

Negotiations with the Indians were unsuccessful throughout the summer of 1865. The Indians had learned that it was to their advantage to roam the plains during the spring and summer months when grass for their horses was plentiful, enjoying the freedom of movement to which they were accustomed and pursuing the dwindling buffalo herds. But, with the approach of the winter season, it was advantageous for them to conclude a "peace treaty" and receive rations from the government. They could always break the treaty the following spring, or at least they could until sufficient troops were present to keep them on their assigned reservations. With this pattern of behavior beginning to appear, it was no surprise that most of the Indians were ready to accept a treaty in the autumn of 1865.

On August 15 and 18, at the mouth of the Little Arkansas River, twenty-four chiefs of the Arapaho, Cheyenne, Apache, Kiowa, and Comanche tribes met with Indian Agent Leavenworth and Major General John B. Sanborn, new commanding officer of the District of the Upper Arkansas, and they agreed to cease all hostilities immediately. They promised to remain at peace and to meet in council at Bluff Creek on October 4 to negotiate and sign a treaty settlement.[104]

Following this agreement, the soldiers along the Trail, at that

[104] *Annual Report of Commissioner of Indian Affairs*, 1865, 39 Cong., 1 sess., *House Exec. Doc.* 1, pp. 578-79.

time being rapidly reduced in numbers as volunteer companies were mustered out of service, could relax the careful vigilance they had been maintaining. The threat of an Indian war was over, and hostilities subsided except for small bands of Indians who either disagreed with the decision to make peace or did not know about it.

The Bluff Creek council opened on the appointed date, with representatives of all the above-named tribes in attendance. A United States commission comprised of Leavenworth, Sanborn, Carson, William S. Harney, Thomas Murphy, William Bent, and James Steele negotiated and signed treaties with the Indians by October 18. All were assigned reservations south of the Arkansas River, where they were to receive annuities for forty years. They agreed not to encamp within ten miles of any town, military post, or main-traveled road without permission from proper authorities, and they promised perpetual peace and to arbitrate future disputes.[105] The treaties of the Little Arkansas, as they were called, were later violated and did not, by any means, bring lasting peace to the plains, but they were the beginning of the end of Indian hostilities and the need for soldiers along the Santa Fe Trail. The remainder of 1865 was peaceful along that route.

[105] *Indian Affairs, Laws and Treaties* (ed. by Kappler), II, 887–95.

6

The Soldiers' Life on the Trail, 1865-1880

THE POST-CIVIL WAR ERA, which formed the last phase of the military history of the Santa Fe Trail, was highlighted by the elimination of the Indian threat throughout its length. It was an era in which the forts and organized campaigns dominated the military activities along the route. It will be instructive to consider the physical development of these posts and to observe the expeditions. In addition to the regular garrison duty, protecting the road, and engaging in campaigns, the soldiers provided guards for the construction crews of the Atchison, Topeka and Santa Fe Railroad, which followed the route, and protected railroad stations threatened by Indians.

The factors leading to the establishment of each of the forts have been described above. From east to west along the Trail, the following posts were garrisoned during part or all of this last phase of the route's history: Fort Zarah, established July 28, 1864, at Walnut Creek; Fort Larned, occupied October 22, 1859, at Pawnee Fork; Fort Dodge, at a point just west of where the Wet and Dry Routes rejoined, founded April 10, 1865; Fort Lyon, established as Fort Wise on September 1, 1860, about half a mile west of Bent's New Fort; and Fort Union, oldest post along the Trail, first occupied on July 26, 1851, near the Río Mora where the Mountain and Cimarron routes rejoined. A more detailed description of these posts follows below, in order of geographical listing.

First, however, it should be mentioned that the forts along the Santa Fe Trail were not fortifications in the strict sense of the word. Unlike the walled structures providing a defensive position, these forts were more properly called posts, and, like most others on the plains, were primarily designed to provide a dwelling place for troops and storage facilities for supplies in the region of real or anticipated Indian attacks. As distinguished from the stockaded fort, those along the Trail were comprised of quarters for officers, barracks for soldiers, stables, military storehouses, hospital, headquarters office, and a sutler's store, all grouped around a parade ground (with the exception of Fort Zarah), but with no protective wall around the outside. In short, rather than resembling defensive positions, they were bases of operations for soldiers serving along the Trail.

At Fort Zarah the first quarters were tents and dugouts with dirt and brush roofs, along the bank of Walnut Creek. According to one of the soldiers living in these holes in the ground, "There is nothing tasty nor fanciful about them, but they are comfortable."[1] W. H. Ryus, express messenger along the Trail during the 1860's, later gave the following description of the officers' quarters in 1864:

> Their quarters was a little dugout in the side of the hill along the river bank. They had a gunny sack for the door, and I went into the first room which was used for a kitchen, and the cook told me to go to the next room, it had a gunny sack door, too, the First and Second Lieutenant were in the other room.[2]

Soon after the post was established, a corral with a capacity of 250 animals was built nearby.

Early in 1865 a small blockhouse, a guardhouse, and a bridge across the Walnut were completed, and an adobe sutler's store was erected. This first site was abandoned—for what reason is not clear—and the post was moved closer to the Arkansas River in December of 1867 when a large stone structure was completed there. It measured 160 by 60 feet, and included two hexagon-

[1] Quoted in Ellen Williams, *Three Years and a Half in the Army: History of the Second Colorados*, 142.
[2] W. H. Ryus, *The Second William Penn*, 162.

The Soldiers' Life on the Trail, 1865-1880

shaped towers fifteen feet high, at opposite corners and adjoining the ends of the main building. This facility contained quarters for one company of troops, soldiers' kitchen, mess room, orderly room, officers' kitchen, and two storerooms for quartermaster and commissary stores. Officers were quartered in one tower, and the dispensary, medical storeroom, and hospital ward were located in the other.[3] This compact unit apparently was well adapted to serve the purposes for which it was built.

There was neither guardhouse nor quarters for married officers within the building. Both these facilities were provided in tents behind the fort, and consequently, the guardhouse usually had to be surrounded by a six-man guard. A bakehouse and blacksmith shop were located between the stone structure and the tents, while the horses were kept in corrals beyond the latter.[4] All these structures together constituted Fort Zarah, from late 1867 until it was abandoned two years later.

The primary duty of the garrison, as stated above, was to provide escorts. The post was located where the road from Fort Riley joined the Santa Fe Trail, so the troops stationed there were required to furnish escorts for mail coaches and government supply trains traveling both routes. During one month of routine duty, the soldiers traveled a combined distance of 1,220 miles on escorts and never went more than forty-five miles from the post.[5] The little garrison obviously kept busy, for, besides serving as escorts, the troops were required to fulfill the duties of guard, teamster, hospital steward, butcher, gardener, mechanic, blacksmith, and hay cutter at the post.

Fort Zarah was instrumental in activities connected with the Indians until after the winter campaign of 1868-69, then it was too far from the scene of Indian hostilities to participate in sup-

---

[3] Fort Zarah, Medical History, Army Post Records, MSS, AGO, AACB, NA; Livingston to Easton, October 14, 1867, CCF, MSS, QMGO, AACB, NA.

[4] Fort Zarah, Medical History, Army Post Records, MSS, AGO, AACB, NA.

[5] Fort Zarah, Post Returns, January, 1865, MSS, *ibid.*

pressing them. The post was abandoned at the close of 1869, having served the purpose for which it had been founded. By that time the immediate region had become safe for travelers and settlers.

Fort Larned was located within a loop of Pawnee Fork, so that the west, north, and east sides were bounded by that stream, providing some natural protection. The sod and adobe buildings constructed there during 1859 and 1860 served as quarters, hospital, and warehouses until after the Civil War. The first stone structure was a hexagon-shaped blockhouse, located at the southeast corner of the parade ground to help protect the exposed side of the post, completed in February, 1865, under orders issued by General G. M. Dodge the previous summer.[6]

Other stone buildings were erected around the square parade ground during 1866-68. On the north side were two sets of barracks, each containing quarters for two companies, a kitchen, mess room, orderly room, and storage rooms. Dormitory space for each company was forty feet square. Along the east side of the parade ground were two buildings, each eighty-four and one-half by thirty feet. The one on the north housed the blacksmith, wheelwright, and harness repair shops. The other held the bakery and included a general mess room. On the south side were the commissary and quartermaster buildings. These two structures, along with the blockhouse, guarded the side which was exposed to open prairie.

An underground tunnel connected the blockhouse with the commissary building and the bakery, and from the latter another tunnel ran to the bank of the Pawnee Fork so that water could be ob-

[6] Fort Larned, at the time of this writing, was one of the best-preserved frontier forts in America. Information about the physical development of the fort was taken from Surgeon General's Office, "A Report on Barracks and Hospitals with Descriptions of Military Posts," *Circular No. 4, 299-300;* Surgeon General's Office, "A Report on the Hygiene of the United States Army with Descriptions of Military Posts," *Circular No. 8,* 271-72; William E. Unrau, "The Story of Fort Larned," *Kansas Historical Quarterly,* Vol. XXIII (Autumn, 1957), 263, 268-71; the author's observations at the site of the post, where all the stone structures erected after the Civil War, with the exception of the blockhouse which disappeared sometime after 1886, still stand.

The Soldiers' Life on the Trail, 1865–1880

tained if the fort were under siege.[7] Almost all the water for the post was obtained from the stream; the wells that were dug at the post contained water too sulfurous for human use.

Along the west side of the parade ground stood the officers' quarters, consisting of three buildings, with the commanding officer's in the center. The latter contained four rooms, each fourteen by sixteen feet, a kitchen, nineteen by sixteen feet, and servants' quarters above the kitchen. The other two officers' buildings were alike, each containing four sets of quarters designed to accommodate two captains and four lieutenants.

One of the old adobe quarters built in 1860 served the post as a hospital until 1874 when, because of the reduced size of the garrison, the eastern half of the east barracks was converted to that purpose. The blockhouse served as the guardhouse. Whenever more than four companies were stationed at the post (and that never happened except for short periods of time), the additional soldiers were quartered in tents. Some quarters were erected for civilian employees at the fort, and several civilian-owned structures were also built, including sutler's stores, saloon, dry goods store, trading post, and others. There were, of course, corrals for both military and civilian animals located nearby. Fort Larned, with its civilian complements, was like a small town upon the plains, as were the others along the Trail.

The post was occupied until July 13, 1878, but the garrison performed few duties other than keeping up the post after the railroad was built beyond that point in 1872. The fort was important in helping to eliminate the Indian threat to that region during the immediate post–Civil War years.

At Fort Dodge the garrison, like that at Fort Zarah, lived in tents and dugouts along the north bank of the Arkansas River initially, as already indicated above. Officers' quarters were built of sod during 1865, as were a mess house, quartermaster and commissary warehouse, and hospital. Construction of stone buildings

[7] The tunnel from the bakery to Pawnee Fork has been restored in recent years.

began in 1866 when a quartermaster storehouse and bakery were erected. The following year two one-company barracks, a hospital, and a commissary storehouse of the same material were completed. The commanding officer's quarters, officers' quarters, additional company barracks, stables, and other necessary buildings were finished during the summer and autumn of 1868. Some of these were of stone and others of adobe brick.[8]

By 1870, three barracks for enlisted men had been erected, two of native stone and one of adobe. The dormitory in each contained twenty-two double two-tier bunks, providing sleeping space for eighty-eight men. Opposite doors and windows provided ventilation, and the quarters were heated by wood stoves during the winter. There was a water well behind each of the barracks. A wooden shed attached to the kitchens contained a trough where the men could wash. The latrines were located about thirty yards from the quarters.[9]

The residence of the commanding officer consisted of a story-and-a-half stone building. Quarters for the other officers of the garrison in 1870 were insufficient to accommodate all the officers, and some lived in tents. There were several quarters under construction, however, and it was hoped that when they were completed the fort would have adequate housing for all the officers.

Two stone storehouses, each 130 by 30 feet, were located on the west side of the parade ground. They were used by the commissary and quartermaster departments. At the north end of each storehouse two rooms were partitioned off as offices. One of these served as the post headquarters. Between the two buildings was a wooden shed, 110 by 27 feet, used as a forage house.

The post hospital was located at the northwest corner of the parade ground, and the ward contained twelve beds. A frame building located about seventy-five feet west of the hospital served as

[8] Fort Dodge, Medical History, Army Post Records, MSS, AGO, AACB, NA. Much information about Fort Dodge is taken from the author's article in the *1960 Brand Book*, cited above, and is used here with the permission of the publisher.

[9] Surgeon General's Office, *Circular No. 4*, 301–302.

The Soldiers' Life on the Trail, 1865-1880

a ward for Negro troops. There were five beds in this ward, and the building also housed the medical storeroom.

On the west side of the parade ground between the storehouses and the hospital was the guardhouse, in 1870 described by the post surgeon as "a temporary wooden shed, 18 by 24 feet, in very bad condition and poorly adapted for the purpose for which it is used."[10] The same official provided a vivid description of that wretched guardhouse in January, 1875. He revealed that an average of twelve prisoners occupied the little building, and of the living conditions he reported:

> It is badly adapted for the purposes and impossible to keep it in good condition: repeated representations have been made of the necessity for a new guard-house. Hitherto without effect. As there is no convenient latrine, during the night the prisoners are obliged to use a bucket for necessary purposes. At one time during the past year quite an epidemic of diarrhea occurred amongst the prisoners and with the convenience (or rather want of it) above referred to, the conditions of those unfortunates was deplorable; certainly not conducive to health or morals.[11]

The laundresses and married soldiers were housed in the old dugouts and sod buildings in 1870. The post bakery was built of stone and contained two large ovens, affording capacity for baking five hundred rations of bread each day. The buildings and corrals for the animals at the post consisted of the quartermaster corral and the cavalry corral. The former had a sod wall along the north side with a shed extending the entire length of the wall on the inner side. The other three sides consisted of a post and rail fence. The cavalry corral was completely enclosed with a sod wall and had a shed roof along three of the four sides. It was large enough for one troop of cavalry horses.[12]

Construction work continued at Fort Dodge, and in 1875 the new additions were described by the post surgeon:

[10] *Ibid.*, 302.
[11] Fort Dodge, Medical History, Army Post Records, MSS, AGO, AACB, NA.
[12] Surgeon General's Office, *Circular No. 4*, 302-303.

Soldiers on the Santa Fe Trail

> Officers quarters are contained in six one-story buildings, located on the north and west sides of the parade....
>
> Verandas are on the front of each of these buildings. All officers' quarters have good-sized yards, inclosed by a board fence. There is also a small quadrangle inclosure in front of each set of officers' quarters, made with a lattice-work of laths. Inside of those inclosures osage orange has been planted, which will in time make hedges.[13]

The last mention of additional construction at the post was recorded in December, 1875. A new grain house, new shops for both wheelwright and blacksmith, and quarters for the mechanics were completed during that month. New houses for laundresses' quarters were under construction at the time.[14]

Drinking water for Fort Dodge was obtained from wells, while that for washing and extinguishing fires came from the river. The wells furnished a plentiful supply, and the post surgeons reported it to be of excellent quality. During the winter months, ice was cut from the frozen river and stored in ice houses. Enough was obtained to furnish the needs of the garrison for an entire summer.

Drainage of rain water at the post was accomplished by means of a trench dug alongside each of the buildings; these discharged into a larger drain, which emptied into the river. The garbage was dumped into the river below the post and was carried off by the current—or was supposed to be so carried off. When the flow of the river was low, the sewage system was undoubtedly ineffective, perhaps offensively so.

Buildings constructed for civilian use completed the post, and these were similar to others along the Trail. Because of the capacity of the soldiers' barracks, Fort Dodge was usually referred to as a three-company post. When additional troops were present, they were quartered in tents. General Nelson A. Miles told Robert Wright, after the Indian wars were over in the Fort Dodge area,

[13] Surgeon General's Office, *Circular No. 8*, 254.
[14] Fort Dodge, Medical History, Army Post Records, MSS, AGO, AACB, NA.

The Soldiers' Life on the Trail, 1865-1880

that the fort should have been a large post, with at least a ten- or twelve-company garrison. With such a force, Miles explained, the fort could have controlled the Indian tribes to the south, who continually escaped from their agencies and headed north to visit and intrigue with the northern Indians, and could have prevented the northern bands from moving south to engage in similar activities. The troops at Fort Dodge could have intercepted Indians moving in either direction, turned them around, and sent them directly back to their reservations before they could do any harm.[15] Since the post was in the heart of the district where Indian difficulties occurred after the Civil War, evidently such hindsight contained much wisdom.

Fort Lyon, as mentioned above, had a fine set of buildings before the Civil War. The site of the fort had proved to be objectionable, however, for floodwaters from the Arkansas periodically had overflowed the stables and some of the company quarters. A nearby marsh had caused intermittent fever and diarrhea among the men. In addition, the supply of timber, believed abundant when the post was occupied, had rapidly decreased. Repeated requests for permission to move the post were made during the Civil War, but not until 1866 was relocation authorized.[16]

A new site was selected during the autumn of that year, twenty miles west of the original post, on the north side of the Arkansas and two and one-half miles east of where it was joined by the Purgatoire. The new position, 38° 5' 36" north latitude and 103° 3' 30" west longitude, centered on a bluff about two thousand feet wide at the widest point and about fifteen hundred feet long, with a sandstone face about ten feet high. The highest point of the bluff was thirty-six feet above the river, clearly out of danger from flood-

[15] Robert M. Wright, *Dodge City, the Cowboy Capital*, 129-30.
[16] Fort Lyon, Medical History, Army Post Records, MSS, AGO, AACB, NA. Lieutenant General William T. Sherman, after a firsthand observation of Fort Lyon, authorized the move on September 30, 1866. 39 Cong., 2 sess., *House Exec. Doc. 23*, p. 19.

Soldiers on the Santa Fe Trail

ing. There was a gentle slope from the center to the edges of the bluff, making surface drainage "excellent."[17]

Temporary buildings were erected at the new site during the spring of 1867, and the first troops moved in on June 9 that same year. Construction of permanent buildings was begun immediately. By 1870 four sets of company quarters had been completed, three of stone and one of adobe, each building one hundred by thirty-one feet. All had identical floor plans, containing quarters for one company, a mess room, office, and storage room. There were six laundresses' quarters and one house for the forage-master, all wooden structures.

The commanding officer's quarters consisted of an eight-room one-and-a-half-story house, with kitchen attached behind. Eight temporary officers' quarters of limestone and mud were occupied in 1870, and six permanent officers' quarters were then under construction. The remaining post buildings were described by the surgeon on duty there as follows:

> The commissary's and quartermaster's store-houses are 320 feet apart, built of sandstone, and are each 42 by 100 feet, outside measurement, with basements 9 feet deep.... The forage-house is built of wood, 40 by 140 by 12 feet, and well ventilated. Located at a distance from the garrison, and near the edge of the bluff, is the magazine, constructed of sandstone. The ice house is made of logs and poles, in the side of the bluff, (under ground,) with a dirt roof, and a shingle roof above that. It is 45 by 46 by 10 feet, outside measurement, and has a capacity of about 389 tons of ice. The blacksmiths, wheelwrights, and saddlers are occupying temporary frame buildings. The guard-house is a temporary frame building....
>
> The building now occupied as hospital, and situated in the center of the post, is built of gray sandstone.... This building will shortly be occupied for post headquarters, as a new hospital building is now in process of erection, and will be completed before the coming winter. Its location is far more desirable, being placed on the northeast side of the post....

[17] Fort Lyon, Medical History, Army Post Records, MSS, AGO, AACB, NA; Surgeon General's Office, *Circular No. 4,* 313.

The Soldiers' Life on the Trail, 1865-1880

A post bakery is built of sandstone. . . .

The cavalry stables are constructed of wood and designed for three troops of horses. . . . The quartermaster's stable is of wood, 60 by 286 by 10 feet. It is only a temporary building, and will eventually be removed to a site corresponding to the cavalry stables.[18]

In addition to the military structures, there were the post traders' stores, a barber shop, and other civilian buildings. A former officers' quarters had been remodeled and served the garrison as a theater and concert room. Fort Lyon was the only post along the Trail with a facility of this kind.

Construction and remodeling continued, and by 1875 the former company quarters had been renovated so that all had come to serve only as barracks, giving the soldiers more living space. In addition, behind each of the barracks a stone building sixty by eighteen feet had been built, each containing a washroom, kitchen, and mess. These were connected to the soldiers' quarters by boardwalks. The old temporary officers' quarters had been converted into houses for laundresses and married soldiers, and new laundresses' quarters were being planned.[19]

Seven adobe officers' quarters were completed along the north side of the parade ground, providing housing for twelve captains, with the commanding officer's residence located in the center. Eight sets of lieutenants' quarters also had been erected. The old hospital, at the south edge of the parade ground, was remodeled and served as post headquarters, containing offices for the post commander and adjutant, the chapel, guardhouse, library, arsenal, and magazine. Fort Lyon was the only post for which a chapel was listed in the records, but religious services were conducted at the other posts, too. It was, also, the only fort listing a separate library, but the others did have library facilities.

In addition to these buildings and the new hospital, new workshops with an adjoining mess hall had been constructed of wood.

[18] *Ibid.*, 314-15.
[19] Surgeon General's Office, *Circular No. 8*, 279-81.

Soldiers on the Santa Fe Trail

A quartermaster stable, similar to the old cavalry stable, also was completed. For a better supply of water, since the Arkansas River was the source of the post's water supply, a canal had been constructed, diverting water from the river six miles above the fort. The main channel ran in front of the officers' quarters, and branches had been dug in front of the soldiers' barracks. Shade trees had been planted along the canal, giving the entire post an attractive appearance. After they could be irrigated, the company gardens were successful, and the troops were assured a supply of fresh vegetables for at least a part of the year.

The railroad reached New Fort Lyon in 1875, bringing the command facilities for rapid communication with the East. The post was occupied until November 15, 1889, long after the Santa Fe Trail had been superseded by the railroad. Indian activities were few around the fort after the Civil War, but the garrison participated in suppressing uprisings which occurred during the 1860's and 1870's and helped to protect the railroad construction crews.

Fort Union was the military post with the longest continuous service along the Trail; it also was the largest such military establishment. The star-shaped earthen fortification erected during the early phases of the Civil War had been abandoned by the close of that conflict, and the garrison had moved into new adobe structures located a few hundred yards to the north. In addition to the post proper, there had been a quartermaster's depot attached to the fort since 1851, and in 1866 a federal arsenal was erected at the original site of Fort Union.[20] It appears that all the permanent buildings were constructed by 1870, the date of the earliest available complete description of the post.[21]

The Fort Union Depot was located just north of and adjacent to the post proper. Six adobe buildings, three which measured

---

[20] The fort itself was moved out into the valley during 1861 when it was feared that an attack would be made on it by the Confederates, as indicated above.

[21] Surgeon General's Office, *Circular No. 4,* 260–61; Surgeon General's Office, *Circular No. 8,* 305–306.

seventy-nine by fifty-seven and the others fifty-six by fifty-five feet, were used as offices and quarters. Five adobe warehouses, four measuring two hundred by forty feet and the other two hundred by twenty, in addition to shops and corrals, completed the depot. The water supply was collected from the roofs of the storehouses into two cisterns. All the buildings had tin roofs.

The arsenal, located one mile west of Fort Union, was enclosed by a wall, forming a square one thousand feet along each side. One set of quarters, one large storehouse, three small storehouses, and several shops comprised the buildings, all of which were constructed of adobe. The water supply came from a well and two cisterns of eighteen thousand gallons capacity each.

The fort itself was a four-company post, arranged on two sides of a rectangular parade ground laid out in a northwest-southeast direction. All buildings were adobe, set on stone foundations. Along the southwest side of the parade ground ranged a row of nine officers' quarters, the commanding officer's in the center. The latter contained eight rooms, the others six; all were divided by a hall running from front to rear. Outhouses were located behind each set of quarters.

On the opposite side of the parade ground stood four sets of soldiers' quarters, each built along three sides of a rectangle, with a courtyard in the center. The front parts of each structure served as dormitories, with facilities for one company. The wings on one side contained orderly and storage rooms, the other wings housed the kitchens and mess rooms. According to the post surgeon, "These quarters are really comfortable dwellings. . . ."[22]

Behind the blocks occupied by these barracks were houses for the laundresses and married soldiers. The guardhouse was in the same row as these buildings, and beyond were located the corrals, stables, warehouses, forage houses, and bakery. The hospital was approximately three hundred yards east of the garrison. It boasted a total capacity of thirty-six beds in six different wards, and contained a large dispensary, kitchen, and dining room, plus several

[22] *Ibid.*, 305.

storerooms. It was apparently the best-equipped hospital to be found in any post along the Trail.

Fort Union was probably the queen of forts on the Santa Fe Trail—at least a comparison of facilities makes it appear so. The railroad did not reach the Fort Union region until 1879, less than a year before it arrived in Santa Fe. Prior to that time, since the post was located on the stage route (as were the others) it had enjoyed fairly rapid communication with the East. A telegraph station was established sometime between 1870 and 1875, connecting the fort with others along the Trail and with Fort Leavenworth. Fort Union was occupied until May 15, 1891, more than a decade after the Santa Fe Trail had fallen into disuse because of the railroad.

All the forts along the Trail, as noted, had comfortable quarters and other facilities to make life easier during the post-Civil War years than in earlier eras. This did not eliminate the factor of loneliness at these outposts, but old Mother Nature posed a less serious threat to the garrisons. The purposes of the soldiers on the Trail during this last phase of the Trail's history were as follows: to protect the route, including the railroad; to protect the settlements which were developing in their respective regions; and, after the Indians were located on the reservations, to keep sufficient armed forces at strategic points to prevent Indians from escaping control by their agencies. All the posts along the Trail, except Fort Zarah, had probably outlived their usefulness several years before they were abandoned, but the citizens of surrounding regions requested that troops remain to provide security from possible Indian outbreaks, and the War Department complied. In the immediate post-Civil War years, however, Indian hostilities continued to occur, and the troops were successful in meeting these threats, finally eliminating serious Indian problems along the Trail.

Following the signing of the Little Arkansas treaties with the Apaches, Arapahoes, Cheyennes, Comanches, and Kiowas in the autumn of 1865, Indian depredations ceased along the Santa Fe

The Soldiers' Life on the Trail, 1865-1880

Trail and other overland routes. The year 1866 was one of the quietest along the Trail in a decade, only minor difficulties occurring. While some observers may have entertained the idea that lasting peace had finally arrived on the plains, those close to the scene were not so optimistic. One of the soldier societies of the Cheyenne tribe, the Dog Soldiers, had not been present at the signing of the Little Arkansas treaties, and they refused to be bound by them. This band was not willing to cede its claims to land in western Kansas. Also, the Indians who had signed the treaties were not immediately located on the assigned reservations, but continued to roam the prairies.[23]

Given this situation, no one knew when some incident might provoke new hostilities and open another war. Since it was impossible to determine whether the Indians would remain quiet throughout 1866, Major General John Pope, commanding the Department of Missouri, established regulations for travel along the Trail similar to those of the previous year. Fort Larned was designated as the rendezvous for all trains moving west. There the traders and travelers were to organize into caravans, elect a captain and other officers, and see that every person with the train was properly armed. No train with less than twenty wagons and thirty men was to be allowed beyond Fort Larned. Trains moving eastward over the Trail were to be organized in the same manner before entering Indian country. In addition, post commanders were authorized to provide an escort whenever such protection was deemed necessary to assure the safe movement of any caravan.[24]

It was seldom necessary to enforce the escort order because there

[23] Annual Report of the Commissioner of Indian Affairs, 1866, 39 Cong.,. 2 sess., *House Exec. Doc. 1*, p. 54; George B. Grinnell, *The Fighting Cheyennes*, 245-46. Lieutenant General W. T. Sherman, after a visit to the posts along the Arkansas during the late summer of 1866, declared: "The Arapahoes and Cheyennes, Kiowas, Comanches and Apaches, Navajoes and Utes, though supposed to be restricted to reservations, will not settle down, but they roam, according to their habits, over the vast plains, and they . . . have done acts of hostility." Annual Report of the Secretary of War, 1866, 39 Cong., 2 sess., *House Exec. Doc. 1*, p. 21.

[24] General Orders, No. 27, Headquarters Department of Missouri, February 28, 1866, 40 Cong., 1 sess., *Sen. Exec. Doc. 2*, pp. 2-4.

were few Indian threats. Indian Agent E. W. Wynkoop, after visiting the tribes along the Arkansas, declared on April 8, 1866, that they all were at peace: "The effect is already plainly visible from the fact of the mail travelling without escort, and small parties of emigrants and freighters pursuing their course in perfect safety and without anticipation of any danger from Indians."[25] This welcome respite continued throughout the year.

During the period of friendlier relations with the Indians along the Trail, the soldiers succeeded in obtaining the surrender of four white prisoners. A band of Kiowas had killed United States citizen James Box in Montague County, Texas, during August, and captured his wife and four daughters. The infant daughter died within a few days, and the Indians threw her into a ravine. The others were taken to the Kiowa camp south of the Arkansas River.[26]

Satanta, a Kiowa chief, came into Fort Larned on September 9 and informed the commanding officer, Major Cuvier Grover, that he had the captives and wished to give them up. Grover reported this to the Indian Agent I. C. Taylor, stationed at Fort Zarah, who came to Fort Larned to secure the release of the prisoners. Satanta demanded a liberal payment in return. Taylor reminded him of the treaty made the previous year and stated that he was authorized to pay nothing. He advised Satanta to bring the whites to Fort Larned and let the Kiowa agent, J. H. Leavenworth, settle with the chief later. Satanta requested, and was granted, several days' time to decide.[27]

Failing to get a ransom there, Satanta traded Mrs. Martha Box and one of the girls to the Apaches and later sent members of his band to Fort Dodge to negotiate the release of the other two girls. Captain Andrew Sheridan, commander of that post, agreed to a trade, offering the Kiowas some guns, powder, lead, coffee, sugar,

[25] 39 Cong., 2 sess., *House Exec. Doc. 1*, p. 278.
[26] Statement of Mrs. Martha Box to Captain Andrew Sheridan, October 20, 1866, 40 Cong., 1 sess., *Sen. Exec. Doc. 13*, pp. 100–101.
[27] Annual Report of the Commissioner of Indian Affairs, 1866, 39 Cong., 2 sess., *House Exec. Doc. 1*, pp. 280–81.

The Soldiers' Life on the Trail, 1865-1880

flour, and a few trinkets. The Indians requested that the goods be delivered to their camp, and this condition was granted.[28]

Two wagons were loaded with the trade items and an ambulance was readied for the trip. A detachment of eight soldiers, under command of Lieutenant G. A. Hesselburger, and the interpreter, Fred Jones, delivered the ransom. The trade was made without incident at the Kiowas' camp, and the girls, aged fourteen and seventeen, were taken back to Fort Dodge. Both had been treated badly, passed from one chief to another, and subjected to cruel and degrading punishment.

It was hoped that when the Apaches heard of the successful trade, they would offer to deliver the mother and sister of these girls by a similar arrangement. General W. T. Sherman, touring the posts along the Arkansas at the time, arrived at Fort Dodge immediately after the return of the two captives, and he instructed Captain Sheridan not to send any more details on so hazardous a mission and not to trade any more goods for prisoners. Such action, he declared, would only encourage the Indians to capture more whites.

A few days later a small party of Apaches appeared at the post as expected and offered to trade Mrs. Box and her child for supplies. Sheridan informed them that he could not send supplies to their camp, but urged them to bring the captives to the post. He would then meet with the chiefs in council to determine what could be done. The chiefs came into the post a few days later, and Sheridan informed them that they were prisoners and would be held until the whites were released. This was a dangerous experiment, because a large body of Apaches were encamped nearby, but it was successful. The chiefs were allowed to inform their people of their predicament, and in less than an hour Mrs. Box and the child were safe inside the fort.

[28] Information concerning the rescue of the Box family was provided by Corporal Leander Herron, Company A, Third U.S. Infantry, who was with the detail that returned part of the family to safety; quoted in Wright, *Dodge City*, 120-29.

Soldiers on the Santa Fe Trail

Indian attacks on the northern plains and in Texas during 1866 gave rise to fears in Kansas that another Indian war was imminent. The large encampments of Indians within short distances of the Santa Fe Trail made the route potentially dangerous if another uprising should occur, and throughout the winter of 1866–67 there were rumors that the coming spring would bring an end to peace.[29]

During this period conflicts arose between Indian agents and military authorities concerning the trading of arms and ammunition to the Indians. Major Henry Douglass, commanding at Fort Dodge in January, 1867, believed the rumors of a renewed uprising the following spring, and he complained that the Indians were laying in large supplies of carbines, revolvers, powder, and lead from the licensed Indian traders. His fears were transferred to the new commander of the Department of Missouri, Major General Winfield S. Hancock, who ordered, on January 26, 1867, that no arms or ammunition would be sold or bartered to the Indians by any person within the limits of the District of the Upper Arkansas, except at Forts Dodge and Larned. At these posts ammunition could be sold only by authorized traders, in such quantities as the post commanders deemed necessary for hunting purposes.[30]

In February, Major Douglass supplied Hancock with further disturbing information. He communicated a statement by the post interpreter, Fred Jones, that Satanta had told Jones to inform the commanding officer at the post that the Indians wanted all military posts and troops removed from the plains. Satanta demanded that Santa Fe Trail traffic be stopped at Council Grove and the railroad be terminated at Junction City. If the roads were not closed and the troops withdrawn, Satanta threatened to join with other Indians and chase the soldiers out of the country. To top off his demands, Satanta arrogantly reported that his own stock was getting poor and tired, and he wanted the government

[29] Grinnell, *Fighting Cheyennes*, 246; Leckie, *Military Conquest of Southern Plains*, 32–37.

[30] 40 Cong., 1 sess., *Sen. Exec. Doc. 13*, p. 53; General Orders, No. 16, Headquarters Department of Missouri, January 26, 1867, *General Orders and Circulars, Department of Missouri, 1867*.

stock fed up a little better, because in a few days he would be at the post to get the animals.³¹ Jones's statement was later proved to be an outright lie, but Major Douglass did not tell that to General Hancock.

This report and similar ones from other sources caused Hancock to believe that another Indian uprising was approaching. Without visiting the frontier to investigate, the general acted upon the information he had received.³² He began concentrating a force at Fort Riley, preparing for an expedition along the Santa Fe Trail, and he instructed Leavenworth and Wynkoop, Indian agents for the Kiowas, Comanches, Arapahoes, Cheyennes, and Apaches, to inform their tribes that a large military force was coming. Its purpose was, in Hancock's words:

> ... to show the Indians within the limits of this department that we are able to chastise any tribes who may molest people who are travelling across the plains. It is not our desire to bring on difficulties with the Indians, but to treat them with justice and according to our treaty stipulations.³³

Before he left Fort Riley with his command of about fourteen hundred troops, Hancock set forth the purpose of the expedition in terms more belligerent than his messages to the Indian agents:

> It is uncertain whether war will be the result of the expedition or not; it will depend upon the temper and behavior of the Indians with whom we may come in contact. We go prepared for war, and will make it if a proper occasion presents. We shall have war if the Indians are not well disposed toward us. If they are for peace, and no sufficient ground is presented for chastisement, we are restricted from punishing them for past grievances which are recorded against them; these matters have been left to the Indian department for adjustment. No insolence will be tolerated from any bands of Indians whom we may encounter. We wish to show them that the govern-

[31] 40 Cong., 1 sess., *Sen. Exec. Doc. 13*, p. 102.
[32] According to Grinnell, *Fighting Cheyennes*, 246–47, the reports were not substantiated by evidence.
[33] 40 Cong., 1 sess., *Sen. Exec. Doc. 13*, p. 78.

Soldiers on the Santa Fe Trail

ment is ready and able to punish them if they are hostile, although it may not be disposed to invite war.[34]

The ill-advised expedition marched to Fort Zarah and on to Fort Larned, arriving there April 7, 1867.[35] After a council with several Cheyenne chiefs at Fort Larned, at which the Indians declared their desire for peace, Hancock determined to march his entire command to the Indians' camp, consisting of about three hundred lodges of Cheyennes and Brulé Sioux, located approximately thirty miles up Pawnee Fork. The approach of the soldiers frightened the Cheyenne women and children, who perhaps suspected another Sand Creek, and the encampment was hastily abandoned.[36] The flight of the Indians convinced Hancock that they must be hostile, and he ordered the village, tipis and all other property, destroyed. Accordingly, the encampment was burned.

Lieutenant Colonel George A. Custer, commanding the battalion of Seventh Cavalry with the expedition, had been dispatched in pursuit of the Indians, but all of the approximately fifteen hundred men, women, and children made good their escape. Custer marched on to Fort Hays on the Smoky Hill route, and Hancock and the remaining force proceeded to Fort Dodge. There he met with several Kiowa chiefs, who proclaimed their peaceful behavior and intentions. General Hancock then abandoned the expedition and returned to his headquarters at Fort Leavenworth.

Following the unprovoked destruction of the Cheyenne and Sioux village, the anticipated Indian uprising became a reality. Hancock had succeeded in bringing on another war where relative

[34] General Field Orders, No. 1, Headquarters Department of Missouri, March 26, 1867, *ibid.*, 83. Grinnell, *Fighting Cheyennes*, 248, declared: "The tone of this order clearly shows Hancock's ignorance of things relating to these Indians." It is interesting to note, in the light of Hancock's statement, that his later attack upon the Cheyennes was justified as "punishment for depredations and murders previously committed." Annual Report of the Secretary of War, 1867, 40 Cong., 2 sess.,. *House Exec. Doc. 1*, p. 34.

[35] Documents relating the Hancock expedition are located in 40 Cong., 1 sess., *Sen. Exec. Doc. 13*, pp. 84–109.

[36] Grinnell, *Fighting Cheyennes*, 249.

peace had existed. The soldiers garrisoned along the Trail were busy once again with escort duties and investigations of reported Indian attacks. Outrages continued throughout the summer months.

The renewed hostilities on the plains prompted Congress to take action, and the Indian Peace Commission was created in July.[37] The government played into the hands of the Indians by offering to make peace in the autumn, a practice which was advantageous for the Indians, as noted above. The commission was created on the premise that war was inevitable as long as Indians occupied lands which the whites wanted. The solution offered was the same as two years earlier—settle the Indians on reservations.

The results were the Medicine Lodge treaties, negotiated between United States Commissioners, Nathaniel G. Taylor, William S. Harney, C. C. Augur, Alfred Terry, John B. Sanborn, Samuel F. Tappan, and John B. Henderson, and the chiefs of the Cheyennes, Apaches, Kiowas, Comanches, and Arapahoes. Signed at Medicine Lodge Creek on October 21 and 28, the treaties provided that all war would immediately cease, offenders against both Indians and whites would, in the future, be punished, and reservations would be set up and their boundaries determined. The Indians agreed to stay on their reservations and give up all claims to lands north of the Arkansas River. The United States government was to provide educational facilities and teachers, hospitals and doctors, blacksmiths, and agricultural implements. The Indians agreed to withdraw all opposition to the railroads, emigrants, travelers, wagon trains, and military posts, and promised not to hunt north of the Arkansas.[38]

Peace once more settled over the plains, and the Trail was free from hostilities. Those who lived, traded, or traveled in the Indian regions were skeptical that the Indians would keep their word. The following article, which appeared in the *Rocky Mountain Daily News* soon after the treaties were signed, illustrates that feeling:

> Lieutenant General Sherman has promulgated the official order which announces peace with the Kiowas, Comanches, Apaches, Chey-

[37] *United States Statutes at Large*, XV, 17.
[38] *Indian Affairs, Laws and Treaties* (ed. by Kappler), II, 977-89.

Soldiers on the Santa Fe Trail

ennes, and Arapahoes. He directs that their rights be respected. Confidence in indian treaties has long since ceased to be a virtue with our people. . . . The present so-called peace is nothing more than a truce in which the United States government, through its commissioners, has agreed to furnish a sufficient amount of subsistence to savages, to enable them to live during the winter, and to renew their hostilities next spring. Let the treaties be preserved, but we warn *every man* to relax no vigilance.[39]

The prediction proved to be correct, for with the coming of spring and green grass in 1868, the Indians broke the treaty agreements and crossed the Arkansas River. Before the year was over, Indian depredations had increased over what they were in 1867, before the treaties were signed.

The Medicine Lodge treaties were not approved by the Senate until July, 1868, and were not signed by the President until the following month. The Indians were left to roam until that time because they could not be located on reservations nor adequately subsisted until money was appropriated. Meanwhile, the Indian War of 1868 began.

In the early spring of that year the Plains Indians began moving from their winter camps and locating near Forts Dodge and Larned, as was their usual custom, to draw government rations until the buffalo migration reached the Kansas plains. Some of the Kiowas, Comanches, and a few Cheyennes located near Larned, while a few Kiowas and Comanches, the remainder of the Cheyennes, and the Arapahoes encamped near Dodge. Most of the Kiowas and Comanches remained in Indian Territory and raided into northern Texas until early July, when they encamped near Fort Larned.[40] When the rations provided were not sufficient, these Indians became restless and began stopping trains on the Trail to obtain supplies.[41]

[39] *Rocky Mountain Daily News* (Denver), November 6, 1867.

[40] Annual Report of the Secretary of War, 1868, 40 Cong., 3 sess., *House Exec. Doc.* 1, p. 10; Marvin Garfield, "Defense of the Kansas Frontier, 1868-1869," *Kansas Historical Quarterly*, Vol. I (November, 1932), 451.

[41] The commissioner of Indian affairs, Nathaniel G. Taylor, explained that the

The Soldiers' Life on the Trail, 1865-1880

Major General Philip H. Sheridan, who had replaced Hancock as department commander, visited these posts during the early spring to observe the situation. At Fort Dodge he found great numbers of Indians encamped. When the Indians learned that a "Big" General was at the post, they sent a delegation requesting an interview with him. Sheridan refused, stating that he was there only to learn of the conditions of the fort and the men stationed there, and that he was not authorized to talk with Indians or to make any agreements with them. He refused to talk for fear that he might compromise the efforts of the Indian Peace Commission. Sheridan later recalled: "My refusal left them without hope of securing better terms, or of even delaying matters longer; so henceforth they were more than ever reckless and defiant."[42]

He learned at Fort Dodge that the Indians were outspoken in their dissatisfaction with the idea of removing to the reservations assigned to them, that they had no intention of removing there permanently, and that they considered the treaty of importance only in so far as it got them annuities. Sheridan declared that the Indians were "insolent and overbearing, and so manifest [with their discontent] as to cause me to take all the precautions in my power to protect . . . [the] lines of travel in the district of the upper Arkansas."[43] He appointed scouts to keep him informed of the Indians' movements and then returned to headquarters.

Indian uprising of 1868 resulted from "the fact that the department, for want of appropriations, was compelled to stop their supplies, and to permit them to recur to the chase for subsistence." Annual Report of the Commissioner of Indian Affairs, 1868, 40 Cong., 3 sess., *House Exec. Doc. 1*, p. 463. In addition, when some hostilities occurred with the Indians subsisting themselves, the guns and ammunition which the Peace Commision had declared those tribes should have were withheld. This further angered the Indians. Believing that the government was not upholding its end of the Medicine Lodge treaties, the Indians concluded they were free to violate them, too. *Ibid.*, 462.

[42] Annual Report of the Secretary of War, 1868, *ibid.*, 10; General Philip Sheridan, *Personal Memoirs*, II, 285-86.

[43] Annual Report of the Secretary of War, 1868, 40 Cong., 3 sess., *House Exec. Doc. 1*, p. 10.

It was relatively quiet along the Trail until June, except that trains were occasionally halted by Indians who demanded coffee, sugar, and food before allowing them to proceed. Sometime in June, a party of Cheyennes attacked the Kansas Indians, traditional enemies, near Council Grove, and from there the fighting spread. The main bodies of Kiowas and Comanches arrived near Fort Larned in early July, as indicated above, to collect their annuities. These supplies had not yet arrived from the East, and the result was a greater number of hungry, dissatisfied Indians along the Trail. Hostilities quickly increased, but Sheridan, with a limited number of troops under his command, was unable to do more than take defensive measures during the summer months.[44]

Sheridan estimated that within the District of the Upper Arkansas the Kiowas, Comanches, Cheyennes, and Arapahoes were able to put about six thousand well-mounted and well-armed warriors into the field, with from two to ten spare horses for each. The total number of troops in the district consisted of approximately twelve hundred cavalry and fourteen hundred infantry. After distributing these troops for the protection of the railroad, military posts, and settlements, there were about eight hundred men available for the field. Insufficient for adequate offensive operations, this force was divided and stationed at Fort Dodge and the crossing of Walnut Creek on the Fort Hays–Fort Dodge road.[45]

Before reinforcements could be obtained to launch an offensive campaign, the Indian attacks became more frequent and deadly. The alarming depredations led General Sheridan to declare war on the Indians, August 24:

> In consequence of the recent open acts of hostility on the part of the Cheyenne and Arrappahoe Indians, embracing the murder of twenty unarmed citizens of the State of Kansas, the wounding of many more, and acts of outrage on women and children, too atro-

[44] For a list of hostilities committed between August 3 and October 24, 1868, see *ibid.*, 13–16.
[45] *Ibid.*, 17–18.

The Soldiers' Life on the Trail, 1865–1880

cious to mention in detail; the Major General Commanding under the authority of the Lieutenant General [W. T. Sherman] Commanding the Military Division, directs the forcible removal of these Indians to their Reservations South of the State of Kansas, and that they be compelled to deliver up the perpetrators of the guilty acts.

All persons whomsoever are hereby forbidden to hold intercourse [with], or give aid or assistance to these Indians, until there is due notice given hereafter that the requirements of this order have been carried out.[46]

The Indian War of 1868 was officially opened.

Brevet Brigadier General Alfred Sully, commanding the District of the Upper Arkansas, began offensive operations in September. He hoped to harass the Indians with a small force until he could collect a larger one. Sully had arrived at Fort Dodge on September 1, where his command, reinforced with troops from Fort Lyon, was to be organized.[47] The expedition was to move south of the Arkansas and strike the Indian villages reportedly located on the Cimarron River.[48]

While this force was concentrating at Fort Dodge, a band of Comanches and Kiowas had the audacity to make a direct attack upon the post on September 3. They were driven off after a hard-fought battle, during which four soldiers were killed and seventeen wounded. The Indians' losses were not known.[49] Because the num-

---

[46] General Field Orders, No. 1, Headquarters Department of Missouri, August 24, 1868, *General Orders and Circulars, Department of Missouri, 1868*. The Kiowas and Comanches were not included in this order, apparently because it was believed they had moved south of the Arkansas after finally receiving their annuities early in August. It was soon discovered, however, that they had moved their women and children into camps south of the Arkansas, but the warriors had returned to plague the Trail.

[47] Sully's force consisted of nine companies of the Seventh Cavalry and three of the Third Infantry, in all between five and six hundred men.

[48] Annual Report of the Secretary of War, 1868, 40 Cong., 3 sess., *House Exec. Doc. 1,* p. 18.

[49] *Rocky Mountain Daily News* (Denver), September 9, 1868.

Soldiers on the Santa Fe Trail

ber of troops along the Trail was inadequate to suppress hostilities, the Indians had become extremely bold in engaging the soldiers.

Sully's expedition left Fort Dodge on September 7 and marched to the Cimarron. They discovered that the Indians had received advance warning and moved southward, and the troops followed the fresh trail. A running fight took place until they had crossed the north fork of the Canadian River. There the Indians made a determined attack and were driven off. The expedition, running short of supplies, then moved back toward Fort Dodge and went into camp about sixty-five miles south of the post to await supplies and reinforcements. Meanwhile, General Sully, who had been injured in a minor accident, returned to Fort Dodge for medical care and rest. In this series of skirmishes, the Indians lost between seventeen and twenty-two killed and an unknown number wounded. The expedition lost one killed, two wounded, and one missing.[50] The campaign had succeeded in harassing the Indians, but had not ended hostilities along the Trail.

General Sheridan requested and received reinforcements to launch a more effective operation. Therefore, twelve companies of troops arrived from the East during late September and early October. Additional reinforcements were provided when a regiment of volunteer cavalry was raised in Kansas. In the meantime, Sully had requested that General Custer be sent to undertake a reorganized campaign. The request was granted, and on October 9 Custer assumed command of the troops encamped south of Fort Dodge. As soon as he arrived there he began aggressive operations against the Indians, who had repeatedly attacked the camp without success.[51]

Three days later he was ordered to move his command north and

---

[50] Fort Dodge, Medical History, Army Post Records, MSS, AGO, AACB, NA; Annual Report of the Secretary of War, 1868, 40 Cong., 3 sess., *House Exec. Doc. 1*, p. 18.

[51] *Ibid.*, 19; Brigadier General E. S. Godfrey, "Some Reminiscences, including the Washita Battle, November 27, 1868," *The Cavalry Journal*, Vol. XXXVII (October, 1928); Fort Dodge, Medical History, Army Post Records, MSS, AGO, AACB, NA.

The Soldiers' Life on the Trail, 1865-1880

scour the area between Fort Zarah and Medicine Lodge Creek, while supplies were accumulated at Fort Dodge for a second move against the Indian encampments to the south. Custer's command found small bands of Indians while scouting in the assigned region, but no villages were located. In the many skirmishes which occurred, two Indians were killed.[52]

Meanwhile, Sheridan was planning a campaign to be launched against the Indians whenever they went into camp for the winter months. Catching the Indians at the time it was most difficult for them to operate, the soldiers could force them onto reservations and punish those who refused to go.[53] Sheridan asked Sherman to obtain permission from headquarters in Washington for the winter campaign and to request that no peace be made with the Indians during the autumn as in previous years. Sherman secured authorization for the plan, and so informed Sheridan during October. Preparations were made to march three columns, one each from Fort Dodge, Fort Lyon, and Fort Bascom in New Mexico, to converge upon the Indians' winter camps in Indian Territory.

The details of the winter campaign of 1868-69 are not related here, since the action took place far from the Santa Fe Trail.[54] It should be noted, however, that several battles were fought, the most important being the Battle of Washita, and severe punishment was inflicted upon the Indians. Beaten into submission, the Indians were forced onto their reservations and remained there, with few exceptions, during the following years. The soldiers, including many from the garrisons along the Trail, had finally been successful where the peace commissions had failed. This method was destructive; nevertheless it was effective.

Only small bands of Indians appeared along the Trail after the winter campaign, and only occasionally did they commit serious hostilities. Troops were maintained at the posts, except Fort Zarah,

[52] Annual Report of the Secretary of War, 1868, 40 Cong., 3 sess., *House Exec. Doc.* 1, p. 19.
[53] See Leckie, *Military Conquest of Southern Plains*, 88.
[54] For details of the campaign, see *ibid.*, 88-132; Grinnell, *Fighting Cheyennes*, 298-309.

Soldiers on the Santa Fe Trail

to deal with these small parties of hostiles and to prevent large groups from escaping their reservations and returning north of the Arkansas. Another expedition was organized at Fort Dodge in 1874, under the command of General Nelson A. Miles, but again the action was far south of the Trail.

During the decade of the 1870's the troops, in addition to garrisoning the posts and helping keep the Indians on the reservations, provided protection for the Atchison, Topeka and Santa Fe Railroad.[55] Whenever a possible Indian threat was feared, survey parties, construction crews, and stations were given protection. The guards usually were small, ranging from five to ten soldiers under the command of a non-commissioned officer. In addition to these direct guards, cavalry forces were often kept scouting south of the Arkansas to check any Indian movements from the reservations, thus providing indirect protection for the railroad. As sections of the railroad were completed, the troops could travel additional distances over the old Trail by rail, making their movements fast and comfortable.

A look at the daily life of the troops at the posts and on the Trail is instructive. Soldiering, whether on garrison duty or in the field, was lonely, hard, and demanding. It was not a glorious adventure, but basically a monotonous, routine life. Isolated as they were from large settlements, the soldiers welcomed any diversion.

The previously-described improvements of facilities, completed at the forts during the post–Civil War years, made garrison life more comfortable than before. Simultaneously, the men had become better protected from the elements, and the addition of well-stocked traders' stores, saloons, and even schools for the troops improved their living conditions. But in the field the same difficulties plagued them as before—high winds which made tenting unpleasant if not impossible, blowing sand and dust, extreme heat in

[55] Information concerning the protection of the railroad is found in numerous pieces of correspondence and orders contained in the post files of Forts Dodge, Larned, and Lyon retained in the Army and Air Corps Branch, National Archives.

The Soldiers' Life on the Trail, 1865-1880

summer and cold in winter, and the scarcity of grass, wood, and good water.

The daily activities of post garrisons were organized within the framework of a rigid schedule. While the exact time allocations varied slightly from post to post and from season to season, one typical schedule, that of Fort Dodge in 1874, will serve for purposes of illustration.[56] All calls were executed by the trumpeters, sounded first from the adjutant's office and immediately repeated by the trumpeter of each company comprising the garrison. The trumpeters assembled just before time for reveille, which was sounded at 5:00 A.M. The other routines were scheduled as follows: 5:10, assembly (roll call), with stable call immediately afterward (cavalrymen to groom and care for mounts); 6:00, breakfast; 6:45, sick call; 7:15, fatigue call; 8:30, mounting of the guard; 9:00, drill for recruits and signal instruction for officers; 9:30, recall from signal instructions; 10:30, recall from drill; 11:45, orderly call; 12:00 noon, recall from fatigue; and 12:30, dinner.

The remainder of the day was as follows: 1:30 P.M., fatigue call; 2:00, target practice (infantry on Tuesday and Thursday, cavalry on Wednesday) and drill (Monday and Friday); 3:30, recall from target practice and drill; 4:00, recall from fatigue; 4:15, stable call; no evening mess call except by gongs and bells; fifteen minutes before sunset, assembly of garrison (except guards) in full dress uniforms; sunset, retreat and roll call; 8:45, tattoo; and 9:00, taps. The Sunday morning inspection was at 9:00 A.M. with guard mounting immediately following. When not answering these various calls, the soldiers were usually free to do whatever they wished, so long as they were within bugle call.

All enlisted men had to serve on guard duty and fatigue details periodically, and they were usually assigned to these chores by a system of rotation. When so engaged they were exempt from drill and other activities occurring at the same time. The mounting of the guard, according to Don Rickey, Jr., in his recent study of

[56] General Orders, No. 13, Headquarters Fort Dodge, May 11, 1874, Fort Dodge Order Book, MSS, USAC, AACB, NA.

the daily life of soldiers on the western frontier, was one of the highlights of each day's activities.[57]

Fatigue details were assigned all types of work, including repairing and constructing buildings, serving in the kitchen, policing the stables, assisting as a room orderly, disposing of garbage, cutting weeds, hauling water, tending post garden, cutting ice during the winter, and cleaning buildings, quarters, and the post in general. The work usually was not difficult physically, but it led to the grumbling and complaining common to most soldiers when assigned the so-called "menial tasks." Those with special skills were often detailed as carpenters, blacksmiths, wheelwrights, stonemasons, and the like. Recruits were usually sent to the forts without training, thus the need for special drills to prepare them for their places in the companies. Each soldier was responsible, of course, for proper maintenance of his weapons and accouterments.

The material benefits to soldiers serving along the Trail were not extraordinary, but apparently they were sufficient. Enlisted men were paid on a basic salary scale as follows: for privates the rate was thirteen dollars per month during the first two years of service, fourteen dollars the third year, fifteen the fourth, sixteen the fifth, and thereafter, while in continuous service, eighteen dollars per month for the next five years, with an additional one dollar per month for each additional five years. The pay for corporals ranged from fifteen to twenty dollars per month, depending upon the length of service. The range for first sergeants was from twenty-five to thirty dollars per month. After twenty-five years of continuous service a soldier could retire with two-thirds pay for the remainder of his life.[58]

A traveling paymaster visited the post periodically, approximately every two months, and paid the troops in cash. In spite of the isolated locations, the soldier's pay usually did not last long. After paying his debts to the post sutler, company laundress, bar-

[57] Don Rickey, Jr., *Forty Miles a Day on Beans and Hay: The Enlisted Soldier Fighting the Indian Wars*, 91-92.
[58] Brigadier General George A. Forsyth, *The Story of the Soldier*, 94.

The Soldiers' Life on the Trail, 1865-1880

ber, cobbler, and tailor, the remainder went principally for food, whisky, and gambling.

Clothing was supplied to the men in addition to their salary, and unless they were extremely hard on wearing apparel the allowances were sufficient.[59] If a soldier did not draw all his clothing allowance, he received cash for the unused portion at the time of his discharge. Dress uniforms were worn only for retreat, weekly inspection, and special occasions such as funerals or visits from dignitaries. Thus they lasted for a considerable length of time. Some soldiers purchased the used clothing of men who were being discharged, and so saved a considerable portion of their clothing allowance.

Food rations were more important than clothing supplies because food had a more direct effect upon the physical and mental health of the soldier. It is impossible to determine the exact food rations because of the variations in types and amounts from post to post and while serving in the field.[60] The staples were beef, salt pork, beans, bread, and coffee. Milk, butter, and eggs were not part of the regular rations, but were often purchased, if available, with

[59] According to Forsyth, the total allowance of clothing for a private during his first three years of enlistment was as follows: "One overcoat, two uniform dress coats, three woollen blouses, three canvas fatigue blouses, seven pairs uniform trousers, seven pairs kersey trousers, three pairs canvas fatigue trousers, three pairs overalls, seven dark blue woolen shirts, nine undershirts, nine pairs drawers, thirty-six linen collars, twelve pairs cotton and twelve pairs woollen socks, nine pairs shoes for infantry and two pairs boots and five pairs shoes for cavalry, four fatigue caps, three campaign hats, two helmets, two pairs woolen blankets, twenty-four pairs white gloves, three pairs suspenders. In addition to the above, the cavalry have furnished them two pairs leather gauntlets and two stable frocks." *Ibid.*, 95.

[60] The food allowances for soldiers, although the actual rations may not always have been full rations, were described by Forsyth as follows: "In quarters, and as far as possible in the field, the daily meat ration of the soldier consists of a pound and a quarter of fresh beef or mutton, or three quarters of a pound of fresh pork and bacon, or one pound and six ounces of salt beef. When it is possible to furnish fish, the daily ration of fourteen ounces of dried fish, or eighteen ounces of pickled or fresh fish. The bread ration is one pound and two ounces of soft bread or one pound of hard bread (hard biscuit), or in lieu thereof one pound and two ounces of flour, or one pound and four ounces of cornmeal. For vegetables, there is potatoes or onions. In winter canned tomatoes, cabbage, beets, etc., are also furnished. The allowance of roasted coffee is one ounce and seven twenty-fifths of an ounce, and of tea eight twenty-fifths of an ounce—ample to make each day three pints of strong coffee or the same amount of strong tea. . . ." *Ibid.*, 95-96.

company funds. Food supplies were frequently supplemented with purchases at the sutler's store, where a wide range of canned goods, fresh and dried fruits, vegetables, delicacies, and many other items could be obtained. The council of administration at each post, comprised of the commanding officer and the next three highest-ranking line officers (if there were less than three line officers they formed a council), set the prices that the sutler or post trader could charge for all items sold.[61] Each post was expected to cultivate a garden to provide fresh vegetables. With few exceptions, such as Fort Lyon, as noted above, these efforts failed.

The health of the soldiers appears to have been surprisingly good, especially since maintenance of proper cleanliness and sanitation was a problem. The men could bathe in the streams during

[61] The following is a partial list of items and prices for the sutler's store at Fort Larned, illustrative of the kinds of products offered and the cost of living at the posts (the size of cans, bottles, and boxes listed is unknown):

Potatoes, per bushel	$2.25	Beer, per gallon	$1.00
Apples, per bushel	3.50	Whiskey, per gallon	1.50
Flour, per sack	4.75	Crackers, per pound	.13
Tomatoes, per can	.60	Corn Meal, per pound	.04
Peaches, per can	.85	Butter, per pound	.25
Strawberries, per can	.85	Chocolate, per pound	.50
Oysters, per can	.75	Brown Sugar, per pound	.18
Lobsters, per can	.50	Cheese, per pound	.22
Pineapple, per can	.85	Tea, per pound	1.25
Jelly, per can	.75	Chewing Tobacco, per pound	.90
Coffee, per box	.45	Mixed Candy, per pound	.60
Clothes Pins, per box	2.50	Soap, per pound	.30
Cigars, per box	4.50	Playing Cards, pack	.25
Eggs, per dozen	.30	Diaper Pins, @	.25
Tomato Catsup, per bottle	.20	Neckties, @	.30
Castor Oil, per bottle	.25	Candles, @	.25
Cologne, per bottle	.25	Wash Boards, @	1.00
Blue Jean Pants, per pair	4.75	Hoop Skirts, @	2.50
Canvas, per yard	.25	Lead Pencils, @	.10
Blankets, @	11.00–15.00	Smoking Pipes, @	1.10–7.50

Other items included song books, fishhooks, coffee pots, guitar strings, saddles, lanterns, epsom salt, cloth, pots and pans, hats, matches, needles and thread, spices, nails, revolvers, buttons, sulphur, hair dye, turpentine, wallets, tin buckets, molasses, axes, padlocks, scissors, mirrors, beads, and horse liniment. Proceedings of Council of Administration, Fort Larned, October 15, 1863, MS, USAC, AACB, NA.

The Soldiers' Life on the Trail, 1865–1880

the summer months, but during the remainder of the year adequate bathing facilities did not exist. The latrines were located near the barracks and, unless lime was used constantly, tended to become unsanitary. The most common diseases at the forts were diarrhea, dysentery, scurvy, rheumatism, phthisis, catarrhal afflictions (including laryngitis, bronchitis, pneumonia, and pleurisy), malarial fevers, and venereal diseases. The last named was the most prevalent during the decade of the 1870's.[62]

During 1867 a cholera epidemic swept down the Santa Fe Trail as far as Fort Lyon. Several companies of the Thirty-Eighth Regiment United States Infantry were marched from Jefferson Barracks at St. Louis to serve in New Mexico during the summer of that year. Some members of the battalion had contracted cholera before the command left St. Louis, but no further cases occurred until after four companies had reached Fort Harker, between Forts Riley and Zarah, June 22 and 25, 1867. There cholera broke out again, and the disease claimed twenty-one lives from the garrison during the remainder of the summer.[63]

On June 28, the date of the first cholera case at Fort Harker, two companies of the Thirty-Eighth Infantry had already departed for New Mexico. Yet one man with the squadron died of cholera on the evening of the first day's march. Cases then occurred almost daily until the troops reached Fort Lyon. Furthermore, they spread the dreaded disease to troops at Forts Zarah, Larned, and Dodge as they passed those posts. During the march, twenty-nine infantrymen were attacked by the ailment and ten died. Six lives were lost from the garrisons at Fort Larned and Fort Zarah, while at Fort Dodge twenty-five cases and fourteen deaths occurred. Major Henry Douglass, commanding officer, his wife, and ten-month-old baby were all stricken, and all recovered. Fort Lyon suffered no losses, although the Thirty-Eighth Infantry lost

---

[62] Surgeon General's Office, *Circular No. 4*, 259–61, 284–315; Surgeon General's Office, *Circular No. 8*, 253–57, 266–87, 303–10.

[63] Surgeon General's Office, "Report on Epidemic Cholera and Yellow Fever in the Army of the United States, during the Year 1867," *Circular No. 1*, 28–49.

Soldiers on the Santa Fe Trail

one man near that post and another south of the Arkansas. The affliction then subsided, and, after a week's isolation in camp after crossing Raton Pass, no new cases were reported.[64]

Because of the isolated positions of the garrisons, the need for relaxation and recreation was not easily satisfied at the posts along the Trail. The army did not provide much in the way of social diversion, and the troops usually had to improvise their own methods of amusement and entertainment.[65] The major form of relaxation in the barracks was visiting with other soldiers. Reading was popular with some men, and every post ultimately had a small library, containing popular novels, biographies, military histories, newspapers, journals, and magazines. Playing cards, singing, dancing (with other soldiers as partners), and playing practical jokes were other common diversions.

Some athletic sports were engaged in, such as foot racing, horseshoe pitching, jumping, and baseball. Musical instruments were another source of enjoyment, especially the guitar, banjo, violin, and mouth organ. Amateur theatricals were sometimes produced with satisfactory results. Hunting and fishing occupied the spare time of some of the men.

Drinking beer and whisky was an important form of relaxation, and many soldiers spent most of their pay for such refreshments. Drunkenness sometimes became a problem, resulting in strict regulations upon the sale of spiritous beverages, but drinking was allowed and tolerated, according to Rickey, "because officers realized that liquor provided an escape or, at least, an artificial and temporary amelioration of the dull, hard, and lonely lives of the men."[66] Gambling was another form of amusement, poker being

[64] In addition to the losses of the soldiers, the disease took the lives of an undetermined number of quartermaster employees. The affliction also spread from Fort Harker, along the Smoky Hill route as far as Fort Wallace in western Kansas.

[65] Data on the social life of the soldiers is found only indirectly in the military records. Some information for these paragraphs was taken from Rickey, *Forty Miles a Day,* 185–213. This recent study provides the only thorough treatment of the daily life of the frontier soldiers.

[66] *Ibid.,* 200.

The Soldiers' Life on the Trail, 1865-1880

the most popular game. Telling tall tales and relating humorous true stories also helped to pass idle hours.

It is known that the men stationed at a number of western forts organized chapters of fraternal societies, such as Freemasons, Odd Fellows, and the International Order of Good Templars. No evidence has been found to show that any of these lodges were located at posts along the Santa Fe Trail, but this does not rule out the possibility.

It is almost impossible to assess the religious life at the forts along the Trail. Forts Larned, Dodge, Lyon, and Union had chaplains, but the relation of these officers to the soldiers cannot be determined from available records. Chapel services were held, but usually only the officers and their families attended, although enlisted men were welcome.

Garrison life had improved during the post-Civil War years, but duty in the field, whether scouting, patrolling, campaigning, or escorting mail coaches, supply trains, merchants' caravans, or the paymaster's train, was little changed from earlier eras. Marching, riding on horses or in wagons, making or breaking camp, standing guard, and other duties in the field were often welcome changes from the monotonous garrison duty, but they, too, were routine and lonely. Whether one looks at life in garrisons or on the march, the soldiers' lot along the Santa Fe Trail was not an enviable one. Like most frontiersmen, the troops must have been hardy fellows.

The Santa Fe Trail was truly a military road, as well as a route of commerce and emigration, and the troops who served on it made significant and valuable contributions to the westward expansion of the nation and the acquisition, retention, and development of the American Southwest. Both the Trail and the soldiers assisted in the building of an empire.

Bibliography

I. MANUSCRIPTS

A. *National Archives, Washington*

Adjutant General's Office, Army and Air Corps Branch (Record Group No. 94):
  Adjutant General's Office General Order Book, Vol. 14.
  Army Post Records, Medical Histories: Fort Dodge, Fort Larned, Fort Lyon, Fort Union, and Fort Zarah.
  Compiled Data on Fort Larned.
  Departmental Commands, Selected Letters and Orders, 1848-80.
  Headquarters of the Army, General Orders, No. 44, December 16, 1850; No. 1, January 8, 1851; No. 5, September 6, 1854; No. 2, May 16, 1859; No. 8, June 30, 1860.
  Orders and Special Orders of the Sixth and Seventh Military Departments, Vol. 247 (1848-50); Vol. 248 (1851-52).
  Outline Description of Fort Union.
  Outline Summary of Fort Aubrey and Fort Zarah.
  Post Returns: Camp Mackay, 1850; Fort Atkinson, 1850-54; Fort Aubrey, 1865-66; Fort Dodge, 1866-80; Fort Larned, 1859-78; Fort Union, 1851-80; Fort Wise (Lyon) 1860-80; and Fort Zarah, 1864-69.
  Secretary of War, Selected Letters Sent, 1846.
  Selected Letters Received, 1833-80.
  Selected Letters Sent, 1846-80.
Quartermaster General's Office, Army and Air Corps Branch (Record Group No. 92):
  Consolidated Correspondence File, Selected Letters, 1851-80.

Bibliography

State Department, Diplomatic, Legal, and Fiscal Branch (Record Group No. 59):
> John Quincy Adams to James Wiley Magoffin, March 3, 1825, Consular Dispatches, Secretary of State.
> Manuel Alvarez to James Buchanan, February 9, 1846, Consular Reports, Santa Fe.

United States Army Commands, Army and Air Corps Branch (Record Group No. 98):
> Fort Dodge: Order Book; Selected Letters Received, 1865–80; Selected Letters Sent, 1866–80.
> Fort Larned: Proceedings of Council of Administration, October 15, 1863; Selected Letters Received, 1867–78; Selected Letters Sent, 1860–78.
> Fort Lyon: Order Book; Selected Letters Sent, 1868–80.
> Fort Union: Selected Letters Received, 1860–80; Selected Letters Sent, 1860–80.
> Ninth Military Department Orders, Vol. 36.
> Ninth Military Department Special Orders, Vol. 37.

B. *Missouri Historical Society, St. Louis*

Stephen Watts Kearny Letter Book, 1846–47.
Ruff, Charles F. "Notes of the Expedition to Santa Fe."
Henry S. Turner Collection, Journal of Henry S. Turner, 1846–47.

C. *State Historical Society of Colorado, Denver*

Alexander Barclay Papers. Transcript.

II. GOVERNMENT PUBLICATIONS

American State Papers: *Military Affairs.* Vols. IV, V, VII. Washington: Gales and Seaton, 1860–61.
Headquarters Department of Missouri. *General Orders and Circulars, Department of Missouri, 1867.* [n.p.]: Government Printing Office, [n.d.].

Soldiers on the Santa Fe Trail

———. *General Orders and Circulars, Department of Missouri, 1868.* Fort Leavenworth: Government Printing Office, 1869.

Heitman, Francis B. *Historical Register and Dictionary of the United States Army, 1789–1903.* 2 vols. Washington: Government Printing Office, 1903.

Kappler, Charles J. (ed.). *Indian Affairs, Laws and Treaties.* 3 vols. Washington: Government Printing Office, 1913.

Missouri House *Journal,* 14 General Assembly, 1 sess.

Surgeon General's Office. "Report on Epidemic Cholera and Yellow Fever in the Army of the United States, during the Year 1867," *Circular No. 1.* Washington: Government Printing Office, 1868.

———. "A Report on Barracks and Hospitals with Descriptions of Military Posts," *Circular No. 4.* Washington: Government Printing Office, 1870.

———. "A Report on the Hygiene of the United States Army with Descriptions of Military Posts," *Circular No. 8.* Washington: Government Printing Office, 1875.

United States Congress, *House of Representatives, Documents:*
- 18 Cong., 2 sess., *No. 79* (Serial 116).
- 21 Cong., 1 sess., *No. 2* (Serial 195).
- 22 Cong., 2 sess., *No. 2* (Serial 233).
- 24 Cong., 1 sess., *No. 181* (Serial 289).
- 26 Cong., 1 sess., *No. 2* (Serial 363).
- 28 Cong., 2 sess., *No. 2* (Serial 463).
- 29 Cong., 1 sess., *No. 2* (Serial 480).

United States Congress, *House of Representatives, Executive Documents:*
- 29 Cong., 2 sess., *No. 4* (Serial 497).
- 29 Cong., 2 sess., *No. 19* (Serial 499).
- 30 Cong., 1 sess., *No. 8* (Serial 515).
- 30 Cong., 1 sess., *No. 41* (Serial 517).
- 30 Cong., 1 sess., *No. 60* (Serial 520).
- 30 Cong., 2 sess., *No. 1* (Serial 537).

Bibliography

    31 Cong., 1 sess., *No. 17* (Serial 570).
    31 Cong., 1 sess., *No. 24* (Serial 576).
    31 Cong., 2 sess., *No. 1* (Serial 595).
    32 Cong., 1 sess., *No. 2* (Serial 634).
    33 Cong., 1 sess., *No. 1* (Serial 711).
    33 Cong., 2 sess., *No. 1* (Serial 778).
    37 Cong., 3 sess., *No. 1* (Serial 1157 & 1159).
    38 Cong., 1 sess., *No. 1* (Serial 1182).
    38 Cong., 2 sess., *No. 1* (Serial 1220).
    39 Cong., 1 sess., *No. 1* (Serial 1248).
    39 Cong., 2 sess., *No. 1* (Serial 1284 & 1285).
    39 Cong., 2 sess., *No. 23* (Serial 1288).
    40 Cong., 2 sess., *No. 1* (Serial 1324 & 1326).
    40 Cong., 3 sess., *No. 1* (Serial 1366 & 1367).
    41 Cong., 2 sess., *No. 1* (Serial 1412 & 1414).
    41 Cong., 3 sess., *No. 1* (Serial 1446 & 1449).
    42 Cong., 2 sess., *No. 1* (Serial 1503 & 1505).
    42 Cong., 3 sess., *No. 1* (Serial 1558 & 1560).
    43 Cong., 1 sess., *No. 1* (Serial 1597).
    43 Cong., 2 sess., *No. 1* (Serial 1635 & 1639).
    44 Cong., 1 sess., *No. 1* (Serial 1674 & 1680).
    45 Cong., 2 sess., *No. 1* (Serial 1794).
    45 Cong., 3 sess., *No. 1* (Serial 1843).
    46 Cong., 2 sess., *No. 1* (Serial 1903).
    46 Cong., 3 sess., *No. 1* (Serial 1952).
United States Congress, *House of Representatives, Miscellaneous Documents:*
    33 Cong., 1 sess., *No. 47* (Serial 741).
United States Congress, *House of Representatives, Reports:*
    26 Cong., 1 sess., *No. 540* (Serial 372).
    35 Cong., 2 sess., *No. 154* (Serial 1018).
United States Congress, *Senate Documents:*
    18 Cong., 2 sess., *No. 7* (Serial 108).
    20 Cong., 2 sess., *No. 52* (Serial 181).

Soldiers on the Santa Fe Trail

21 Cong., 1 sess., *No. 1* (Serial 192).
21 Cong., 1 sess., *No. 46* (Serial 192).
21 Cong., 2 sess., *No. 39* (Serial 203).
22 Cong., 1 sess., *No. 90* (Serial 213).
24 Cong., 1 sess., *No. 400* (Serial 283).
24 Cong., 2 sess., *No. 1* (Serial 297).
26 Cong., 1 sess., *No. 472* (Serial 360).
28 Cong., 1 sess., *No. 1* (Serial 431).
28 Cong., 1 sess., *No. 339* (Serial 435).
28 Cong., 2 sess., *No. 1* (Serial 449).
29 Cong., 1 sess., *No. 1* (Serial 470).
29 Cong., 1 sess., *No. 438* (Serial 477).

United States Congress, *Senate Executive Documents:*
29 Cong., 2 sess., *No 1* (Serial 493).
30 Cong., 1 sess., *No. 1* (Serial 503).
30 Cong., 1 sess., *No. 7* (Serial 505).
32 Cong., 1 sess., *No. 1* (Serial 611).
32 Cong., 2 sess., *No. 1* (Serial 659).
33 Cong., 1 sess., *No. 1* (Serial 691).
34 Cong., 1 sess., *No. 1* (Serial 811).
34 Cong., 3 sess., *No. 5* (Serial 876).
35 Cong., 2 sess., *No. 1* (Serial 974 & 975).
36 Cong., 1 sess., *No. 1* (Serial 1024 & 1025).
36 Cong., 2 sess., *No. 1* (Serial 1079).
37 Cong., 2 sess., *No. 1* (Serial 1117).
39 Cong., 2 sess., *No. 26* (Serial 1277).
40 Cong., 1 sess., *No. 2* (Serial 1308).
40 Cong., 1 sess., *No. 13* (Serial 1308).

United States Congress, *Senate Reports:*
39 Cong., 2 sess., *No. 156* (Serial 1279).

United States Statutes at Large. Vols. IV, XV.

United States War Department. *The War of the Rebellion: A Compilation of the Official Records of the Union and Confederate Armies.* 128 vols. Washington: Government Printing Office, 1880–1901.

Bibliography

III. PUBLISHED DIARIES, LETTERS, JOURNALS, MEMOIRS, AND CONTEMPORARY NARRATIVES

A. Articles

Becknell, Thomas. "The Journals of Captain Thomas [William] Becknell from Boone's Lick to Santa Fe and from Santa Cruz to Green River," *Missouri Historical Review*, Vol. II (January, 1910), 65-84.

Bliss, Robert S. "Journal of Robert S. Bliss, with the Mormon Battalion," *Utah Historical Quarterly*, Vol. IV (July, October, 1931), 67-96, 110-28.

Boone, Nathan. "Captain Nathan Boone's Journal," ed. by W. Julian Fessler. *Chronicles of Oklahoma*, Vol. VII (March, 1929), 58-105.

Cooke, Philip St. George. "A Journal of the Santa Fe Trail," ed. by William E. Connelley. *Mississippi Valley Historical Review*, Vol. XII (June, September, 1925), 72-98, 227-55.

Evans, Hugh. "The Journal of Hugh Evans, Covering the First and Second Campaigns of the United States Dragoon Regiment in 1834 and 1835," ed. by Grant Foreman and Fred S. Perrine. *Chronicles of Oklahoma*, Vol. III (September, 1925), 175-215.

Godfrey, General E. S. "Some Reminiscences, Including the Washita Battle, November 27, 1868," *The Cavalry Journal*, Vol. XXXVI (October, 1928), pages not numbered.

Lowe, Percival G. "Kansas as Seen in the Indian Territory," *Kansas Historical Society Transactions*, Vol. IV (1886-90), 360-66.

———. "Recollections of Fort Riley," *Kansas Historical Collections*, Vol. VII (1901-1902), 101-13.

Moore, Horace L. "The Nineteenth Kansas Cavalry," *Kansas Historical Collections*, Vol. VI (1897-1900), 35-52.

Perrine, Fred S. "Military Escorts on the Santa Fe Trail," *New Mexico Historical Review*, Vol. II (April, July, 1927), 175-93, 269-304; Vol. III (July, 1928), 265-300.

Waldo, William. "Recollections of a Septuagenarian," Missouri Historical Society, *Publications,* Nos. II and III (St. Louis, 1881), 1–18.

B. Books

Benton, Thomas Hart. *Thirty Years' View.* 2 vols. New York, D. Appleton and Company, 1854–56.

Cooke, Philip St. George. *Conquest of New Mexico and California.* New York, Putnam's Sons, 1878.

———. *Scenes and Adventures in the Army, or Romance of Military Life.* Philadelphia, Lindsay and Blakiston, 1857.

Cutts, James Madison. *The Conquest of California and New Mexico, by the Forces of the United States, in the Years 1846 and 1847.* Philadelphia, Carey and Hart, 1847.

Davis, W. W. H. *El Gringo, or New Mexico and Her People.* Santa Fe, The Rydal Press, 1938.

Edwards, Frank S. *A Campaign in New Mexico with Colonel Doniphan.* Philadelphia, Carey and Hart, 1847.

Forsyth, General George A. *The Story of the Soldier.* New York, D. Appleton and Company, 1905.

Fowler, Jacob. *The Journal of Jacob Fowler, 1821–1822.* Ed. by Elliott Coues. New York, Francis P. Harper, 1898.

Garrard, Lewis H. *Wah-to-Yah and the Taos Trail.* Vol. VI of *The Southwest Historical Series,* ed. by Ralph P. Bieber. Glendale, The Arthur H. Clark Company, 1938.

Gibson, George Rutledge. *Journal of a Soldier under Kearny and Doniphan, 1846–1847.* Vol. III of *The Southwest Historical Series,* ed. by Ralph P. Bieber. Glendale, The Arthur H. Clark Company, 1935.

Gregg, Josiah. *Commerce of the Prairies.* Ed. by Max L. Moorhead. Norman, University of Oklahoma Press, 1954.

———. *Diary and Letters of Josiah Gregg.* Ed. by Maurice Garland Fulton. 2 vols. Norman, University of Oklahoma Press, 1941, 1944.

Hafen, LeRoy R. and Ann W. Hafen (eds.). *Relations with the Indians of the Plains, 1857–1861: A Documentary Account.* Vol.

Bibliography

IX of *The Far West and Rockies Series,* ed. by LeRoy R. Hafen. Glendale, The Arthur H. Clark Company, 1959.

Hildreth, James. *Dragoon Campaigns to the Rocky Mountains.* New York, Wiley and Long, 1836.

Hollister, Ovando J. *Boldly They Rode: A History of the First Colorado Regiment of Volunteers.* Lakewood, Colorado, The Golden Press, 1949.

Hughes, John T. *Doniphan's Expedition.* Cincinnati, J. A. and U. P. James, 1848.

Inman, Colonel Henry. *The Old Santa Fe Trail.* Topeka, Crane and Company, 1899.

James, Thomas. *Three Years among the Indians and Mexicans.* Waterloo, Illinois, printed at the office of the "War Eagle," 1846.

Johnston, Abraham Robinson, Marcellus Ball Edwards, and Philip Gooch Ferguson. *Marching with the Army of the West.* Vol. IV of *The Southwest Historical Series,* ed. by Ralph P. Bieber. Glendale, The Arthur H. Clark Company, 1936.

Kendall, George W. *Narrative of the Texan Santa Fe Expedition.* 2 vols. New York, Harper and Brothers, 1844.

Magoffin, Susan Shelby. *Down the Santa Fe Trail and into Mexico; the Diary of Susan Shelby Magoffin, 1846-1847.* Ed. by Stella M. Drumm. New Haven, Yale University Press, 1963.

Meriwether, David. *My Life in the Mountains and on the Plains.* Ed. by Robert A. Griffen. Norman, University of Oklahoma Press, 1965.

Pike, Zebulon Montgomery. *The Expeditions of Zebulon Montgomery Pike.* Ed. by Elliott Coues. 3 vols. New York, Francis P. Harper, 1895.

———. *The Journals of Zebulon Montgomery Pike, with Letters and Related Documents.* Ed. by Donald Jackson. 2 vols. Norman, University of Oklahoma Press, 1966.

Polk, James Knox. *Polk: The Diary of a President, 1845-1849.* Ed. by Allan Nevins. New York, Longmans, Green and Company, 1929.

Richardson, William H. *Journal of William H. Richardson.* New York, William H. Richardson, 1848.

Robinson, Jacob S. *A Journal of the Santa Fe Expedition under Colonel Doniphan.* Reprinted from the 1848 edition with introduction by Carl L. Cannon. Princeton, Princeton University Press, 1932.

Ryus, W. H. *The Second William Penn.* Kansas City, Missouri, Frank T. Riley Publishing Company, 1913.

Sheridan, General Philip H. *Personal Memoirs.* 2 vols. New York, Charles L. Webster Company, 1888.

Webb, James Josiah. *Adventures in the Santa Fe Trade, 1844-1847.* Vol. I of *The Southwest Historical Series,* ed. by Ralph P. Bieber. Glendale, The Arthur H. Clark Company, 1931.

Williams, Ellen. *Three Years and a Half in the Army: History of the Second Colorados.* New York, Fowler and Wells Company, 1885.

Wilson, Richard L. *Short Ravelings from a Long Yarn, or Camp March Sketches of the Santa Fe Trail.* Ed. by Benjamin F. Taylor. Santa Ana, California, Fine Arts Press, 1936.

Wright, Robert M. *Dodge City, the Cowboy Capital.* Wichita, The Wichita Eagle Press, 1913.

IV. NEWSPAPERS

Missouri Democrat (Fayette), July 1, September 2, 1846.

Missouri Intelligencer (Fayette), May 1, 1829.

Niles' Weekly Register (Baltimore), March 23, 1833; August 19, 1843.

Rocky Mountain Daily News (Denver), November 6, 1867; September 9, 1868.

The St. Louis Weekly Republican, August 10, 1846.

The St. Louis Weekly Reveille, May 25, June 22, July 6, 20, August 17, 1846.

The Santa Fe Republican, May 3, June 28, July 19, August 1, 1848.

Bibliography

V. SECONDARY STUDIES

A. Articles

Beers, Henry Putney. "Military Protection of the Santa Fe Trail to 1843," *New Mexico Historical Review,* Vol. XII (April, 1937), 113-33.

Bieber, Ralph P. "Some Aspects of the Santa Fe Trail, 1848-1880," *Chronicles of Oklahoma,* Vol. II (March, 1924), 1-8.

Binkley, William Campbell. "New Mexico and the Texan Santa Fe Expedition," *The Southwestern Historical Quarterly,* Vol. XXVII (October, 1923), 85-107.

———. "The Last Stage of Texan Military Operations against Mexico, 1843," *The Southwestern Historical Quarterly,* Vol. XXII (January, 1919), 260-72.

Carroll, H. Bailey. "Steward A. Miller and the Snively Expedition of 1843," *The Southwestern Historical Quarterly,* Vol. LIV (January, 1951), 261-86.

Culmer, Frederic A. "Marking the Santa Fe Trail," *New Mexico Historical Review,* Vol. IX (January, 1934), 78-93.

"Early Military Posts, Missions and Camps," *Kansas Historical Society Transactions,* Vols. I and II (1875-78), 263-70.

Garfield, Marvin. "Defense of the Kansas Frontier, 1864-1865," *Kansas Historical Quarterly,* Vol. I (February, 1931), 140-52.

———. "Defense of the Kansas Frontier, 1858-1869," *Kansas Historical Quarterly,* Vol. I (November, 1932), 451-73.

Hafen, LeRoy R. "Thomas Fitzpatrick and the First Indian Agency of the Upper Platte and Arkansas," *Mississippi Valley Historical Review,* Vol. XV (December, 1928), 374-84.

Hill, Joseph J. "An Unknown Expedition to Santa Fe in 1807," *Mississippi Valley Historical Review,* Vol. I (March, 1920), 560-62.

Loyola, Sister Mary, S. H. N. "The American Occupation of New Mexico, 1821-1852," *New Mexico Historical Review,* Vol. XIV (January, April, July, 1939), 34-75, 143-99, 230-86.

Marshall, Thomas Maitland. "Commercial Aspects of the Texan

Santa Fe Expedition," *The Southwestern Historical Quarterly*, Vol. XX (January, 1917), 242-59.

Oliva, Leo E. "Fortification on the Plains: Fort Dodge, Kansas, 1864-1882," *1960 Brand Book*. Denver, Denver Westerners, (1961), 137-79.

"Report of Committee Appointed to Prepare a Correct Map of the Old Santa Fe Trail across the State of Kansas," Kansas State Historical Society, *Eighteenth Biennial Report of the Board of Directors* (1911-12), 107-25.

Stephens, F. F. "Missouri and the Santa Fe Trade," *Missouri Historical Review*, Vol. X (July, 1916), 233-62; Vol. XI (April, July, 1917), 289-312.

Thomas, Alfred B. "The First Santa Fe Expedition, 1792-1793," *Chronicles of Oklahoma*, Vol. IX (June, 1931), 195-208.

Unrau, William E. "The Story of Fort Larned," *Kansas Historical Quarterly*, Vol. XXIII (Autumn, 1957), 257-80.

Utley, Robert M. "Fort Union and the Santa Fe Trail," *New Mexico Historical Review*, Vol. XXXVI (January, 1961), 36-48.

Wood, Henry. "Fort Union: End of the Santa Fe Trail," *1949 Brand Book*. Denver, Denver Westerners, (1950), 205-56.

Young, Otis E. "Dragoons on the Santa Fe Trail in the Autumn of 1843," *Chronicles of Oklahoma*, Vol. XXXII (Spring, 1954), 42-51.

———. "Military Protection of the Santa Fe Trail and Trade," *Missouri Historical Review*, Vol. XLIX (October, 1954), 19-32.

———. "The United States Mounted Ranger Battalion, 1832-1833," *Mississippi Valley Historical Review*, Vol. XLI (December, 1954), 453-70.

B. Books

Bancroft, Hubert Howe. *History of Arizona and New Mexico, 1530-1888*. San Francisco, The History Company, 1889.

Bender, Averam B. *The March of Empire, Frontier Defense in*

Bibliography

the Southwest, 1846-1860. Lawrence, University of Kansas Press, 1952.

Billington, Ray Allen. *The Far Western Frontier, 1830-1860.* New York, Harper and Brothers, 1956.

Brackett, Albert Gallatin. *History of the United States Cavalry, from the Formation of the Federal Government to the First of June, 1863.* New York, Harper and Brothers, 1865.

Chittenden, Hiram Martin. *The American Fur Trade of the Far West.* 2 vols. New York, Barnes and Noble, Inc., 1935.

Clarke, Dwight L. *Stephen Watts Kearny.* Norman, University of Oklahoma Press, 1961.

Colton, Ray C. *The Civil War in the Western Territories: Arizona, Colorado, New Mexico, and Utah.* Norman, University of Oklahoma Press, 1959.

Dick, Everett. *Vanguards of the Frontier.* New York, D. Appleton-Century Company, 1941.

Duffus, Robert L. *The Santa Fe Trail.* New York, Longmans, Green and Company, 1930.

Golder, Frank Alfred, Thomas A. Bailey, and J. Lyman Smith. *The March of the Mormon Battalion from Council Bluffs to California, Taken from the Journal of Henry Standage.* New York, The Century Company, 1928.

Gregg, Kate L. (ed.). *The Road to Santa Fe.* Albuquerque, University of New Mexico Press, 1952.

Grinnell, George B. *The Fighting Cheyennes.* Norman, University of Oklahoma Press, 1956.

Hafen, LeRoy R. *The Overland Mail, 1849-1869.* Cleveland, The Arthur H. Clark Company, 1926.

——— and W. J. Ghent. *Broken Hand, the Life Story of Thomas Fitzpatrick, Chief of the Mountain Men.* Denver, Old West Publishing Company, 1931.

Hall, Martin Hardwick. *Sibley's New Mexico Campaign.* Austin, University of Texas Press, 1960.

Hayes, A. A. *New Colorado and the Santa Fe Trail.* New York, Harper and Brothers, 1880.

Hodge, Frederick Webb (ed.). *Handbook of American Indians North of Mexico.* 2 vols. New York, Pagent Books, Inc., 1959.

Hollon, W. Eugene. *The Southwest: Old and New.* New York, Alfred A. Knopf, 1961.

Hunt, Aurora. *Major General James Henry Carleton, 1814–1873: Western Frontier Dragoon.* Glendale, The Arthur H. Clark Company, 1958.

Hunt, Elvid. *History of Fort Leavenworth, 1827–1937.* Second Edition. Fort Leavenworth, The Command and General Staff Press, 1937.

Leckie, William H. *The Military Conquest of the Southern Plains.* Norman, University of Oklahoma Press, 1963.

Loomis, Noel M. *The Texan–Santa Fe Pioneers.* Norman, University of Oklahoma Press, 1958.

Marshall, James. *Santa Fe: The Railroad that Built an Empire.* New York, Random House, 1945.

Moorhead, Max L. *New Mexico's Royal Road: Trade and Travel on the Chihuahua Trail.* Norman, University of Oklahoma Press, 1958.

Pride, W. F. *The History of Fort Riley.* [n.p.], United States Army, 1926.

Rickey, Don, Jr. *Forty Miles a Day on Beans and Hay: The Enlisted Soldier Fighting the Indian Wars.* Norman, University of Oklahoma Press, 1963.

Settle, Raymond W. and Mary L. Settle. *Empire on Wheels.* Palo Alto, Stanford University Press, 1949.

Singletary, Otis A. *The Mexican War.* Chicago, University of Chicago Press, 1960.

Stanley, F. *Fort Union, New Mexico.* [n.p.], F. Stanley, 1953.

Twitchell, Ralph Emerson. *The Leading Facts of New Mexican History.* 5 vols. Cedar Rapids, Iowa, The Torch Press, 1911–17.

———. *The Story of the Conquest of Santa Fe, New Mexico, and the Building of Old Fort Marcy, A.D. 1846.* Santa Fe, Historical Society of New Mexico Publications No. 24, 1921.

Bibliography

Vestal, Stanley. *The Old Santa Fe Trail*. Boston, Houghton Mifflin Company, 1939.

Waters, L. L. *Steel Trails to Santa Fe*. Lawrence, University of Kansas Press, 1950.

Whitford, William Clarke. *Colorado Volunteers in the Civil War: The New Mexico Campaign in 1862*. Denver, The State Historical and Natural History Society, 1906.

Young, Otis E. *The First Military Escort on the Santa Fe Trail, 1829*. Glendale, The Arthur H. Clark Company, 1952.

———. *The West of Philip St. George Cooke, 1809–1895*. Glendale, The Arthur H. Clark Company, 1955.

Index

Abert, Lt. J. W.: 18, 63
Adams-Onís Treaty (1819): 6
Adkin's Ranch, Kans.: 163
Adobe (used for construction of forts): 110, 123, 168, 170–72, 176–78
Adobe Fort (on Canadian River): 159
Alexander, Capt. Edmund B.: 105
Allen, Capt. James: 61, 77–78
Allison, Bill: 116n.
Allison's Ranch (on Walnut Creek): 116–17
Almonte, Juan: 44
Alvarez, Manuel: 57
Angney, Capt. William Z.: 63
Annuities (for Indians): 142, 144, 146, 149, 190
Anthony, Maj. Scott J.: 148–49, 154, 156, 158–59
Apache Canyon, battle of: 132–36
Apache Indians: 16, 54, 85–86, 89, 106, 126, 129, 139, 147–48, 180, 182–83; hostile acts by, 143; campaign against, 185; treaties with, 165–66, 187–88
Apache Pass: 75
Arapaho Indians: 16, 85–86, 126, 129, 147–50, 152, 158, 180; hostile acts by, 141, 143, 161, 190; campaigns against, 157, 160, 185; treaties with, 165–66, 187–88
Archuleta, Diego: 74
Arkansas Crossing: 28, 35, 140; *see also* Cimarron Crossing, Upper Crossing, etc.
Arkansas River: 9, 15–19, 21, 23, 27–30, 32, 36, 38, 40–41, 44–46, 48–50, 53–54, 73, 84–88, 90, 112–13, 124, 152, 163, 165, 175, 187–88
Armijo, Gov. Manuel: 42, 44–45, 53, 64–65, 72–75
Army of the West: 15, 18, 22, 77, 79, 91; organization, 55–68; march to Santa Fe, 68–76
Arrow Rock, Mo.: 7, 12
Artillery: 10, 32, 36, 39, 63, 66, 77, 84–85, 87, 134–37
Ash Creek: 16, 48
Atchison, Topeka and Santa Fe Railroad: 23, 167, 194
Atkinson, Gen. Henry: 35
Augur, C. C.: 187
Austin, Stephen F.: 3n.

Baird, James: 9
Barclay, Alexander: 104n.
Barclay's Fort: 104n.
Barton, Sen. David: 12
Bayard, Lt. George D.: 117
Becknell, William: 7–9
Bell, Lt. David: 121–23
Bent, Charles: 28, 36, 44–45, 52
Bent, William: 124n., 129, 159, 166; spy for Army of the West, 56n., 73; Indian agent, 113, 125
Benton, Sen. Thomas Hart: 12, 26, 33–34
Bent's Fort: 17–19, 44, 49, 53, 80, 85, 124n.; in Mexican War, 56, 60, 65–67, 69–73; recommended for military post, 92, 95
Bent's New Fort: 124 & n., 125, 127, 167
Bergmann, Capt. E. H.: 155

217

Bernal Springs, N.M.: 133, 135
Beysacher, Dr. A. L.: 122
Big Bend of the Arkansas River: 15, 36, 144
Big Coon Creek: 119
Big Timbers (Colo.): 18, 53, 95, 113, 126
Black Hawk War: 34
Black Kettle (Cheyenne chief): 158
Blue Mills, Mo.: 13
Bluff Creek Council (1865): 165-66
Blunt, Gen. James G.: 143, 153, 157-58
Boone, A. G.: 142
Boone, Capt. Nathan: 43-44
Boonville, Mo.: 13
Box family, rescued: 182-83
Box, James: 182
Box, Mrs. Martha: 182-83
Brooke, Lt. Francis J.: 28n., 31
Brooke, Gen. George M.: 59
Brulé Sioux Indians: 186
Bryant, Maj. Thomas S.: 87
Buchanan, Sec. of State James: 57
Buckner, Lt. Simon B.: 99-101, 107
Buffalo: 15-16, 29-32, 68, 140, 142, 146, 165, 188
Burgwin, Lt. John Henry K.: 37
Butze, William: 115

Caches: 10, 17, 46, 80
Caddo Indians: 147 & n.
Calhoun, Gov. James S.: 107
California: 55, 57-58, 66, 76, 77-78, 93; gold rush, 21; volunteers, 163
Camp Alert: *see* Fort Larned
Camp Center: *see* Fort Riley
Camp Mackay: 95-96
Camp Nichols: 162-64
Camp on Pawnee Creek: *see* Fort Larned
Camp Wynkoop: 152, 164
Campaigns (military): 140, 164, 167; against Kiowas and Comanches (1860), 113, 123-26; against Indians along Santa Fe Trail (1865), 164-65; winter of 1868-69, 193
Canadian River: 7, 18, 34, 40-41, 85-86, 90, 92, 109, 159
Canby, Lt. Col. E. R. S.: 132, 139-41, 145
Caravans (traders): 10, 13-17, 19-21, 25-26, 28-30, 32, 36-37, 39-40, 44-51,

54, 57-58 & n., 60, 63-65, 77, 79-81, 106, 116, 119, 122, 155, 161-63, 181; *see also* Santa Fe traders
Carleton, Capt. (Gen.) James H.: 101, 106-107, 145-46, 155, 159, 161, 163
Carson, Christopher "Kit": 141, 159, 163-64, 166
Cass, Sec. of War Lewis: 34-35, 36n.
Cats: 98
Cattle: 30, 80, 87, 129, 155
Cavalry: 27, 31, 34, 77, 99-100, 116, 136-37, 146, 151, 155, 190, 192; First U. S. Regt., 114-15, 119, 123, 125-27, 132n., 135, 159; Third U. S. Regt., 132n.; Fourth Texas Regt., 135; Seventh Texas Regt., 135; Second Colo. Vol. Regt., 144; Ninth Kans. Vol. Regt., 144; First Colo. Regt., 150, 151n., 153; Third Colo. Regt., 159; Eleventh Kans. Regt., 163; Seventh U. S. Regt., 186, 191n.; *see also* Dragoons
Chambers, Samuel: 9
Chapel, Fort Lyon: 177
Chaplains, military posts: 201
Chapman, Maj. William: 140-41
Chávez, Antonio José: 43
Chavez, Lt. Col. Manuel: 138
Cheyenne Indians: 16, 85-86, 126, 129, 147-49, 152n., 158, 180; hostile acts by, 101, 150-51, 161, 190; campaigns against, 157, 160, 185-86; treaties with, 165-66, 187-88
Chihuahua (city), Mexico: 4, 6
Chihuahua (state), Mexico: 11, 55, 75, 86
Chilton, Capt. R. H.: 97-98, 100-101, 111
Chivington, Maj. (Col.) John M.: 133, 135-36, 138, 151n., 152, 156, 157n., 159
Cholera epidemic: 199-200 & n.
Chouteau, Pierre: 6 & n.
Chouteau's Island: 17 & n., 29-30, 124-25
Cimarron Crossing: 17, 38, 40, 45-46, 48, 50-51, 65, 80-81, 92, 95, 98, 120, 122, 141, 148, 153, 155, 157; *see also* Arkansas Crossing, Upper Crossing, etc.
Cimarron Desert: 9, 17
Cimarron River: 17-19, 29, 32, 45, 84,

218

Index

87, 89, 90, 112, 121, 124, 144, 146, 191–92
Cimarron Route: 17, 77–78, 80, 105–106, 141, 145, 161–63, 167
Civil War: 22, 24, 93, 110, 120, 123, 129–31, 139, 175, 178; *see also* battles of Apache Canyon and Glorieta Pass
Claflin, Lt. Ira W.: 132n.
Clark, Maj. Meriwether Lewis: 63
Clarke, Gen. N. S.: 100, 111
Cold Spring (Cimarron River): 18, 45, 109–10, 126, 141, 162–63
Cole, William H.: 118
Cole County, Mo.: 63
Colley, S. G.: 144, 147, 150, 157
Collins, James L.: 138
Colorado: 8, 17, 23, 120, 129, 131–32, 139, 150, 157; gold rush, 21, 113; volunteers, 132 & n., 135, 145n., 151
Colorado, Dist. of: 153
Comanche Indians: 16, 38–39, 85–86, 98, 106, 115–16, 129, 141–42, 147, 152, 160, 180, 191 & n.; hostile acts by, 79, 84, 87–88, 109–10, 112–14, 148, 154, 190; campaigns against, 89–90, 123–26, 159, 185; treaties with, 165–66, 187–88
Confederate invasion of New Mexico: 131–139
Connelly, Henry: 74–75
Conrad, Sec. of War C. M.: 106n., 111
Cooke, Lt. (Capt.) Philip St. George: 25, 28n., 31, 42, 44, 46–52, 54, 59, 66, 72–75, 78
Coon Creek: 88
Cooper, Benjamin: 9
Cooper, Braxton: 9
Cooper, Adj. Gen. Samuel: 119
Cooper, Stephen: 9
Cottonwood Creek: 15, 23, 37, 48
Council Bluffs, Iowa, Mormons at: 57, 77–78
Council Grove, Kans.: 14–16, 18, 23, 28–29, 36, 44, 50, 52, 80, 84, 95, 151, 152, 161–62, 184, 190
Cow Creek: 15, 37, 116, 121–22, 142–43, 147, 151, 153
Crawford, Sec. of War G. W.: 94–95
Creek Indians: 35
Crittenden, Lt. Col. George B.: 110
Crocker, Lt. W. D.: 150

Curtis, Gen. Samuel R.: 152–54, 156, 160
Custer, Lt. Col. George A.: 186, 192

Davis, Capt. Nicholas S.: 155
Davis, W. W. H.: 21
DeCourcey, Lt. James A.: 72
Delaware Indians: 60
De Mun, Jules: 6 & n.
Denver, Colo.: 124, 128, 157
Departments (military): *see* Kansas, Dept. of, Ninth Mil. Dept., etc.
DeSaussure, Capt. W. D.: 114–18, 125
Diamond Spring: 15, 23, 36
Diana (steamboat): 27
Diseases: 199
Districts (military): *see* Colorado, Dist. of, etc.
Dodge City, Kans.: 9, 23
Dodge, Maj. (Col.) Henry: 26n., 35, 37–38
Dodge, Gen. Grenville M.: 162–63, 165, 170
Dog Soldiers (Cheyennes): 181
Donaldson, Maj. J. L.: 116
Doniphan, Col. Alexander W.: 61
Donkeys: 5, 19
Dorr, Lt. Gustavus: 28n.
Douglass, Maj. Henry: 184–85, 199
Downing, Maj. Jacob: 150
Doyle, W. B.: 104 n.
Dragoons: 82–84, 103; First U. S. Regt., 25, 36n., 37, 39–41, 43–44, 46, 48–55, 58–59, 61–64, 66, 68, 72, 98, 100–101, 105–106, 111; Second U. S. Regt., 123, 125; *see also* cavalry
Drinkard, Sec. of War William R.: 115
Drunken Creek: 30
Dry Route: 16–17 & n., 36, 46, 95, 162, 167
Dugouts (used as soldiers' quarters): 163, 168, 171
Duncan, Capt. Matthew: 25, 34–35
Duncan, Capt. Thomas: 141

Easton, Lt. Col. Alton R.: 78
Easton, Capt. L. C.: 104, 111
Eaton, Sec. of War John H.: 33 & n.
Eayre, Lt. George S.: 151–152n.
Edmonson, Maj. Benjamin B.: 77

219

Soldiers on the Santa Fe Trail

Edwards, Gov. John C.: 56 & n.
Ellsworth, Kans.: 23
Emory, Lt. William H.: 63
Escorts (Mexican troops): 25n., 40, 44, 49, 64; in 1829, 31–32, 40; in autumn of 1843, 40, 51
Escorts (U. S. troops): 10, 25–26, 65, 80, 92–94, 106, 110, 140, 143, 151, 161–62, 169, 181, 187; in 1829, 26–33, 35, 44, 111; in 1833, 33–36; in 1832, 34 n.; in 1834, 36–41; in spring of 1843, 41–49; in autumn of 1843, 49–52; for mails, 101, 108–109 & n., 112, 119–21, 130, 142, 152, 155
Eustis, Capt. William: 58, 59n.
Evans, Gov. John: 157

Fauntleroy, Col. Thomas Turner: 109–10
Ferguson, Philip Gooch: 79
Fillmore, Pres. Millard: 107
Fischer, Capt. Woldemar: 63
Fitzpatrick, Thomas: 82n., 86n., 91–93, 112
Ford, Capt. (Col.) James H.: 132n., 162–63, 165
Fort Arbuckle, I. T.: 126
Fort Atkinson, Iowa: 59
Fort Atkinson, Kans.: 94, 96–103, 106–107, 110–11, 114–15, 146, 148, 155, 162–63
Fort Aubrey, Kans.: 162, 164
Fort Bascom, N. M.: 193
Fort Cobb, I. T.: 126
Fort Crawford, Wis.: 59
Fort Dodge, Kans.: 17 & n., 162–63, 167, 171–75, 182–84, 186, 188–95, 199, 201
Fort Gibson, I. T.: 36–37, 41, 43, 50, 52, 59n.
Fort Harker, Kans.: 199, 200 n.
Fort Hays, Kans.: 186
Fort Hays–Fort Dodge road: 190
Fort Kearny, Neb.: 123, 126
Fort Laramie, Wyo.: 53, 100–101
Fort Larned, Kans.: 17n., 113–14, 119–28, 130, 141, 143–48, 150–54, 156–57, 161–63, 165, 167, 170, 181–82, 184, 186, 88, 190, 199, 201
Fort Larned–Fort Riley road: 151
Fort Leavenworth, Kan.: 13, 25, 27, 29, 32, 34–36, 48–49, 51–56, 58–64, 66–68, 77–84, 87, 91, 94–101, 112, 120, 154, 186
Fort Lyon (Wise), Colo.: 113, 126–30, 141–42, 144–46, 148, 152–55, 157–59, 162–64, 167, 175–78, 191, 193, 199, 201
Fort Mann, Kans.: 21, 80–90, 94–95
Fort Marcy, N. M.: 80 n., 105
Fort Osage, Mo.: 12–14
Fort Riley, Kans.: 102, 110–16, 119–20, 123, 125, 127, 143–45, 151, 153, 161, 165, 169, 185, 199
Fort Scott, Kans.: 49–50, 52, 58
Fort Sod: *see* Fort Atkinson
Fort Sodom: *see* Fort Atkinson
Fort Union, N. M.: 101, 105–110, 121–23, 126, 130, 132, 134–35, 139–41, 144–45 & n., 161–62, 167, 178–80, 201
Fort Union Arsenal: 178–79
Fort Union Depot: 178
Fort Wallace, Kans.: 200 n.
Fort Washita, I. T.: 126
Fort Wise, Colo.: *see* Fort Lyon
Fort Wise Treaty, with Arapahoes and Cheyennes (1861): 129–30
Fort Zarah, Kans.: 153 & n., 161, 165, 167–71, 180, 182, 186, 193, 199
Forts: 93–94, 130, 167–68, 180; *see also* military posts
Fowler, Jacob: 8–9
Franklin, Mo.: 9, 12–13
Franklin, Lt. W. B.: 54
Fraternal societies at forts: 201
Freighting: 22; *see also* caravans, Santa Fe traders, & supply trains
Fur traders: 6
Furs: 5–6, 19, 45

Gaines, Gen. Edmund P.: 49, 51
Galisteo, N. M.: 135–36
Garland, Col. John: 109
Garrard, Lewis H.: 81–82
Georgetown, Texas: 45
Gilpin, Maj. (Lt. Col.) William: 21, 61, 84–87, 89, 91–93
Glenn, Hugh: 8–9
Glorieta Pass, N. M.: 18, 132, 134; battle of, 136–39
Gold: 5, 19
Granada, Colo.: 23
Gray's Ranch, N. M.: 155

Index

Great Bend, Kans.: 116n.
Great Plains: 3, 10, 28, 67
Gregg, Josiah: 4, 10, 14, 22, 26n., 37–40
Griffin, Capt. John C.: 89
Grover, Maj. Cuvier: 182
Guadalupe Hidalgo, treaty of: 91

Hall and Co. (mail contractor): 102, 114
Hall, Jacob: 21, 114–15, 119
Hamilton County, Kans.: 164
Hancock, Gen. Winfield S.: 184–86, 189
Hancock Expedition: 185–87
Harney, William S.: 166, 187
Harvey, Thomas H.: 91
Hay (at forts): 99, 120, 122, 128, 129
Hayden (wagonmaster): 83
Hayden, Capt. Julius: 141–43
Hays, Kans.: 23–24
Henderson, John B.: 187
Herron, Corp. Leander: 183n.
Hesselburger, Lt. G. A.: 183
Heth, Lt. Henry: 98, 101
Hidalgo, Miguel: 6
Hoffman, Capt. William: 95–96, 98
Holt, Postmaster Gen. Joseph: 114
Horses: 7, 10, 16, 27n., 28, 30–31, 41, 50, 60–61, 69, 73, 87–88, 110, 120, 169, 190
Hospitals, military posts: Fort Lyon, 128, 176–77; Fort Zarah, 169; Fort Larned, 170–71; Fort Dodge, 171–72; Fort Union, 179–80
Houston, Sam: 42–43
Howard, George Thomas: 57–58, 63–64, 69–71
Howard County, Mo.: 62
Howitzers: 44, 47, 71, 132 & n., 137, 155, 159
Howland, Capt. George W.: 132n.
Hudson, Capt. Thomas B.: 63
Huerfano Creek: 145n.
Hughes, John T.: 70, 79

Illinois volunteers: 78
Independence, Mo.: 13–14, 16, 18–19, 21–22, 63–64, 71, 102, 107, 115, 117
Independence-Santa Fe mail: 93, 108
Indian Battalion: 84–92, 94
Indian Peace Commission: 187, 189
Indian Territory: 25, 48, 188, 193
Indian traders: 184

Indian War of 1868: 188, 189n., 191–93
Indians: 4–5, 7, 12, 15–16, 21, 24, 36, 40, 52, 67–68, 76, 91–92, 94, 97, 99–101, 103–104, 108, 128–30, 139, 141, 144–47, 164, 167, 184, 189, 193; hostilities along Trail, 10, 26, 29–32, 34, 79–84, 93, 121, 123, 131, 140, 142, 149–53, 155–56; confined to reservations, 23; engaged by soldiers, 157, 160; treaties with, 165–66, 187; *see also* Apache, Arapaho, etc.
Infantry: 27, 30, 33, 35, 63, 68–69, 73, 78, 84–85, 98–99, 101, 111, 123, 137, 142, 155, 190; Sixth U. S. Regt., 25–26, 35, 95, 99, 103, 111–12; First Illinois Vol. Regt., 78; Missouri Vol. Battalion, 78; Third U. S. Regt., 105, 191n.; Second U. S. Regt., 122; Tenth U. S. Regt., 126, 128; Fifth U. S. Regt., 132n.; Second U. S. Vol. Regt., 163; Thirty-Eighth U. S. Regt., 199
Interior Dept.: 114
Irrigation at Fort Lyon: 178
Iturbide, Agustín de: 7
Izard, Lt. James Farley: 28n.

Jackson, Pres. Andrew: 26, 42
Jackson County, Mo.: 62
Jackson, Capt. Hancock: 62n.
James, Thomas: 7–9
Jefferson Barracks, Mo.: 27, 199
Jefferson City, Mo.: 59
Jesup, QM Gen. T. S.: 61, 80–81
Jicarilla Apache Indians: 159
Johnson's Ranch, N. M.: 132, 134–36, 138
Jones, Fred (interpreter): 183–85
Jones, Adj. Gen. Roger: 55, 70, 94–95
Jones, Capt. Thomas: 89–90
Junction City, Kans.: 184

Kansas: 23, 131, 139, 147, 181, 184, 190, 192
Kansas, Dept. of: 143, 152
Kansas, Dist. of: 146
Kansas City, Mo.: 23, 156
Kansas Indians: 16, 37–38, 41, 44, 143, 190
Kansas militia: 152, 154
Kansas Pacific Railroad: 23

221

Kansas River: 14, 111
Kansas Stage Company: 151
Kansas volunteers: 144
Kaskaskia, Ill.: 4
Kearny, Col. (Gen.) Stephen Watts: 22, 25, 43–44, 52–79
Kiowa Indians: 16, 54, 85–86, 98, 106, 115–17, 129, 142, 147, 149, 160, 180, 183, 190, 191 & n.; hostile acts by, 34, 84, 109–10, 112–14, 118–20, 122, 143, 148, 150, 152, 154, 182, 191; campaigns against, 123–26, 157, 159, 185–86; treaties with, 165–66, 187–88
Kit Carson, Colo.: 23
Kozlowski's Ranch, N. M.: 133–37, 139

Laclede Rangers: 63, 66
La Lande, Jean Baptiste: 4
Lamar, Colo.: 124 n.
Lamar, Mirabeau B.: 42
Lamme, Samuel C.: 26, 30
Lamy, N. M.: 24
Lane, William Carr: 107
Larned, Col. Benjamin Franklin: 119
Las Animas, Colo.: 23
Las Vegas, N. M.: 18, 23–24, 73, 75, 80, 84, 94, 104–105, 133
Laundresses: 78, 173, 177, 179
Leavenworth, Gen. Henry: 36–37
Leavenworth, J. H.: 144, 146, 148, 164–66, 182, 185
Leitensdorfer, Eugene: 72
Lewis, Capt. W. H.: 132n.
Liberty, Mo.: 60
Libraries at forts: 177, 200
Linn, Sen. Lewis F.: 30n.
Little Arkansas River: 15, 16, 32, 41, 50, 143, 165
Little Arkansas River Treaties: 166, 180–81
Little Osage Indians: 41
Little Raven (Arapaho chief): 149
Long Route: 162
Lost River: *see* Cimarron River
Louisiana Purchase: 6
Love, Lt. John: 46, 82–83, 88
Lovell, Capt. Charles S.: 111
Lower Crossing: 17, 36, 124; *see also* Arkansas Crossing, Cimarron Crossing, etc.
Lower Spring (Cimarron River): 17–18, 146, 154–55
Lyon, Gen. Nathaniel: 126–27n.

McDaniel, David: 43
McDaniel, John: 43
McFerran, Col. J. C.: 155–56
Mackay, Col. E. A.: 95
McKissack, Capt. William: 80–81
McKnight, John: 8
McKnight, Robert: 6, 8
Macomb, Gen. Alexander: 27n., 33
Macomb, Capt. J. N.: 121
Magoffin, James Wiley: 12, 72 & n., 73–74
Magruder, Lt. W. T.: 108
Mail service on Trail: 21, 93, 106, 142, 143, 162, 169
Mail stations on Trail: 102–103, 114, 116, 119–20, 152, 162
Majors, Russell and Waddell Co.: 22, 119
Mann, Daniel P.: 81
Marcy, Sec. of War William L.: 56–57, 59, 80, 91
Marmaduke-Storrs Expedition (1824): 10–11
Matamoros, Mexico: 20
Maxwell's Ranch, N. M.: 155
Medicine Lodge Creek: 187, 188, 193
Medicine Lodge Creek Treaties: 187–88, 189n.
Melgares, Gov. Facundo: 7
Meriwether, David: 6
Mexican Revolution: 6, 7, 8
Mexican soldiers: 7, 8, 12, 25, 31, 45, 64, 65
Mexican War: 12, 18, 20–22, 24, 28, 41, 52, 54–55, 84, 91–93; *see also* Army of the West
Mexico: 5, 29, 40, 42, 56
Mexico City, Mexico: 51
Middle Crossing: *see* Cimarron Crossing
Middle Spring (Cimarron River): 18
Mier, Mexico: 42
Miles, Gen. Nelson A.: 174, 194
Military posts: 10, 22, 25, 92–93, 112, 126, 140, 161–62, 167–68, 190, 193; *see also* forts
Miller, Gov. John: 26, 27n.

Index

Miller, Robert: 112–13
Mississippi River: 6, 131
Missouri: 5–7, 9, 12, 18–20, 24–25, 33–34, 37, 43–45, 70, 76, 107; furnishes vols. for Mexican War, 59, 61, 62n., 63, 76–78; furnishes vols. to serve on Trail, 84
Missouri, Dept. of: 162, 181, 184
Missouri legislature: 26
Missouri militia: 61
Missouri Mounted Vols.: First Regt., 61, 62 & n., 64, 66, 84; Second Regt., 76–77, Third Regt., 78
Missouri River: 13, 25, 27, 51, 58
Mitchell, Col. David D.: 77
Montague County, Texas: 182
Moore, Capt. Benjamin D.: 44, 58, 64–65, 67, 69
Mora, N. M.: 42, 45, 85, 105
Mora Creek: *see* Río Mora
Mora Land Grant: 105
Mormons, Mormon Battalion: 57, 76–78
Morrison, William: 4
Moss, Capt. Oliver Perry: 62n.
Mt. Vernon, Mo.: 10
Mountain Route: 18–19, 78, 105, 110, 141, 161, 167
Mounted Riflemen: 100–101, 110, 126, 141
Mulberry Creek: 17, 89
Mules: 5, 9, 10, 14, 19, 28, 34, 60–61, 68–69, 79, 87–88, 102, 109, 118, 145, 151
Munroe, Maj. John: 104
Murphy, Thomas: 166
Murphy, Capt. William S.: 63

Narrows: 14, 23
Nauvoo, Ill.: 57
Navaho Indians: 129, 139
Neosho River: 14
New Mexico: 4–8, 15, 17, 20–22, 29, 37, 42–45, 50, 53, 55–58, 60, 64, 66, 69–72, 74–76, 78–80, 82, 91, 93, 98, 102, 104, 107, 116, 119, 121, 131, 134, 139–141, 143, 145, 159, 199
New Mexico, Dept. of: 132, 145, 155
New Mexico volunteers: 138, 140–41, 155, 163
New Orleans, La.: 20
New Spain: 3

Newby, Capt. (Col.) E. W. B: 78, 115–16, 119
Nicoll, William H.: 28n.
Ninth Mil. Dept.: 104
Noble, Lt. Patrick: 64
North Canadian River: 124, 192
North, Robert: 149n.

O'Connell, Lt. J. B.: 122
Ogden, Capt. E. A.: 111
Oklahoma: 17
110-Mile Creek: 14
Onís, Don Luis de: 8
Ordnance: 87
Oregon Territory: 52–53
Oregon Trail: 14, 25, 52–53, 68, 101
Osage Indians: 15–16, 86, 89
Osage River: 14
Otero, Don Miguel Antonio: 24
Otis, Lt. (Capt.) Elmer: 117–18, 142
Oxen: 14, 28, 30, 32, 60, 61, 68, 69, 73, 79, 82, 83

Parke, Lt. John G.: 104
Parmetar, Capt. J. W.: 151–52
Parsons, G. A.: 56n.
Parsons, Capt. Monroe M.: 62n.
Patrols: 93–94, 100–101, 106–107, 140, 143–45 & n., 148
Paul, Col. G. R.: 132
Pawnee (Kiowa chief): 116–17
Pawnee Fork: 16, 17n., 36, 46, 65, 69, 82, 83, 87, 92, 95, 97, 107, 113–25, 157, 167, 170, 186
Pawnee Indians: 16, 39, 41, 54, 79, 84, 89–90, 129
Pawnee Rock: 16
Peck, Lt. William G.: 63
Pecos Village, N. M.: 18
Pelzer, Capt. William: 85
Pentland, Capt. Joseph: 28n.
Pfeiffer, Maj. Albert H.: 164
Pierce, Capt. Henry: 163
Pigeon's Ranch, N. M.: 134–36, 139
Pike, Lt. Z. M.: 5
Pikes Peak emigrants killed: 119
Platte County, Mo.: 63
Platte River: 150
Platte River Route: 149, 157
Point of Rocks: 18

Polk, Pres. James K.: 55–56 & n., 66, 71–72, 76
Pope, Gen. John: 181
Post Office Dept.: 108
Price, Col. Sterling: 77
Pueblo, Colo.: 8
Purgatoire River: 19, 73, 125, 155, 175
Pyron, Maj. Charles L.: 132, 134

Quartermaster Dept.: 104, 111, 116

Ralls, Col. John: 78
Raton Pass: 9, 18–19, 23, 73, 86, 145n., 200
Red River: 39
Reid, Capt. John W.: 62n.
Rencher, Gov. Abraham: 140
Republican River: 111, 126
Riley, Maj. (Gen.) Gennet: 25–33, 35, 111
Río Grande: 20, 42–43, 74
Río Mora: 73, 105, 108, 167
Ritter, Capt. John F.: 132n.
Robidoux, Antoine: 59
Rodgers, Capt. Charles E.: 62n.
Round Grove: 14, 23, 27, 36
Round Mound: 18
Royall, Lt. William B.: 87–88
Rucker, Lt. Daniel Henry: 47
Ruff, Lt. Col. Charles R.: 61
Ryus, W. H.: 168

St. Louis, Mo.: 6, 8, 13, 27, 43, 59, 60, 62, 63, 122, 199
St. Vrain, Céran: 44–45, 52, 141
Salina, Kans.: 151–52
Saltillo, Mexico: 12
San Miguel, N. M.: 9, 18, 75
Sanborn, Gen. John B.: 165, 187
Sand Creek (Colo.): 154, 157n., 158–60
Sand Creek Affair ("Massacre"): 159–60, 165, 186
Sanderson, Maj. W. S.: 100–101
Sangre de Cristo Mountains: 19
Santa Anna: 51
Santa Clara Spring: 19
Santa Fe, N. M.: 3–10, 12, 14–22, 24, 26–28, 32, 34, 40, 42–45, 48, 49–51, 55–58, 64, 68, 70–71, 73–78, 80, 82–83, 86, 102, 105, 107, 119, 131–32, 156, 163

Santa Fe trade: 4–5, 7, 9, 11–14, 19–20, 22–24, 26, 33–34, 40, 42–44, 65
Santa Fe traders: 6–7, 9–10, 14–20 & n., 24–26, 29–31, 34–35, 37–39, 41–44, 48, 54–55, 57–58 & n., 63, 82, 92
Santa Fe Trail: established, 3 & n., 5, 7, 9–11; survey, 12; description, 12–19; in Mexican War, 21, 75–78, 91–92; in Civil War, 23, 131, 133, 136, 139–40, 146; mentioned, 24, 26, 32–34, 36–37, 46, 49, 52–54, 68, 79, 81–82, 84–97, 91, 93–95, 98–105, 110, 120, 123, 126, 130, 143, 145, 150, 156–57, 160, 164–67, 169, 180–81, 184–85, 187, 189–90, 199; military road, 55, 201
Sapello Creek: 75, 105
Satank (Kiowa chief): 116, 125
Satanta (Kiowa chief): 182, 184
Scott, Gen. Winfield: 56, 96
Scurry, Col. William R.: 135–36, 138–39
Sedgwick, Maj. John: 124–28
Sevier, Lt. Robert: 28n.
Shawnee Indians: 60
Sheridan, Capt. Andrew: 182–83
Sheridan, Gen. Philip H.: 189–90, 192–93
Sherman, Gen. William T.: 183, 188, 193
Shoup, Col. George L.: 159
Sibley, Gen. Henry Hopkins: 131–33, 139
Silver: 5, 19
Sixth Mil. Dept.: 111
Slough, Col. John P.: 132, 135–37, 139
Sioux Indians: 149
Smith, I. G.: 40
Smith, Jedediah, killed: 34
Smith, Lawrence: 118
Smith, Michael: 117–18
Smoky Hill River: 111, 125
Smoky Hill Route: 186, 200n.
Snively Expedition: 43, 45–49, 52, 54, 72
Snively, Jacob: 43, 45–48
Sod (used for construction of forts): 96, 98, 120, 122, 170–71
Somervell, Alexander: 42
Sonora (state), Mexico: 11
South Kansas, Dist. of: 153
South Pass: 25, 52–53
South Pass Expedition (1845): 52–54
Spain: 5, 7
Spanish troops: 5
Speyer, Albert: 64

224

Index

Stagecoach service: 21–22, 93, 162–63
Steele, James: 166
Steele, Capt. William: 124–25
Steen, Capt. Enoch: 50
Stephenson, Capt. John D.: 62n.
Steuart, Capt. George N.: 119–21
Stone (used for construction of forts): 96–97, 103, 123, 128, 163–64, 168, 170–72, 176
Storrs, Augustus: 10, 12
Stremmel, Lt. Philip: 87
Stuart, Lt. J. E. B.: 125, 127
Sturgis, Capt. Samuel Davis: 126
Sully, Gen. Alfred: 191–92
Sully Expedition (1868): 191–92
Sumner, Capt. (Col.) Edwin V.: 59, 66, 70, 95–97, 104–106 & n., 115, 119–20, 122, 127
Supply trains (for army): 20, 22–23, 79, 82, 89, 92–93, 114, 135, 137, 138, 140–41, 143, 155, 162, 169
Supply wagons (Confederate) destroyed: 138–39
Surgeons: 63
Sutlers: 63
Sutler's store: Fort Zarah, 168, Fort Larned, 171, 198n.

Table Creek: 58
Taos, N. M.: 8, 9, 12, 19, 32, 58, 70, 72, 81
Taos Pueblo: 72
Taos Revolt: 76
Tappan, Lt. Col. Samuel F.: 132, 187
Taylor, I. C.: 182
Taylor, Nathaniel G.: 187, 189n.
Taylor, Gen. Zachary: 59
Tecolote, N. M.: 75
Tents (soldiers' quarters): 163, 168, 171
Terrett, Capt. Burdett A.: 47–48
Terry, Alfred: 187
Texan–Santa Fe Expedition (1841): 42–43, 57
Texans: threaten Santa Fe trade in 1843, 42–49; mentioned, 50, 140, 142; invade N. M. in Civil War, 131–39
Texas: 3n., 20, 42, 45, 48, 53, 131, 139, 184
Theater, Fort Lyon: 177
Thomas, Adj. Gen. Lorenzo: 146
Thompson, Sec. of Int. Jacob: 114

Timber (used for construction of forts): 96, 128, 175
Timpas Creek: 19, 73
Topeka, Kansas.: 23
Topographical Engineers: 18, 54, 63, 104, 111, 121
Traders: *see* Santa Fe traders
Trading-post ranches: 143
Trinidad, Colo.: 23
Tunnel, Fort Larned: 170–71 & n.
Turkey Creek: 15
Turkey Mountains: 105
Turner, Lt. Henry S.: 59

Union Pacific Railroad, Eastern Division: *see* Kansas Pacific Railroad
U. S. Mounted Rangers: 25, 31, 33–35, 36n.
U. S. volunteers: 152–53
Updegraff, Maj. Joseph: 155
Upper Arkansas, Dist. of the: 153, 162, 165, 184, 190, 191
Upper Crossing: 17, 29, 92; *see also* Arkansas Crossing, Cimarron Crossing, etc.
Upper Spring (Cimarron River): 18, 155
Ute Indians: 129, 159

Van Buren, Ark.: 26n.
Van Swearingen, Lt. Joseph: 28n.
Vera Cruz, Mexico: 5
Vizcarra, Col. José Antonio: 32, 33n.

Wagons: 9, 14, 16–21, 27–28, 31, 36, 41, 44–45, 50, 60–61, 64–65, 67–68, 77, 80–84, 102
Waldo, David: 26, 62n., 64–65
Waldo, Hall and Co. (mail contractor): 21
Walker, Capt. W. T.: 114, 116–17, 129
Wallen, Maj. H. D.: 145
Walnut Creek: 16, 37, 44–46, 84, 87, 98, 102, 113–14, 116–17, 143–44, 147–48, 153, 167–68, 190
Walton, Capt. William P.: 62n.
War Department: 33, 44, 52–53, 55, 57–59, 61, 70, 84, 91–94, 103, 113, 115, 123, 126, 180
Ward, Gen. Thompson: 61

225

Soldiers on the Santa Fe Trail

Warfield, Charles A.: 42–43, 45
Warner, Lt. William H.: 63
Washita, battle of: 193
Waters, Lt. George W.: 28n.
Watrous, N. M.: 105
Webb, James J.: 58n.
Weightman, Capt. Richard H.: 63
Wessels, Capt. H. W.: 119, 124
West, Dept. of the: 35, 49, 59, 115
Westport, Mo.: 13, 68
Wet Route: 16–17 & n., 95, 124, 162, 167
Wharton, Capt. (Col.) Clifton: 37–41, 91

Wickliffe, Capt. William N.: 25, 28n., 31, 35–36
Willock, Maj. David: 77
Willow Bar (Cimarron River): 18
Wilson, Lt. Luther: 159
Wise, Gov. Henry A.: 126 & n.
Wolf Creek: 124
Woodruff, Lt. J. C.: 111
Wright, Robert: 174
Wynkoop, E. W.: 157–58, 182, 185

Yellow Buffalo (Kiowa chief): 149
Young, Lt. Gov. James: 59

The text for *Soldiers on the Santa Fe Trail* has been set on the Linotype in 11-point Old Style No. 7, for years one of the most popular book faces. This popularity is traceable to the splendid, even color of the type, its uncommon legibility, and compact fit. The paper on which the book is printed bears the watermark of the University of Oklahoma Press and has an effective life of at least three hundred years.